Learning With Technology
A Constructivist Perspective

David H. Jonassen
Pennsylvania State University

Kyle L. Peck
Pennsylvania State University

Brent G. Wilson
University of Colorado, Denver

Merrill,
an imprint of Prentice Hall
Upper Saddle River, New Jersey   Columbus, Ohio

Library of Congress Cataloging-in-Publication Data

Jonassen, David H., 1947–
    Learning with Technology: a constructivist perspective / David H.
  Jonassen, Kyle L. Peck, Brent G. Wilson.
      p.   cm.
  Includes bibliographical references and index.
  ISBN 0-13-271891-X
  1. Educational technology.   2. Teaching--Aids and devices.
  3. Learning. 4. Constructivism (Education)   I. Peck, Kyle L.
  II. Wilson, Brent G. (Brent Gayle)   III. Title.
  LB1028.3.J63   1999
  371.33--dc21   98-8508
                                                    CIP

Editor: Debra A. Stollenwerk
Production Editor: Mary Harlan
Photo Coordinator: Anthony Magnacca
Design Coordinator: Diane C. Lorenzo
Text Design and Production Supervision: Custom Editorial Productions, Inc.
Cover Design: Rod Harris
Cover Photo: © Super Stock, Inc.
Production Manager: Pamela D. Bennett
Illustrations: Custom Editorial Productions, Inc.
Director of Marketing: Kevin Flanagan
Marketing Manager: Suzanne Stanton
Marketing Coordinator: Krista Groshong

This book was set in Palatino by Custom Editorial Productions, Inc., and was printed and bound by R.R. Donnelley and Sons, Company, Harrisonburg, VA. The cover was printed by Phoenix Color Corp.

Photo Credits: Scott Cunningham/Merrill/Prentice Hall, pp. 51, 58, 61, 85, 115; Anthony Magracca/Merrill/Prentice Hall, pp. 1, 19, 62, 151, 193; Anne Vega/Merrill/Prentice Hall, p.217.

Printed in the United States of America

10 9 8 7 6

ISBN: 0-13-271891-X

Prentice-Hall International (UK) Limited, *London*
Prentice-Hall of Australia Pty. Limited, *Sydney*
Prentice-Hall of Canada, Inc., *Toronto*
Prentice-Hall Hispanoamericana, S. A., *Mexico*
Prentice-Hall of India Private Limited, *New Delhi*
Prentice-Hall of Japan, Inc., *Tokyo*
Pearson Education Asia Pte. Ltd., *Singapore*
Editora Prentice-Hall do Brasil, Ltda., *Rio de Janeiro*

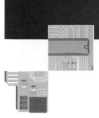

PREFACE

Constructivism is a relatively new idea to education. It is an even newer idea to educational technology. It is so new to some educational circles that some people perceive it as a fad. We think not. Constructivism is an old idea to sociology and art. And as a way of understanding the learning phenomenon, it is ageless. People have always constructed personal and socially acceptable meaning for events and objects in the world. Since evolving from the primordial ooze, humans have interacted with the world and struggled to make sense out of what they saw. The popular Chinese proverb about forgetting what you tell me and understanding what I do bears witness to the ageless belief that knowledge/meaning/understanding do not exist outside of meaningful, intentional activity. People naturally construct meaning. Formal educational enterprises that rely on the efficient transmission of prepackaged chunks of information are not natural. Yet they are pandemic. The modern age values understanding less than it does the efficient transmission of culturally accepted beliefs. It doesn't have to be that way. Modernism can support meaning making as well. This book looks at how modern technologies, such as computers and video, can be used to engage learners in personal and socially co-constructed meaning making.

For many, constructivism represents a new way of conceiving the educational experience. Yet constructivism, as a philosophy and as a pedagogy, is now widely accepted. This is a time of theoretical foment, where nearly all of the contemporary theories of learning (constructivism, situated learning, social cognition, activity theory, distributed cognition, ecological psychology, and case-based reasoning) all share very convergent beliefs about how people naturally come to know. This book is not about theory, but it shares the beliefs of these theories.

Learning With Technology is about how educators can use technologies to support constructive learning. In the past, technology has largely been used in education to learn *from*. Technology programs were developed with the belief that they could convey information (and hopefully understanding) more effectively than teachers. But constructivists believe that you cannot convey understanding. That can only be constructed by learners. So this book argues that technologies are more effectively used as tools to construct knowledge *with*. The point of this book is that technology is a tool to think and learn *with*.

How can technologies be used as meaning-making tools? After describing the assumptions of constructivism in Chapter 1, we describe six ways (in six chapters) that technology can support personal and social meaning making. In Chapter 2, we show how learners who articulate a personally meaningful goal or intention can explore the Internet in search of ideas that help them to construct their own understanding. Sharing their own understanding by constructing personal and group Web sites completes the knowledge construction cycle.

Chapter 3 describes numerous activities in which students can use video cameras, editors, and digitizers to represent their ideas. Constructing video presentations requires that learners articulate an idea well enough to represent it through video. In this chapter, video is used not to teach students, but rather as a tool that learners can teach and learn with. Students are natural video producers.

From video, Chapter 4 adds sound, graphics, and multimedia computers as tools that students can use to represent what they know. While producing multimedia programs, students become sensitive to the needs and desires of the audience for whom they are producing. And they work harder using more skills without complaint than they ever would with pencil and paper. Multimedia represents a new form of literacy that students will only learn by participating in the production of multimedia.

This book assumes that intentional learners are effective learners. When students declare an intention and desire to learn, they become a force. This force emerges most naturally in learning communities. Chapter 5 describes some of the ways that technologies can be used to support the development of learning communities. Conferencing systems are tying students together into a potentially massive, singular community of learners. They can communicate with any other students at any time anywhere in the world.

Chapter 6 briefly describes how technologies can be used as knowledge reflection and representation tools. It is an updated distillation of many of the ideas presented originally in *Computers in the Classroom: Mindtools for Critical Thinking* (Merrill/Prentice Hall, 1996).

Chapter 7 integrates all of the other technologies into constructivist learning environments, which are problem- or project-based activities that use all of the technologies to engage students in the most meaningful kinds of learning possible.

Chapter 8 stimulates the reader to reflect on the ideas presented in the rest of the book and to consider the knottiest of questions for most educators: How do we assess the constructive learning that learners do? To help answer that question, we provide a number of rubrics for assessing constructive learning with technology.

We live in the information age. In order to function in that world, students must learn how to be information producers, not just consumers. This book provides a new look at how educational technologies can support the knowledge construction process rather than the knowledge reproduction process. When educational technologies are used as knowledge construction tools, students are naturally and necessarily engaged in meaningful learning, which should be the goal of all educators.

Acknowledgments

The author would like to thank the following reviewers: Kara Dawson, University of Virginia; Peggy Ertmer, Purdue University; R. Scott Grabinger, University of Colorado at Denver; Joan Hanor, California State University, San Marcos; W. Michael Reed, West Virginia State University; Gregory C. Sales, University of Minnesota; Edna O. Schack, Morehead State University; Mark Schack, Morehead State University; Sharon Smaldino, University of Northern Iowa; Neal Strudler, University of Nevada, Las Vegas; Nancy H. Vick, Longwood College; and Connie Zimmer, Arkansas Tech University.

CONTENTS

LEARNING WITH TECHNOLOGY:
TECHNOLOGIES FOR MEANING MAKING

LEARNING WITH TECHNOLOGY

This book is about learning. The question that it seeks to answer is, how can technology best enhance meaningful learning? Traditionally, technologies have been used to teach students. That is, they have been used to deliver and communicate messages to students who, it is hoped, comprehend those messages and learn from them. The underlying assumption is that people learn *from* technology—that is, students learn from watching instructional films and television, responding to programmed instruction or computer-assisted instruction frames, just as they learn from listening to a lecture by the teacher. This view assumes that knowledge can be transmitted from the teacher to the student and that knowledge can be embedded in technology-based lessons and transmitted to the learner. Thus, students learn *from* technology what the technology knows or has been taught, just as they learn *from* the teacher what the teacher knows.

In this book, we argue that students cannot learn *from* teachers or technologies. Rather, students learn from *thinking*—thinking about what they are doing or what they did, thinking about what they believe, thinking about what others have done and believe, thinking about the thinking processes they use—just thinking. Thinking mediates learning. Learning results from thinking.

Thinking is engaged by activity. Different activities engage different kinds of thinking. That is, different kinds of thinking are required to memorize a list, read a book, understand a lecture, solve a problem, design a new product, or argue for a belief. These activities can be presented and supported by teachers and technologies. But teachers and technologies do not necessarily cause thinking, so they do not necessarily cause learning. They may, if the learner has a need or desire to learn, but they may not, if the learner is thinking about something else. How many lectures have you endured while your thoughts drifted to the weekend coming up or the celebration last night? The important point is that the role of teachers and technologies in learning is indirect. They can stimulate and support activities that engage learners in thinking, which may result in learning, but learners do not learn directly from the technology; they learn from thinking about what they are doing. Technologies can foster and support learning, we argue in this book, if they are used as tools and intellectual partners that help learners to think. What are the assumptions underlying this role for technology?

OUR ASSUMPTIONS ABOUT LEARNING

We learn from experiencing phenomena (objects, events, activities, processes), interpreting those experiences based on what we already know, reasoning about them, and reflecting on the experiences and the reasoning. Jerome Bruner (1990) called this process *meaning making*. Meaning making is at the heart of a philosophy of learning called *constructivism* that is relatively new to the field of educational technology. What is constructivism, and what do constructivists believe?

Constructivists believe that knowledge is constructed, not transmitted. Individuals make sense of their world and everything with which they come in contact by constructing their own representations or models of their experiences. Knowledge construction is a natural process. Whenever humans encounter something they do not know but need to understand, their natural inclination is to attempt to reconcile it with what they already know in order to determine what it means. Toddlers are archetypal constructivists. They constantly explore their worlds and frequently encounter phenomena that they do not understand. So they continue to explore it, familiarizing themselves with its possible functions and limitations. Parents try to intervene by teaching them lessons, but toddlers prefer to explore and learn for themselves.

Constructivists believe that knowledge cannot be simply transmitted by the teacher to the student or from us to you. In this book, we cannot "teach" you what we know. You cannot know what we know, because you have not experienced all that we have (nor us what you have), and so even if we now share an experience, our interpretation will be different from yours because we are relating it to a different set of prior experiences. In this book, we state our beliefs about learning and technology. You will interpret those beliefs in terms of your own beliefs and knowledge. You may accept them as valid or reject them as heresy (as many of our colleagues do). Teaching is not a process of imparting knowledge, because the learner cannot know what the teacher knows and what the teacher knows cannot be transferred to the learner. We believe that teaching is a process of helping learners to construct their own meaning from the experiences they have by providing those experiences and guiding the meaning-making process.

Knowledge construction results from activity, so knowledge is embedded in activity. We cannot separate our knowledge of things from our experiences with them. We can only interpret information in the context of our own experiences, so the meaning that we make emerges from the interactions that we have had. We might make meaning (constructed knowledge) about the things that we experienced. We might not. We can (and frequently do) memorize ideas that we have not experienced. Nearly every child in American schools is required to memorize the states and capitals. But they probably do not make much meaning for those facts, if they have not experienced them in a rich way. If, however, students attend a field trip to the state capital, then they construct some meaning for it, although not always the meaning that the teacher intends.

Knowledge is anchored in and indexed by the context in which the learning activity occurs. The knowledge of phenomena that we construct and the intellectual skills that we develop include information about the context of the experience (Brown, Collins, and Duguid 1989; Lave and Wenger 1991). Information about the context is part of the knowledge that is constructed by the learner in order to explain or make sense of the phenomenon. If we had an embarrassing experience while learning about something, that embarrassing feeling becomes an important part of the knowledge that we construct. The knowledge that a learner constructs consists of not only the ideas (content) but also knowledge about the context in which it was acquired, what the learner was doing in that environment, and what the knower intended to get from that environment. This means that abstract rules and laws (like mathematical formulae), divorced from any context or use, have little meaning for learners (except skilled mathematicians, who have used those formulae in other contexts). The meaning that we construct for ideas includes information about the experiences and the settings in which they were applied or learned. So, the more directly and interactively we experience things, the more knowledge about it we are likely to construct.

What we really understand about skills and knowledge is the application of them. When we learn how to use a skill, we store that use as a story, which is a primary medium of conversation and meaning making among humans (Schank 1986). We later recall those stories when faced with similar experiences and attempt to use those to guide activity. Constructivism argues that skills will have more meaning if they are acquired initially and consistently in meaningful contexts to which they can be related. Teaching facts and explaining concepts without using them in some context probably does not result in much meaning making.

Meaning is in the mind of the knower.   The meaning-making process produces perceptions of the external, physical world that are unique to the knower, because each individual has a unique set of experiences that have produced a unique combination of beliefs about the world. The sense that *we* make of the world is necessarily somewhat different from the sense that you make of it, but we can share our meaning with others. This does not mean that we cannot share parts of our reality with others. We do so by socially negotiating shared meanings. That is, we converse with others and agree on the relative importance and meanings for things. The important point is that knowledge is not an external object that is acquired by the learner; it can only be constructed. You can experience our realities vicariously, if we tell you about them, you can even construct meaning for them, but that understanding will be your personal interpretation of our experiences that are based on your own experiences.

Therefore, there are multiple perspectives on the world.   Since no two people can possibly have the same set of experiences and perceptions of those experiences, each of us constructs our own knowledge, which in turn affects the perceptions of the experiences that we have and those we share. Those perceptions and beliefs about the world affect our perspectives and beliefs about any subject. Why else would discussions of politics or religion evoke such strongly different perspectives about the specific subject being considered (a particular candidate, a piece of legislation, or a religious practice)? In Western societies, for instance, we have trouble understanding or accepting many of the practices of Eastern cultures because those practices rely on different perspectives and beliefs about the world that are endemic to that culture.

Meaning making is prompted by a problem, question, confusion, disagreement, or dissonance (a need or desire to know) and so involves personal ownership of that problem. What produces the knowledge construction process is a dissonance between what is known and what is observed in the world. Meaning making often starts with a problem, a question, a discrepant and inexplicable event, a curiosity, wonderment, puzzlement (Duffy and Cunningham 1996), a perturbation (Maturana and Varela 1992), expectation violations (Schank 1986), cognitive dissonance, or a disequilibrium. We can memorize ideas that others tell us, but to actively seek to make meaning about phenomena involves the desire to make sense of things. When learners seek to resolve that dissonance, it becomes their problem, not the teacher's. Resolving dissonance ensures some ownership of the ideas and the problem on the part of the learner (a point that we will return to often in this book). That ownership makes what is learned (the knowledge that is constructed) more relevant, important, and meaningful to the learner.

Knowledge-building requires articulation, expression, or representation of what is learned (meaning that is constructed). Although activity is a necessary condition for knowledge construction, it is not sufficient. It is possible (and even common) for humans to engage in activities from which no knowledge is constructed. Why? Because they did not reflect on or think about the experience that gave rise to the knowledge construction process. For usable knowledge to be constructed, learners need to think about what they did and articulate what it meant. Usually that articulation process is verbal, but learners can construct a variety of visual or auditory representations of their experiences or understandings. Chapter 6 describes a number of computer-based tools that support this reflective process.

Meaning may also be shared with others, so meaning making can also result from conversation. Just as the physical world is shared by all of us, so is some of the meaning that we make from it. Humans are social creatures who rely on exchanges with fellow humans to determine their own identity and the viability of their personal beliefs. Social constructivists believe that meaning making is a process of negotiation among the participants through dialogues or conversations. Learning is inherently a social-dialogical process (Duffy and Cunningham 1996). Recall a conversation that you had at the last party you attended. Probably, you were exchanging stories about your experiences. Those stories were an attempt to share understanding. This social dialogue occurs most effectively within knowledge-building communities (Scardamalia and Bereiter 1993/94) or discourse communities (described in Chapter 5) where people share their interests and experiences. These people have similar experiences and enjoy discussing similar topics, so they can learn from each other because the stories they tell evoke similar experiences. These conversation communities can be a valuable source of meaning making and are described in Chapter 5.

So, meaning making and thinking are distributed throughout our tools, culture, and community. As we interact with others in knowledge-building communities, our knowledge and beliefs about the world are influenced by that community and their beliefs and values. Through participating in the activities of the community (Lave and Wenger 1991), we absorb part of the culture that is an integral part of the community, just as the culture is affected by each of its members. Communities of learners, like communities of practitioners, can be seen as a kind of widely distributed memory with each of its members storing a part of the group's total memory. Distributed memory—what the group as a whole knows—is clearly more capacious than individual memories; sharing those memories makes the community more dynamic. Just as the cognitive properties of individuals vary, the cognitive attributes and accomplishments of communities also vary, depending on differences in the social organization of the groups (i.e., the ways in which members distribute cognitive responsibilities) (Hutchins 1991).

As we interact, discourse communities change our knowledge and beliefs. Just as our knowledge of the world is influenced by activities, our knowledge and beliefs are also influenced by the beliefs of our fellow practitioners. Our knowledge is naturally influenced by those with whom we converse. That is why we associate with like-minded people in social or professional groups. Learning can also be conceived of as changes in our relation to the culture(s) to which we are connected (Duffy and Cunningham 1996). As we spend more time in a club, we become more influenced by its beliefs and culture, because the group's knowledge is distributed among the participants (Salomon 1993). Members of the group will contribute what they know when a complex task has to be performed.

Not all meaning is created equally.   Constructivists do not subscribe, as many claim that they do, to the view that all meaning is equally valid because it is personally constructed (Savery and Duffy 1995).

The litmus test for the knowledge that individuals construct is its viability (Duffy and Cunningham 1996). Within any knowledge-building community, shared ideas are accepted and agreed upon. That is, meaning is reflected in the social beliefs that exist at any point in time. If individual ideas are discrepant from community standards, they are not regarded as viable unless new evidence supporting their viability is provided. Individuals are regarded as more knowledgeable because their understanding is constructed from a richer and more varied set of experiences. Bransford (1994) asked, "Who 'ya gonna call?" if your dog is misbehaving: a plumber, dog trainer, or brain surgeon? Presumably, the dog trainer has more viable knowledge about your dog's behavior, while the neurosurgeon better understands your cerebral activity. Assessing the viability of anyone's knowledge involves many criteria.

Table 1.1 contrasts fundamental differences between constructivist views of learning and traditional views of learning. We believe that constructivist views of making meaning necessarily engage different kinds of thinking. In order to engage different kinds of thinking, we must rethink the ways that we teach and the ways that we use technology in our teaching. This book is about some of the ways that educators can use technology to engage students in meaningful learning.

Table 1.1   Constructivist Versus Traditional Learning Methods

	Constructivist	Traditional
Knowledge	Constructed, emergent, situated in action or experience, distributed	Transmitted, external to knower, objective, stable, fixed, decontextualized
Reality	Product of mind	External to the knower
Meaning	Reflects perceptions and understanding of experiences	Reflects external world
Symbols	Tools for constructing reality	Represents world
Learning	Knowledge construction, interpreting world, constructing meaning, ill-structured, authentic-experiential, articulation-reflection, process-oriented	Knowledge transmission, reflecting what teacher knows, well-structured, abstract-symbolic, encoding-retention-retrieval, product-oriented
Instruction	Reflecting multiple perspectives, increasing complexity, diversity, bottom-up, inductive, apprentice-ship, modeling, coaching, exploration, learner-generated	Simplify knowledge, abstract rules, basics first, top-down, deductive, application of symbols (rules, principles), lecturing, tutoring, instructor derived and controlled, individual, competitive

MEANINGFUL LEARNING: OUR GOAL FOR SCHOOLS

Our assumption in this book is that the primary goal of education at all levels should be to engage students in meaningful learning, which occurs when students are actively making meaning. While schools play a variety of important social, custodial, and organizational roles in communities, we assume that their primary obligation should be to help students to learn how to recognize and solve problems, comprehend new phenomena, construct mental models of those phenomena, and, given a new situation, set goals and regulate their own learning (learn how to learn). This book is devoted to describing how technology can be used to foster those goals. Figure 1.1 illustrates the interaction of five interdependent attributes of meaningful learning. If we accept that our goal, as technology-using educators, is to support meaningful learning, then we should use technologies to engage students in active, constructive, intentional, authentic, and cooperative learning. These attributes of meaningful learning will be used throughout the remainder of the book as the goals for using technologies, as well as the criteria for evaluating the uses of technology. Let's examine these attributes a little more closely.

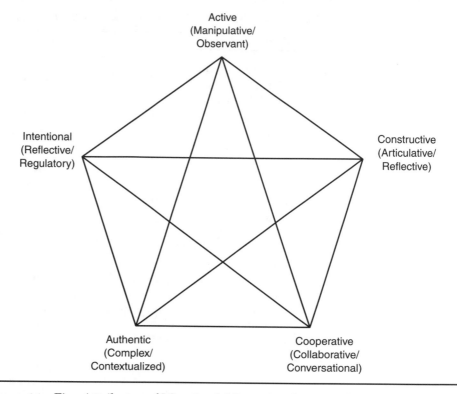

Figure 1.1 Five Attributes of Meaningful Learning Are Interdependent

• **Active (Manipulative/Observant)** Learning is a natural, adaptive human process. Humans have survived and therefore evolved because they were able to learn about and adapt to their environment. Humans of all ages, without the intervention of formal instruction, can develop sophisticated skills and construct advanced knowledge about the world around them when they need to or want to. When learning about things in natural contexts, humans interact with their environment and manipulate the objects in that environment, observing the effects of their interventions and constructing their own interpretations of the phenomena and the results of the manipulation. For instance, before playing sandlot baseball, do kids subject themselves to lectures and multiple-choice examinations about the theory of games, the aerodynamics of orbs, and vector forces of bats? No! They start swinging the bat and chasing fly balls, and they negotiate the rules as they play the game. Through formal and informal apprenticeships in communities of play and work, learners develop skills and knowledge that they then share with other members of those communities with whom they learned and practiced those skills. In all of these situations, learners are actively manipulating the objects and tools of the trade and observing the effects of what they have done. Children who consistently hit foul balls will adjust their stance or handgrip on the bat continuously to manipulate the flight path, and they will observe the effects of each manipulation. Real learning requires *active* learners—people engaged by a meaningful task (not just pressing the space bar to continue) in which they manipulate objects and the environment in which they are working and then observe the results of their manipulations.

- **Constructive (Articulative/Reflective)**   Activity is necessary but not sufficient for meaningful learning. Learners must reflect on their activity and observations to learn the lessons that their activity has to teach. New experiences often provide a discrepancy between what learners observe and what they understand. They are curious about or puzzled by what they see. That puzzlement is the catalyst for meaning making. By reflecting on the puzzling experience, learners integrate their new experiences with their prior knowledge about the world, or they establish goals for what they need to learn in order to make sense out of what they observe. Learners begin constructing their own simple mental models to explain their worlds, and with experience, support, and more reflection, their mental models become increasingly complex. Ever more complex models will enable them to reason more consistently and productively about the phenomena they are observing. The active and constructive parts of the meaning-making process are symbiotic. They both rely on the other for meaning making to occur.

- **Intentional (Reflective/Regulatory)**   All human behavior is goal directed (Schank 1994). That is, everything that we do is intended to fulfill some goal. That goal may be simple, like satiating hunger or getting more comfortable, or it may be more complex, like developing new career skills or studying for a master's degree. When learners are actively and willfully trying to achieve a cognitive goal (Scardamalia and Bereiter 1993/94), they think and learn more because they are fulfilling an intention. Articulating that intention is essential for meaningful learning. Technologies have traditionally been used to support teacher goals, but not those of learners. Technologies need to engage learners in articulating what their learning goals are in any learning situation, and then support them. Technology-based learning systems should require learners to articulate what they are doing, the decisions they make, the strategies the use, and the answers that they found. When learners articulate what they have learned and reflect on the processes and decisions that were entailed by the process, they understand more and are better able to use their constructed knowledge in new situations.

- **Authentic (Complex/Contextual)**   The greatest intellectual sin that educators commit is to oversimplify ideas in order to transmit them more easily to learners. In addition to removing ideas from their natural contexts for teaching, we also strip ideas of their contextual cues and information and distill the ideas to their "simplest" form so that students will more readily learn them. But what are they learning? That knowledge is divorced from reality, and that the world is a reliable and simple place? However, the world is not a reliable and simple place, and ideas rely on the contexts they occur in for meaning. At the end of chapters, textbooks insert the ideas taught in the chapter into some artificial problem context. However, learners often fail to solve the problems because the ideas were learned as algorithmic procedures without any context, so they have no idea how to relate the ideas to new contexts. Additionally, these textbook problems are constrained, practicing only a limited number of activities that were introduced in the chapter, so when they are faced with complex and ill-structured problems, students do not know where to begin.

A great deal of recent research (described in Chapters 3, 4, and 7) has shown that learning tasks that are situated in some meaningful real-world task or simulated in some case-based or problem-based learning environment are not only better understood, but also are more consistently transferred to new situations. Rather than presenting ideas as rules that are memorized and then applied to other canned problems, we need to teach knowledge and skills in real-life, useful contexts and provide new and different contexts for learners to practice using those ideas. And we need to engage students in solving complex and ill-structured problems as well as simple problems (Jonassen 1997). Unless learners are required to engage in higher-order thinking, they will develop oversimplified views of the world.

• **Cooperative (Collaborative/Conversational)**   Humans naturally work in learning and knowledge-building communities, exploiting each others' skills and appropriating each others' knowledge. In the real world, humans naturally seek out others to help them to solve problems and perform tasks. Then why do educators insist that learners work independently all of the time? Schools generally believe that learning is an independent process, so learners seldom have the opportunity to "do anything that counts" in collaborative teams, despite their natural inclinations. When students collaborate without permission, they may even be accused of cheating. However, we believe that relying solely on independent methods of instruction cheats learners out of more natural and productive modes of thinking. Often, educators will promote collaborative methods of learning, only to resort to independent assessment of learning. Learners, they believe, must be accountable for their own knowledge, so even if you agree, at least in principle, with collaborative learning principles, the hardest part of applying your beliefs will be assessing learners. Throughout this book, we will provide vignettes on how groups as well as individuals may be assessed. We cannot forget that most learners are strategic enough to know "what counts" in classrooms, so if they are evaluated individually, collaborative instruction may fail because students realize that group outcomes are not important.

Collaboration most often requires conversation among participants. Learners working in groups must socially negotiate a common understanding of the task and the methods they will use to accomplish it. Given a problem or task, people naturally seek out opinions and ideas from others. Technologies can support this conversational process by connecting learners in the same classroom, across town, or around the world (see Chapter 5). When learners become part of knowledge-building communities both in class and outside of school, they learn that there are multiple ways of viewing the world and multiple solutions to most of life's problems. Conversation should be encouraged. In classrooms that focus on individual learning, however, it is too often discouraged. In those classrooms, students know that the important views are those espoused by the textbook or the teacher, so conversation may be difficult to foster.

As is depicted in Figure 1.1, these characteristics of meaningful learning are interrelated, interactive, and interdependent. That is, learning and instructional activities should engage and support combinations of active, constructive, intentional, authentic, and cooperative learning. Why? Because we believe that these characteristics are synergetic. That is, learning activities that represent a combination of these characteristics result in even more meaningful learning than the individual characteristics would in isolation.

There are many kinds of learning activities that engage meaningful learning, just as there are teachers who have for years engaged students in meaningful learning. We argue throughout this book that technologies can and should become the tools of meaningful learning. Technologies afford students the opportunities to engage in meaningful learning if used as learning tools. These characteristics of meaningful learning are used throughout the remainder of the book as criteria for evaluating the use of different technologies. In the next section, we describe the assumptions about technologies that underlie their use as learning tools.

OUR ASSUMPTIONS ABOUT TECHNOLOGY

Traditional Conceptions of Educational Technologies

Educational technologies have been traced historically to the advent of movable type in the fifteenth century, to illustrations in seventeenth-century books, and to slate chalkboards in eighteenth-century classrooms. Educational technologies in the twentieth century include first lantern slide projectors, later radio, and then motion pictures. Chapter 3 describes the development of educational television in the 1950s and 1960s. During the same period, programmed instruction emerged as the first true educational technology—that is, the first technology developed specifically to meet educational needs. With every other technology, including computers, educators recognized its importance and debated how to apply each nascent commercial technology for educational purposes. Unfortunately, the most obvious way to use technologies was to have them teach in the same ways that teachers had always taught, making them substitute teachers. That meant that knowledge was embedded in the technology (e.g., the content presented by films and TV programs or the teaching sequence in programmed instruction), and the technology presented that knowledge to the student. The students' role was to learn the knowledge presented by the technology, just as they learned knowledge presented by the teacher. The role of the technology was to deliver lessons that teach learners, just as trucks deliver groceries to supermarkets (Clark 1983). The logic is: If you deliver groceries, people will eat; if you deliver instruction, students will learn.

The introduction of computers in classrooms followed the same pattern of use. Before the advent of microcomputers in the 1980s, mainframe computers were used to deliver drill-and-practice and simple tutorials for teaching students lessons. When microcomputers began populating classrooms, the natural inclination was to use them in the same way. A 1983 national survey of computer uses showed that drill-and-practice was the most common use of microcomputers (Becker 1985), along with learning to program in BASIC. Drill-and-practice represented the *tutor* role for computers, while programming represented the *tutee* role, where students learned by teaching the computer (Taylor 1984). This was a powerful idea, but unfortunately, BASIC was a limited medium and, as we shall argue throughout this book, learners should use technologies as media for representing what they know and for teaching each other.

During the early 1980s, educators began to perceive the importance of computers as productivity *tools*. The growing popularity of word processing, databases, spreadsheets, graphics programs, and desktop publishing were enabling businesses to become more productive. So students in classroom began using word processing, graphics packages, and desktop publishing programs. This tool conception pervaded computer uses, according to a 1993 study by Hadley and Sheingold, which showed that well-informed teachers were extensively using text-processing tools (word processors), analytic and information tools (especially databases and some spreadsheet use), and graphics tools (paint programs and desktop publishing), along with instructional software (including problem-solving programs along with drill-and-practice and tutorials).

The development of inexpensive multimedia computers and the eruption of the Internet in the mid-1990s quickly changed the nature of educational computing. Communications and multimedia, little used in 1993, have dominated the role of technologies in the classroom over the past few years. Unfortunately, their roles in education have been naturally conceived as teachers and sources of knowledge, rather than tools for learning. As we argue in Chapters 4 and 5, multimedia and computer-mediated communications are among the most powerful learning tools that students can use.

Our conception of educational computing and technology use, described in the next section, does not conceive of technologies as teachers. Rather, we believe that in order to learn, students should share the role of representing what they know, rather than memorizing what teachers and textbooks know. Technologies provide rich and flexible media for representing what students know and what they are learning. A great deal of research on computers and other technologies has shown that they are no more effective at teaching students than teachers, but if we begin to think about technologies as learning tools that students learn *with*, not *from*, then the nature of student learning will change.

Our Conception of Educational Technologies

The ways that we use technologies in schools should change, from their traditional roles of technology-as-teacher to technology-as-partner in the learning process. Before, we argued that students cannot learn from technology, but that technologies can support meaning making by students. That will happen when students learn *with* technology. But, how do students learn *with* technologies? How can technologies become intellectual partners with students? If you agree with this role for technologies, then you must make a different set of assumptions about what technologies are and what they do. Throughout this book, we assume that:

• Technology is more than hardware. Technology consists of the designs and the environments that engage learners. Technology can also consist of any reliable technique or method for engaging learning, such as cognitive learning strategies and critical thinking skills.

- Learning technologies can be any environment or definable set of activities that engage learners in active, constructive, intentional, authentic, and cooperative learning.
- Technologies are not simply conveyors or communicators of meaning. Nor should they prescribe and control all of the learner interactions.
- Technologies support learning when they fulfill a learning need—when interactions with technologies are learner-initiated and learner-controlled, and when interactions with the technologies are conceptually and intellectually engaging.
- Technologies should function as intellectual tool kits that enable learners to build more meaningful personal interpretations and representations of the world. These tool kits must support the intellectual functions that are required by a course of study.
- Learners and technologies should be intellectual partners in the learning process, where the cognitive responsibility for performing is distributed to the part of the partnership that performs it the best.

How Technologies Foster Learning

If technologies are used to support learning in the ways that we have described, then they will not be used as delivery vehicles (such as in computer-assisted instruction, tutorials, drill-and-practice) (Jonassen, Campbell, and Davidson 1993). Rather, technologies should be used as engagers and facilitators of thinking and knowledge construction. Some useful roles for technology in learning include:

- Technology as tools to support knowledge construction:
    - for representing learners' ideas, understandings, and beliefs
    - for producing organized, multimedia knowledge bases by learners
- Technology as information vehicles for exploring knowledge to support learning-by-constructing:
    - for accessing needed information
    - for comparing perspectives, beliefs, and world views
- Technology as context to support learning-by-doing:
    - for representing and simulating meaningful real-world problems, situations and contexts
    - for representing beliefs, perspectives, arguments, and stories of others
    - for defining a safe, controllable problem space for student thinking
- Technology as social medium to support learning by conversing:
    - for collaborating with others
    - for discussing, arguing, and building consensus among members of a community
    - for supporting discourse among knowledge-building communities
- Technology as intellectual partner (Jonassen 1996) to support learning-by-reflecting:
    - for helping learners to articulate and represent what they know
    - for reflecting on what they have learned and how they came to know it

for supporting learners' internal negotiations and meaning making
for constructing personal representations of meaning
for supporting mindful thinking

Technologies are applications of human knowledge to real-world problems. They are tools for supporting human needs. Computer technologies such as word processors, spreadsheets, desktop publishing, and computer-assisted design programs all enhance the productivity of their users. Most knowledge construction (and reproduction) requires producing communications, designing materials, or managing resources. Technologies as tools extend humans' functional capabilities.

Computer-based technologies are also used as information access tools. Within a few years, virtually all technical information will be stored online. Literacy for the next generation will require knowing how to use and manipulate these tools to locate and access multiple forms of information (see Chapter 2). Internet search engines enable increasingly sophisticated search strategies. Learners need to know how to use sophisticated search tools in order to access and manipulate information.

Using technologies as context means creating and representing contexts and situations from which learners can problem-solve and construct knowledge. Technologies, such as Case-based learning environments (see Chapter 7) and microworlds (Chapter 6) seek to provide rich and situated problem spaces for learners to investigate while solving meaningful, real-world problems.

Certainly the fastest-growing use of technologies is the interconnection of communities of learners (see Chapter 5). Students are now able to converse and collaborate with other students all over the world. Communal learning experiences are no longer limited to students in the same classroom. Using technologies as social media will increasingly define global learning communities.

However, technologies can do more than extend the capabilities of humans; they can amplify them. Using technologies as cognitive tools extends learners' cognitive functioning by engaging learners in thinking while constructing knowledge of which they would not otherwise have been capable (Pea 1985). Cognitive tools (see Chapter 6) are computational devices that can support, guide, and extend the thinking processes of their users (Derry and LaJoie 1993) if the users are in control of the computers, rather than being controlled by the computers. Computers and videoplayers are knowledge construction tools that engage learners in critical thinking about what they are learning.

Our conception of technologies is broad. In it, the user and the hard technologies (computers, video, etc.) blend together to form a single entity with distributed intelligence, where learners contribute what they do best and technologies contribute what they do best—the learner is in charge. When students learn *from* technology, such as watching instructional television or interacting with computer-assisted instruction, both the technology and the learners assume roles that can better be fulfilled by the other. Technologies present information, ask questions, and judge answers (all of which humans do better), while students receive, store, and retrieve information (all of which computers do better). What results in learners is inert, unusable knowledge. Our goal in this book is to reconceptualize the roles of technologies in learning as tools for learners to construct their own meaning.

Assumptions About Assessing and Evaluating Learning With Technologies

If you agree that learning is or should be an active, constructive, intentional, authentic, and cooperative process, and if you agree that technologies should be used as learning tools for students to learn *with*, then you must probably also challenge your beliefs about how to assess and evaluate learning by students. Why? Because instructional theory insists that if learning is an active, constructive, intentional, authentic, and cooperative process, so should the ways in which we assess learners and the criteria that we use to evaluate them. That is a difficult requirement intellectually, socially, and politically. We traditionally assess students for the amount of knowledge that they have acquired from the teacher and the textbook. Constructivism suggests that we need to assess the meaning that learners have co-constructed from their interactions with the world. How is that different? The meaning and interpretations that individuals and groups construct will all vary somewhat from each other. So what is the right answer? There probably will not be a single correct answer. How can we know when students have learned? Probably by assessing learning while it is occurring. Assessment, from a constructivist perspective, is process-oriented. Assess learning as it is occurring, rather than separating assessment from learning, focusing not only on what students have learned (their knowledge), but also on the ways that students learn. Assessing the strategies and tactics that students use to learn will predict how well they will be able to learn and solve problems in new situations.

If we believe that the ways that we assess learning should change, we also need to rethink the ways that we evaluate that learning. Evaluation places a value on the kinds of learning that has occurred. Traditionally, we assign a letter grade based on the percentage of ideas that are remembered or understood (90 percent is excellent, 80 percent is above average, etc.). From a constructivist perspective, student knowledge must be evaluated based on its viability. Does it make sense, is it well founded and justified by the learners, is it well represented by the learners, can it be applied meaningfully, and is it consistent with the standards (scientific or literary) that are accepted by the field? This form of assessment, described in Chapter 8, is more difficult and time consuming than traditional forms of assessment and evaluation, which seek to commoditize knowledge as something that can be acquired. Traditional assessment asks, how much knowledge did students acquire?

Most evaluation methods argue that more is better. Assessment from a constructivist perspective seeks to know what the learner knows. Because meaning making is a complex and multifaceted phenomenon, assessment of learners' knowledge must should also be multifaceted and multimodal. No single measure can begin to assess the complexity of human understanding, especially a multiple-choice measurement. So, we need to develop more diverse and complex ways of assessing learning. Is this possible? Isn't there already too much to accomplish in a school day or year? It is possible, if you let the technologies provide the means of assessment. That is, you should assess student-constructed knowledge bases produced with technologies.

In Chapter 8, we provide some rubrics for assessing meaningful learning with technologies. As students use technologies as learning tools (as described throughout the remainder of the book), they will produce technology-based arti-facts—student-constructed knowledge bases. These knowledge bases are rich, multimodal indicators of what students have learned. They are activity-based (i.e., embedded in activity). They require learners to articulate and reflect on what they know and believe. They are complex, and given the opportunity, they will usually describe some authentic problem. Student perspectives are necessarily more authentic to them. Assessment does not have to be a separate process that occurs after learning has occurred. Technologies afford student representations of what they know. If you assess those constructions, students will learn quickly that the ways that they use technologies are not only more fun and engaging than tradi-tional recitation methods, they also count. Throughout this book, we will provide boxed recommendations about how to use technologies to assess learning or how to assess what students have constructed.

CONCLUSIONS

An underlying assumption of this book is that the most productive and meaning-ful uses of technology will not occur if technologies are used in traditional ways—as delivery vehicles for instructional lessons. Technology cannot teach students. Rather, learners should use the technologies to teach themselves and others. They learn through teaching with technologies. Meaningful learning will result when technologies engage learners in:

- Knowledge construction, not reproduction
- Conversation, not reception
- Articulation, not repetition
- Collaboration, not competition
- Reflection, not prescription

The remainder of this book describes how technologies can be used to sup-port meaningful learning in schools from a constructivist perspective. Although the focus of the book is K–12, most of the ideas that we present are also valid for universities, corporations, and other learning agencies.

THINGS TO THINK ABOUT

If you would like to reflect on the ideas that we presented in this chapter, consider your responses to the following questions and compare them with the responses of others.

1. If learners cannot know what the teacher knows because they do not fully share a common knowledge and experience base, how can we be certain that students learn important things? For instance, if you want to teach students about the dangers of certain chemical reactions in the lab, how do you ensure that learners know and understand those important lessons?

2. Is it possible to learn (construct personal meaning) without engaging in some overt activity; that is, is it possible to learn simply by thinking about something? What are you thinking about? Can you give an example?

3. When learners construct knowledge, what are they building? How is it possible to observe the fruits of their labor, that is, the knowledge they construct?

4. Recall an event from your childhood. What do you remember? Where did your remembrance occur? What meaning did it have at the time? How has that meaning changed over time?

5. Think about a recent controversial topic that you have heard or read about. What are different sides arguing about? What do they believe? What assumptions do they make about what is causing the controversy? What prompted those beliefs?

6. Radical constructivists argue that reality exists only in the mind of the knower. If that is true, is there a physical world that we live in? Prove it.

7. Some educators argue that we learn much more from our failures than from our successes. Why? They believe that we should put students in situations where their hypotheses or predictions fail. Can you think of a situation in which you learned a lot from a mistake?

8. Recall the last difficult problem that you had to solve. Did you solve it alone, or did you solicit the help of others? What did you learn from solving that problem? Can that learning be used again?

9. Can you learn to cook merely from watching cooking shows on television? What meaning do you make from the experiences that you observe? Will the experience that you have when you prepare a dish be the same as that of the television chef? How will it be different?

10. Technology is the application of scientific knowledge, according to many definitions. Can you think of a teaching technology (replicable, proven teaching process) that does not involve machines?

11. Can you calculate the exact square root of 2,570 without a calculator? Does the calculator make you smarter? Is the calculator intelligent?

12. Describe the difference in thinking processes engaged by a short answer versus a multiple-choice test question. Are they different? Are they assessing knowledge? Is that knowledge meaningful? Why or why not?

13. Have you ever produced your own video, movie, slide show, or computer program? How did it make you think? How did it make you feel?

REFERENCES

Becker, H. J. (1985) *How schools use microcomputers: Summary of a 1983 national survey.* ERIC Document Reproduction Service, ED 257448.

Brown, J. S., A. Collins, and P. Duguid (1989, January–February). Situated cognition and the culture of learning. *Educational Researcher* 32–42.

Bruner, J. (1990) *Acts of Meaning.* Cambridge, MA: Harvard University Press.

Clark, R. (1983). Reconsidering research on learning from media. *Review of Educational Research,* 53(4), 445–459.

Derry, S. J., and S. P. LaJoie (1993). A middle camp

for (un)intelligent instructional computing: An introduction. In S. P. LaJoie and S. J. Derry (eds.), *Computers as cognitive tools.* Hillsdale, NJ: Lawrence Erlbaum Associates.

Duffy, T. M., and D. C. Cunningham (1996). Constructivism: Implications for the design and delivery of instruction. In D. H. Jonassen (ed.), *Handbook of Research on Educational Communications and Technology.* New York: Macmillan.

Gagné, R. M. (1977). *The conditions of learning* (3rd ed.). New York: Holt, Rinehart and Winston.

Hadley, M., and K. Sheingold. (1993). Commonalities and distinctive patterns in teacher interaction of computers. *American Journal of Education,* 101 (3): 261–315.

Hutchins, E. (1991). Organizing work by adaption. *Organizational Science* 2, 14–39.

Jonassen, D. H. (1996). *Computers in the classroom: Mindtools for critical thinking.* Englewood Cliffs, NJ: Merrill/Prentice-Hall.

Jonassen, D. H. (1997). Instructional design models for well-structured and ill-structured problem-solving learning outcomes. *Educational Technology: Research and Development,* 45(1), 65–95.

Jonassen, D. H., J. P. Campbell, and M.E. Davidson (1994). Learning with media: Restructuring the debate. *Educational Technology: Research and Development,* 42(2): 31–39.

Lave, J., and E. Wenger (1991). *Situated learning: Legitimate peripheral participation.* Cambridge, UK: Cambridge University Press.

Maturana, H. R., and A. Varela (1992). *The tree of knowledge: The biological roots of human understanding.* Boston: Shambhala.

Pea, R. D. (1985). Beyond amplification: Using the computer to reorganize mental functioning. *Educational Psychologist,* 20 (4): 167–182.

Salomon, G. (1993). On the nature of pedagogic computer tools. The case of the wiring partner. In S. P. LaJoie and S. J. Derry (eds.), *Computers as cognitive tools.* Hillsdale, NJ: Lawrence Erlbaum Associates.

Savery, J. R., and T. M. Duffy (1995). Problem based learning: An instructional model and its constructivist framework. In B. G. Wilson (ed.), *Designing constructivist learning environments: Case studies.* Englewood Cliffs, NJ: Educational Technology Publications.

Scardamalia, M., and C. Bereiter (1993/94). Computer support for knowledge-building communities. *Journal of the Learning Sciences,* 3(3): 265–84.

Schank, R. C. (1986). *Explanation patterns, understanding mechanically and creatively.* Hillsdale, NJ: Lawrence Erlbaum Associates.

Schank, R.C. (1994). Goal-based scenarios. In R. C. Schank and E. Langer (eds.), *Beliefs, reasoning, and decision making: Psycho-logic in honor of Bob Abelson.* Hillsdale, NJ: Lawrence Erlbaum Associates.

Spiro, R. J., and J. C. Jehng (1990). Cognitive flexibility and hypertext: Theory and technology for the non-linear and multi-dimensional traversal of complex subject matter. In D. Nix and R. J. Spiro (eds.), *Cognition, education, and multimedia: Explorations in high technology.* Hillsdale, NJ: Lawrence Erlbaum Associates.

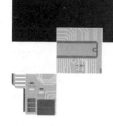

LEARNING BY EXPLORING WITH TECHNOLOGY

In June 1996, in a letter to Congress introducing the report "Getting America's Students Ready for the 21st Century", Secretary of Education Richard Riley said:

> Computers are the "new basic" of American education, and the Internet is the blackboard of the future. But the future is here and now, and we cannot miss this opportunity to help all of our young people grow and thrive. I strongly believe that if we help all of our children to become technologically literate, we will give a generation of young people the skills they need to enter this new knowledge- and information-driven economy. (p. 3)

This conception reflects the beliefs of most computer-literate professionals in the United States. However, after reading this chapter, we hope that you'll agree that "technological literacy" is an inappropriate goal, and the Internet is far more than "the blackboard of the future." Although the Internet is certainly a great source of information (far better than the best of blackboards), its incredible potential as a learning environment to support constructive learning is generally overlooked.

The Internet can immerse students in stimulating, challenging, motivating, vibrant learning environments that provide a context in which computer literacy develops—not as a goal, but as a requirement in order to achieve much higher goals. The skills and attributes of successful professionals in the future [what Ted Sizer (1996) calls "habits of mind"] include, but are not limited to, creativity, problem solving, global awareness, respectful skepticism, cooperation, responsibility, independence, self-discipline, ethics, systems thinking, and (of course) conventional and technological literacy. In "Getting America's Students Ready for the 21st Century", an unnamed high school student succinctly described the real power of technologies:

> Exposure to computers has changed the type of student I am and my methods for attacking problems. I now gain a far better understanding of the topics I pursue, and discover links and connections between them. (p. 20)

We believe that the Internet, if used to engage learners in meaningful learning, has the potential to transform education.

WHAT IS THE INTERNET?

The Internet is a worldwide *network of networks* composed of thousands of smaller regional networks connecting millions of users in more than 90 nations around the globe. These regional networks are composed of still smaller networks that serve institutions, businesses, and individuals who connect their computers to the regional networks via modems and telephone lines. To gain access to the Internet, you need to connect your computer to a network that is part of the Internet, or contact an *access provider* that will allow you to connect to their network (usually via modem and telephone lines) for a monthly or per-hour fee.

The computers on the Internet fall into two main categories: *servers* and *clients*. Servers are computers that offer information to users who access the information using their *client* machines. It's sort of like a high-speed, universal, electronic library system, in which requests from patrons are quickly answered. The servers are like the libraries, and the clients are like the library patrons. Here's how it works.

Each computer on the Internet has a *name*, which may be thought of as an address that uniquely identifies it. Each segment of information made available to the public has a *Universal Resource Locator* (URL) that functions like an address and includes the address of the server on which it is located. You (and the millions of other Internet users) request a certain piece of information by sending a request that contains the address of the desired information to the appropriate server. The server then sends an electronic copy of the information to your computer's address, where software known as *browser* software (like Netscape or Internet Explorer) displays it for you. People talk about the Internet as if they were *going to* an address, using analogies such as *surfing* from one place to another. In reality, the information comes to you. The requests can be made by typing a URL into your browser software, or by clicking on text or images someone has identified as a *link* that will place your request automatically.

Let's look at an example. Figure. 2.1 shows a nice piece of student artwork created by Janice Chow, a third-grade student at Colony Bend Elementary School.

The drawing was part of a document stored at the URL, http://www. fortbend.k12.tx.us/schools/art.htm. The first part of a URL for that document (in this case *http://*) tells you that the document is stored in *hypertext transfer protocol*, the way all documents developed for distribution via the World Wide Web are stored (most of the URLs you will see will start with http://). The next segment of the URL (everything after http:// and before the next slash) is a unique name that identifies the computer acting as the server. In this case the server name is *www.fortbend.k12.tx.us*. The *www.fortbend* is a name given the computer by its owners. Many machine names start with *www* to indicate that they serve information to the World Wide Web.

Figure 2.1   Student artwork on the Internet

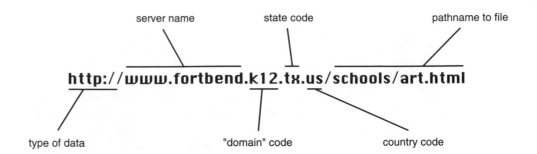

The rest of the server name tells you what kind of organization is providing the service, and often provides information about the nation in which it operates. In the web site shown below, the *k12* tells you that it is a school or district, the *tx* is a state code for Texas, and the *us* is a country code. The rest of the URL is a pathname on the server that identifies the document. In this case, it appears that the document is titled *art.html*, and it is stored in a folder or directory named *schools*.

Table 2.1 is a list of other common domain and country codes:

Table 2.1 Common Domain and Country codes

Code	Type	Code	Country
.com	Commercial	.au	Australia
.edu	Educational	.ca	Canada
.gov	Governmental	.ch	Switzerland
.int	International	.de	Germany
.mil	Military	.dk	Denmark
.net	Internet resource	.es	Spain
.org	Nonprofit organization	.fr	France
.k12	Public school	.il	Israel
		.it	Italy
		.jp	Japan
		.mx	Mexico
		.nz	New Zealand
		.pl	Poland
		.ru	Russia
		.tr	Turkey
		.uk	United Kingdom
		.us	United States
		.va	Vatican

How Large Is the Internet?

It is extremely difficult to estimate the size of the Internet, because it has been growing at the rate of approximately 10 percent per month. According to Classroom Connect (1996), more than 40,000 new Internet services and Internet information locations become available each month, providing services to roughly 20 million users in more than 50 countries. The Internet, as a network of networks, has no owner. Its individual networks have owners, but it is not uncommon for different people and companies to own different parts. Because nobody owns the Internet, there is no single governing body that controls what happens on it or to it.

What's on the Internet?

Physically, the Internet is a worldwide tangle of cables, modems, computers, and other hardware. Most people are less interested in the Internet than they are in the resources and opportunities made available by it. In its early days, the Internet and its ancestors delivered only text. Users sent and accessed text documents only. That has been changing dramatically. Although the majority of information out there is still in the form of text, the Internet is now being used to deliver images (lots and lots of images), animations, sounds and music (and telephone calls), and even short video segments. Access to the Internet usually means access to electronic mail, interactive conferences, information resources, electronic conversations in the form of bulletin boards and network news, and the ability to transfer files from computer to computer and from person to person. These capabilities are being used to inform, to teach, to sell, to connect people, and more.

People talk about the Internet as if it were a place—often a place in space. The term *cyberspace* refers to the places where information is stored; *virtual* refers to a objects in this artificial world. Some people divide the content accessible through the Internet as if it were land to be separated into countries.

The World Wide Web (WWW)

According to Kevin Hughes (1994) in *Entering the World Wide Web: A Guide to Cyberspace*, the World Wide Web is officially described as a "wide-area hypermedia information retrieval initiative aiming to give universal access to a large universe of documents." Think of the WWW as the sum of all documents stored using a multimedia format (hypertext transfer protocol) and made accessible via the Internet. Just as nobody owns the Internet, nobody owns the World Wide Web. Hundreds of thousands of people around the world make information that they create and harvest available to the computer users of the world from their homes, workplaces, and schools.

The Web's vast archive of information of text, image, sound, and video, and its ability to link information together, has captured the attention of educators, while the millions of people (potential consumers) who use the Internet have captured the imagination of businesses. Educators who seek to provide stimulating learning environments to their students are excited by both the resources and the people the Internet brings to the learning enterprise. The connection of millions of people (thinkers, as opposed to consumers) in a real-time environment has opened fantastic potential for human communication and exploration. When combined with a vast array of information at the students' fingertips, the possibilities for exploration and growth seem almost limitless.

What Will We Do with the WWW and the Internet?

What will we do with the power offered us by the Web and Internet? Will it be the blackboard of the future, or will we use it to move beyond blackboards? If it is impossible to transfer knowledge from one person's mind to another's (as we argued in Chapter 1), then the blackboard metaphor breaks down. If the act of exploring and making discoveries in a context rich with challenges results in meaningful learning and the development of cognitive strategies that will serve the learner throughout life, then we need a newer, more powerful metaphor than the blackboard.

Andy Carvin (1996) in *EdWeb: Exploring Technology and School Reform* (http://edweb.cnidr.org:90/web.effects.html) sees four major roles for the WWW in education:

- tutor
- publishing house
- forum
- navigator

While there is power in each of these roles, the Web as *tutor* and Web as *navigator* roles are fairly traditional. In this chapter we will focus largely on the roles of the WWW as *publishing house*, and in Chapter 5 we will look at the WWW as *forum*.

INTERNET LEARNING ACTIVITIES

In Chapter 1, we argued that technologies can help us engage learners in active, constructive, intentional, authentic, and cooperative learning. This chapter will illustrate how the Internet can facilitate that. Most of the ideas in this chapter come from Internet projects initiated by practicing educators responding to calls for collaboration posted on the Internet's *Global Schoolhouse* (http://www.gsh.org/about.htm). The Global Schoolhouse was founded by the Global SchoolNet Foundation through the efforts of some teachers more than a decade ago. With no budget and minimal support, they set out to create an educational information infrastructure starting at the grassroots level—with teachers. A grant from the National Science Foundation in 1992 increased their momentum, and now corporate sponsors help them cover costs of this valuable service to teachers and their students. The Global Schoolhouse is further discussed in Chapter 5.

Supporting Scientific Experimentation

The major premise of this chapter is that the Internet is a tool for facilitating knowledge exploration by learners. Exploration is most effective when learners articulate a clear purpose for their explorations—finding information to solve a problem, resolving an argument, constructing an interpretation, and so on.

Learning Activities   If the Internet is to be more than an electronic baby-sitter, learners must articulate an educational purpose for using it. The following activities show how the Internet can be effectively used.

Following Butterflies.   Several fine examples of Internet use can be found in Mr. Smith's third-grade class at Granger Elementary School, in Granger, Texas (Figure 2.2). We'll use their "Monarch Butterflies" project as an example. Through the Internet, Mr. Smith learned of the efforts of researchers at the University of Kansas, who believe they can understand the migratory patterns of monarch butterflies by figuring out what they had been eating as caterpillars.

Monarch caterpillars eat only milkweed. Since rainwater in different parts of the country contains different levels of an isotope of hydrogen, which changes the characteristics of the milkweed leaves, the researchers believed they could trace monarchs they knew had come from caterpillars that had eaten milkweed grown from rainwater in different parts of the country. The researchers sent milkweed plants on which monarch eggs had been laid to students in different parts of the country, who watered the plant with locally collected rainwater.

As the eggs hatched and the caterpillars grew, the students made careful scientific observations of the caterpillars' size and activities, and they wrote their observations and drew pictures at different stages. Students in Mr. Smith's class exchanged their observations via e-mail with Ms. Lewis's class at Atholton Elementary School in Columbia, Maryland, which they located through the *Teacher to*

Figure 2.2   Butterfly investigation

Teacher link of the Journey North home page. The observations continued from August to December, as the caterpillars turned to adult butterflies, and at the end of the project the students sent two butterflies (one male and one female) back to the University of Kansas for the scientists to study. They kept some adult butter-flies in their classroom, which "laid tons of eggs on milkweed plants inside the cage." From these eggs they got "42 more big fat caterpillars," enough to give away to begin similar activities in two other classes.

During this process, the students created a wonderful Web site, including written observations, drawings, and photographs. They welcome you to visit their site http://www.esc13.tenet.edu/granger/.

Open-Ended, Student-Directed Research Projects. In open-ended and student-directed research projects, students harvest the Internet's vast information bank to learn about topics, generally in order to produce some original work using their new knowledge. *Open-ended* refers to the fact that the students are encouraged to learn as much as they can about the topic, rather than simply to find answers to questions posed by the teacher. Good teachers use these projects to help students develop strategies to determine what information is important—to develop their own set of questions. *Student-directed* implies that the students are in charge, making key decisions about search strategies, about which sites look most promis-ing, about what to collect, about when to initiate conversations with information providers, and so on.

An example of an open-ended research project is Christiansburg Elementary School's TechnoZoo. On their Web site (http://www.bev.net/education/schools/ces/), teacher Cathy Ney reports that the assignment was explained to students in this way: "In order to understand the future survival of many animals, you will design and construct zoo habitats for endangered animals." Teams of four or five students then used the Internet and other resources to find information on the assigned habitats: arctic, South American rainforest, African savannah, American prairie, Australia, and "aquatia." Each team was also given the challenge of saving five animals from extinction, and asked to find certain types of information (habi-tat, predation, enclosure size) on each.

To demonstrate what they had learned, the students built scale models (a great way to incorporate math skills!) of the zoo enclosures they would build to house and preserve the animals, and developed five-minute oral reports describ-ing their work and the thinking behind it. The teams found several Internet data-bases valuable during the project, including animal information databases at Sea World, San Diego Zoo, and Larry's Hotspots.

In another project, classes from different locations conduct simple soil tests and send the results and a class photo to a central site, which analyzes the data, develops maps, and returns the results to participating schools. A similar project dealing with acid rain was sponsored by the National Geographic Society's KIDNET project. Water samples from ponds, streams, and faucets were analyzed locally, then transmitted to researchers who pooled the data and returned them to all sites, where students drew conclusions and compared them with those of other classes. In a similar project, one fifth-grade class asked that students from around the world send actual water samples, rather than data, which the class analyzed.

As another example, consider the National Student Research Center (NSRC) at Mandeville Middle School in Louisiana. The center "facilitates the establishment of Student Research Centers in schools across the country, and it helps students understand and use the scientific method to study problems of interest to them" (contact: John Swang nsrcmms@aol.com).

Although these examples were all scientific in nature, opportunities abound in other subjects as well. Students often use the Internet to collect input for and to distribute magazines, to survey citizens of the world on social issues, and to do research. The goal in all of these projects is to give students an opportunity to *do*, rather than just hear about the subject of study. That is the key to active learning strategies.

Learning Processes   Conducting scientific research is among the most complete intellectual activities that learners can pursue. In defining research problems, seeking evidence using the Internet as well as observing their own studies, and then communicating their results via the Internet, students engage in active, constructive, and intentional learning. Researchers are active because they manipulate environments and observe the results of their manipulations. They are constructive because they are required to articulate the nature of scientific problems, while reflecting on their importance. In order to conduct research, learners must regulate their own performance as well as the activities of that which they are observing. Most of the problems that these students are investigating are authentic. They are complex without a certain answer, and they definitely emerge from the real world. Finally, in order to accomplish most of these activities, student must cooperate with each other in defining and carrying out research topics. Reporting their results via the Internet requires a final and important level of reflection about what they have observed and discovered.

Student Roles   Students as researchers assume a variety of novel roles. They must observe the world and decide what issues interest them. Agreeing on an issue or topic to investigate requires careful negotiation with other students. It is important that no single student or group of students dominates this process. Ownership of learning requires a commitment from all students. Refining the issue or topic into researchable issues requires analysis of the topic for its components and evaluation of each of those components. Having decided on a research topic, students must clarify which issues can be operationalized and how to locate information about each issue. If an experiment is involved, students must operationalize issues into manipulable objects and figure out how to measure their manipulations. Students must then convert their discoveries into some form of communication, which must be represented in text and graphics and converted into html code for the Internet. All of these student activities require a complex set of higher-order thinking skills, independent self-regulation skills, and a lot of practice.

Teacher Roles   Assuming that the teacher is able, his/her primary role will be as coach, prompting the students to consider alternative ideas or views, suggesting appropriate ways of looking at the world and additional ways of operationalizing (e.g., how to find variables and measure them). In some of these projects, the teacher initiated the study, suggesting topics. That may be a useful way to start, but students should assume control of the topics and the issues being investigated. That way, they will have greater ownership of their learning and resulting products. Teachers can also provide tools that scaffold the different tasks involved in the investigation. They may teach students how to use spreadsheets to tabulate data, how to use Web-authoring packages, and so on.

Assessing Learning   Assessing these kinds of learning activities should focus on the investigation itself and on reporting the results of those investigations. You should think about how well the students articulated the issues and conducted the investigation and then how well they communicated it to others. Questions such as these provide assessment criteria:

- How relevant was the topic to the course of study? Did it address issues relevant to your course?
- Were all of the issues identified? Were there redundant issues? How important were the issues to the topic being studied?
- Were the issues carefully articulated? Were variables identified that adequately and accurately described the issues?
- Did students carefully observe and describe these variables?
- Were student investigations of the issues thorough? Did they uncover all of the important issues? Were multiple views and perspectives provided?
- Did students accurately draw conclusions from their observations?
- Did students communicate their results in easily interpretable ways? Were there adequate graphical representations? Was their writing clear?
- Did students develop independent research skills that could be used in other settings?

Creating Home Pages

Constructing knowledge involves attending to and gathering new ideas, comparing those ideas to existing structures, identifying and reconciling apparent discrepancies between what is known and what is becoming known, and modifying the existing knowledge base as required. Papert (1990) has argued that the best way to engender knowledge construction is to support the construction of physical artifacts, building knowledge through building things. Building Web pages is among the most constructivist activities that learners can engage in, primarily because of the ownership that students feel about their products and the publishing effect.

Learning Activities   Most of the activities described in this section resemble those described in Chapter 4, which is about multimedia and hypermedia construction. Since the Internet is including more and more multimedia resources, building Web sites is becoming indistinguishable from building multimedia. So, the learning activities described in this section could have been included in Chapter 4, but were left here because they pertain explicitly to the Internet and so may be more effectively accessed.

Virtual Schoolhouse.   Students at the Andrew Robinson Elementary School in Jacksonville, Florida (with significant guidance from the faculty and administration), have created an amazing Web site (http://www.rockets.org/) that exemplifies a very comprehensive *virtual schoolhouse*. It was created and is maintained by students in collaboration with their teachers and principal, and with significant contributions from local businesses. The site provides an interesting, easy-to-use tour through the school, with lots of information about what goes on and what students are learning. It features lots of student artwork, and many of the drawings of the building are used as clickable maps, so users of the Web site can click on pictures to virtually tour the school. Figure 2.3 shows the lobby.

When you click on a door, you move through it. When you click on the door to the administrative offices, you see a counter, plants, and labeled doors for the principal, assistant principal, counselor. When you click on the principal's door, your screen looks like Figure 2.4.

Each image has many links to other places and information. In the principal's office, for example, clicking on the file drawer labeled Teachers brings up a list of links to information and classrooms of the teachers. Follow the link to the computer teacher's lab, and you'll see artwork of a row of computers, the monitors of which show the names of software the students use (HyperStudio, Digital Chisel, etc.). If you click on one of the monitors, you get information about that software, how the students use it, and more.

Consider the meaning making that went into this project! In addition to the artwork and writing, so many decisions had to be made. "What do we include?

Sketch by Nereus Manning, 5th Grade Student
Please explore our school by clicking on the colored areas.

Figure 2.3   Introduction to a virtual schoolhouse

Figure 2.4   Principal's office in the virtual schoolhouse

What gets linked to what? Who will do what, and by when? How will the work of that group connect to the work of this one?" This project illustrates the results of giving students control over an exciting project. The Internet made it attractive, is the source of lots of feedback on their work, and is the source of many possible extensions of this project.

Where will the students take the project in the future? They saw some Web sites that had developed photographic *virtual reality tours* using a new software product called RealVR. They decided they should add that capability to their site:

> When we decided to add a virtual reality element to our school's Web site this year, we spent a lot of time looking at the various browsers and plugins. We wanted to build with technology that would be friendly to the user and create the feeling of really being there. We chose RealVR because they fulfilled these requirements. We sent them e-mail explaining who we were and what we wanted to do. Very quickly, the CEO was back in touch with us. RealSpace has provided us with their software, and been very generous with their time in answering questions and providing support. (http://www.rockets.org)

The students provided a small sample of what their site will look like when they were done (Figure 2.5). An image in a book does a poor job of conveying what happens on your screen, however. The picture you see moves in any direction. If you hold the mouse button down and drag in any direction, the image

Figure 2.5   Virtual lobby

scrolls. You can turn all the way around (360 degrees) and keep going. You can look up and down, and by using the Shift and Control keys you can zoom in and out.

We look forward to seeing what the students do with this new capability, but we hope they don't use it to replace what they've already done. Their artwork adds personal meaning. They are faced with a series of new decisions to make about how to integrate this new technology with their existing artwork. It is obvious from their Web site that these students are growing intellectually through their use of state-of-the-art tools. This is a great example of how a constructive Internet project gives new meaning to their reading, writing, artwork, communication skills, and computer skills, while causing them to develop in important ways the traditional classroom ignores. Congratulations to the students and their leaders on a great example for us to consider!

Other good ideas that demonstrate the Internet's constructive potential include: creating student Web pages; creating Web pages on topics from the curriculum; creating Web pages on local points or topics of interest; creating Web-based simulations and games; creating collaborative research projects; and conducting open-ended, student-directed WWW-based research. Each of these topics is discussed briefly.

Student Home Pages.   Personal home pages where students describe themselves are very constructive. Most home pages are an individual's attempt to help others get to know the author. They are sort of an informal resume, through which browsers can get a multimedia understanding of someone's interests and accomplishments.

Web pages, whether they are an individual's *home page*, electronic magazines, photo essays, or another form of Web-based publishing, are written in html. HTML was developed to allow multimedia documents to be displayed on a variety of different computers, with different sized screens. This is accomplished by

---

TECHNIQUE

- Obtain a site license to use an HTML editor, like Claris HomePage, HotMetal Pro, or Web Weaver, or use a word processor, desktop publishing program, or multimedia development program that allows you to save as html, such as Microsoft Word, Digital Chisel, or PageMaker.

- Give a home page assignment. Don't be overly directive. There are many sites displaying student home pages in which it is clear that the teachers gave a rather strict assignment, constraining the student's creativity (must have your name at the top, in blue, as a level 1 heading, followed by a hobbies section with three links, etc., etc., etc!). In the best student pages it is evident that students had a lot of freedom and really got excited about it. In the more directive assignments, students seem to get less excited and seem to simply meet the requirements.

- Give students ample opportunity and training necessary to include media, like images, sounds, and perhaps animations and/or short videos.

- Don't let storage space constrain you. Some teachers don't let kids put up a lot of images because they fear they will run out of disk space. The cost of storage space is decreasing rapidly, and it should be relatively easy to get a local business to donate more disk space, perhaps in exchange for some student work.

- Think about and reach consensus about how you will deal with the risks presented by the public nature of the WWW. It is true that there are strange people in the world, and that when students put their work, addresses, and e-mail contact information on the Web, they might be contacted by undesirable people. How will you deal with this? Some schools allow students to put their work up, but not images of themselves (this is a shame, because students really like to have their photos on the Web). Some schools don't allow students to use their last names, or require that all contact come through the teacher's e-mail account. This, too, limits what students get out of the experience. We recommend that you talk about concerns with parents, and train students to report any unusual contacts to their teachers and parents. By doing so, you can leave students open to the much more likely possibility of hearing from the many warm, healthy Internet users whose feedback can enrich their learning experience.

creating a universal *source document* that is a set of instructions interpreted by the browser software (like Netscape or Internet Explorer) designed for each type of computer. The browser software then creates the attractive display that resembles what the author had in mind. HTML is a coding system in which text-only documents are expanded to include *tags* that indicate where to put images, links to other Web sites, changes in text formatting, and more. In the Web's early days we created Web pages by writing the "source document" in a word processor, and manually inserting the hundreds of cryptic tags (a WWW search will reveal many online tutorials that will help you learn to write HTML code). While HTML coding provides lots of opportunities for debugging (a worthwhile cognitive challenge), we are now fortunate to have several HTML editors—for example, Claris HomePage, Page Mill, and Microsoft Front Page—that simplify the process of Web page development and allow us to concentrate on what we want to say and how we want it to appear, avoiding distractions that force us to determine why we didn't get what we had envisioned.

Role-Playing on the Web.   Although home pages usually celebrate the self, students can also create content-oriented Web pages. The primary difference is that the page is about a person other than the student, or is about a topic or place of interest. Why not encourage students to immerse themselves in the topic they are studying by creating a home page for it, as if they were the topic of study? For example, why not have students studying the Colonies during the Revolutionary War develop home pages for famous historical figures or places, in the first person? Imagine Thomas Jefferson's home page (or Ben Franklin's, or George Washington's), through which the world could ask questions that cause students to do research, think from that perspective, and respond. A browser might ask Thomas Jefferson, "What was your quote about government and a coat that was too small, and what did it mean?" or "How did you feel about slavery, and did you think the founding fathers meant the Bill of Rights to mean the way Lincoln interpreted it?" This idea could also be developed to help build a context for students to learn about places and perhaps even concepts ("Hydrogen's home page," or "Water's Web site.)" The appeal of the WWW and its interactive and communicative potential make it a great place to create contexts for learning.   .

Creating Web-Based Simulations and Games.   A relatively new, but powerful option, which gained great momentum with the release of Apple Computer's new product Cocoa, is to create Web games and simulations. With this product, released in its *beta version* in December 1996, Apple may have taken another HyperCard-sized step to release the power of computers to children. Cocoa was designed to offer kids the opportunity to create interactive media, including simulations and games, and deliver their products via the Web.

With Cocoa, elementary students build simple to complex microworlds (see Chapter 6 for a detailed description). These worlds contain objects, and the behavior of these objects is governed by rules. That is, students can create small characters, and then bring them to life. These rule-based worlds and the objects they contain can be used to create games or simulations, which can be used interac-

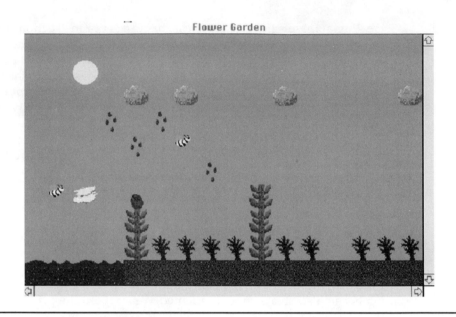

Figure 2.6   Simulation in Cocoa

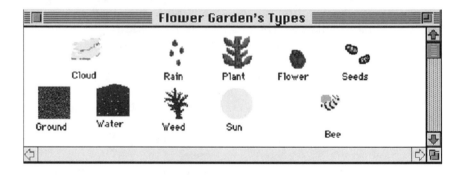

Figure 2.7   Objects in Flower Garden microworld

tively by Internet users with appropriate plugins for their Web browsers. Figure 2.6 is a "Flower Garden," distributed by Apple. On the screen you see what looks like a picture, but it is actually a collage of objects, each of which may have rules that govern its behavior and influence the behavior of other objects. Figure 2.7 shows the types of objects that make up this microworld.

Each of these objects has a series of rules that define how it acts. These rules can specify what happens when, and can range from simple (if there's nothing to the right, move right) to complex (if the object to the right is a flower and if the flower has not yet been pollinated, and if I'm carrying pollen, then pollinate the flower). Many of these rules are established graphically, by dragging objects into proximity of each other, then recording what you want the result to be—by creating *before* and *after* representations. Although it sounds complicated, and in fact it is, it represents an appropriate challenge for upper elementary older kids who find it very motivating and will accept and meet the challenge. Apple makes it sound easier than it really is. They call it Programming by Demonstration, saying "you just show what you want to have happen in a given situation, and Cocoa does the programming for you . . . automagically!" The good news is, it's *not* that easy. It's still a challenge, but one that students can accept and meet. Figure 2.8, for example, is a window displaying the rules that govern the bee in the Flower Garden scenario.

Imagine students working to use this tool to develop a simulation of a simple food chain, or the water cycle, or simply to create a game for others to play. These constructive activities require students to understand the system they are attempting to simulate, and the task of developing a simulation will help them figure out what they don't know.

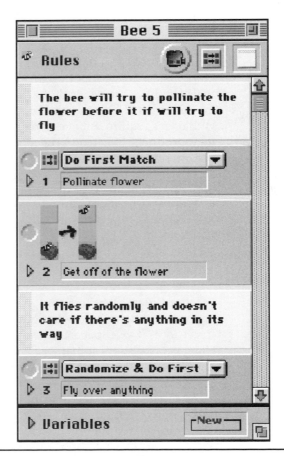

Figure 2.8   Bee controller in Flower Garden simulation

In addition, as students work in this environment they learn (and sometimes even "discover") the basics of object-oriented programming, including important programming concepts like variables, counters, and loops, while having fun and learning content at the same time. Give this exciting new environment a try, but allow lots of time for students to produce projects of value. And remember, the real value is not in the product, but in the process. It's the growth we're after, not the game or simulation itself.

If you're interested in obtaining this product, try Apple's Web site at http://cocoa.apple.com.

Learning Processes   Like multimedia and hypermedia construction, Web-site construction is first and foremost constructive (constructionist, to use Papert's term). In constructing Web sites, students are developing multimedia views of the ideas that they are representing. Web-site construction also involves a lot of intentional learning. Our research with hypermedia construction showed that learners reflect a lot on their designs, making sure that they are desirable and interesting to other students. Finally, Web-site construction normally is complex enough that it requires collaboration among a group of learners. Students will naturally break up into research, authoring, and design teams in order to complete projects.

Student Roles   Student home pages are student initiated and student regulated. Students assume a lot of ownership in their own home pages, probably because their products are available for the entire world to see. They readily assume the myriad research, design, and production roles required to build Web pages. Most Web pages require some research. When students realize that the public will view their products, they tend to be more careful. They must also design the Web pages. Their tendency is to use a lot of graphics, so that their Web sites won't be boring. Most students become very excited over the prospects of including virtual reality in their Web sites. After designing the Web site, they must create the code. Most Web-site production tools make this process easy; however, some html coding is often required. In order to create complex effects, many students (especially in high school) readily learn to use Java and Pearl scripts. Finally, students evaluate and maintain their Web sites, which required reflection on its contemporaneity and effectiveness.

Teacher Roles   Teachers tend to be less prescriptive when students are constructing personal home pages, but our experience has shown that when students construct topical Web pages, it is not uncommon for teachers to play a larger role. However, we suggest that teachers pass this role on to students whenever possible. Suppose, for example, that a sixth-grade class studying the U.S. states and the Canadian provinces decided to make Web pages and then use each others' pages to learn. The teacher might want the pages produced by each group of students to have similar components (say, commerce, population density, etc.) so that students can make comparisons and learn important concepts and principles. Instead of assigning these components, generate a discussion in which the group lists important components. The process of thinking about what is important is a valuable learning experience, and the students might come up with additional useful categories. Don't stifle creativity.

Encourage groups to talk to each other and to create links as appropriate. The Web's ability to support links from one page to another (anywhere in the world) can be a great stimulus to cause students to see relationships they would otherwise have missed, and to explore areas they would have otherwise bypassed. Encourage students to make numerous links to other student-generated work and to work of others out there. Encourage students to contact people who have developed sites to which they are linking. These contacts are often very welcome, and often lead to new friendships and productive learning experiences.

Assessing Learning   Evaluating Web sites can be done analytically or holistically. More often than not, holistic evaluation better reflects student creativity, which is the hallmark of any design project. Merely viewing most Web sites is sufficient for realizing how much effort, how much creativity, and how much mental effort students have committed. If you are looking for some criteria, you might want to try these:

- How is the Web site organized? How complex is that organization? How appropriate is that organization for describing the content of the Web site? Are there adequate buttons for accessing different parts of the Web site?
- What auditory and visual resources were used in the site? How did those resources complement/explain/or illustrate the ideas being conveyed?
- How descriptive were the hyperlinks to different parts of the Web site? Did they describe the information that was being accessed?
- How accurate is the information represented?
- Are all important information sources represented in the Web site?

As you evaluate more Web sites, more criteria should become obvious to you.

Supporting Social Co-Construction of Knowledge Through Collaborative Communication

One of the criticisms of the Internet as a learning tool is that there are so many interesting topics to explore and it is so easy to explore them (they're only a click away), that students are often off-task, following links that take them away from, rather than toward, their learning goal. On the other hand, the information resources made available on the Internet are unparalleled, and a self-regulated learner who keeps the goal in mind, resists temptation, and makes good decisions can find the Internet a fantastic resource during intentional learning. That intentionality is enhanced when a group of learners is committed to the same goals. They regulate each other's performance. There are a number of projects that have maintained students' focus by supporting collaborative meaning making among groups of learners.

Learning Activities   Although we normally think of knowledge construction as an individual process, it can become a social process when students participate in learning communities (see Chapter 5 for a more detailed discussion of learning communities). When people work together and discuss what they are doing and why, participants develop and refine cognitive strategies as well as knowledge. The Internet is an powerful medium for collaboration. The following projects show why.

Surveying Students.   First, consider a project titled *The Milkee Way*. Marva Breden-dick organized this project when she learned that a recent survey suggested that children are not drinking as much milk as they once did. In response to this, she created a project in which students of different ages in many locations around the world will record the amount of milk and other beverages they drink for a week, and will answer questions about their gender, age, and advertising about milk. Students in participating locations will receive the data from all locations, and will be asked to compare their interpretations of the results with the interpretations of other locations. A Web page will be created to communicate the results to the world.

The project leader cites the main purpose of this project as "to help students become aware of the benefits of drinking milk." We are confident that will happen, not because students were told to drink milk, but because they partici-pated in a milk awareness project. In doing so, these students have also learned a lot about how scientific investigations are conducted, as well as about how com-puters work. They will develop reading, writing, and math skills, too, but most importantly, they will wrestle with the processes of interpreting data and turning it into useful information, and making that information available to the public.

Another interesting project, developed at Manor Park Primary School, in Coventry, UK, is called *Birds in the Playground*. The goal of the project is "to observe and record the number and variety of birds that appear in the school grounds and communicate these results with schools in different areas of the world." Participating schools register for the project by providing introductory information about the school (town, country, latitude and longitude, and a general description of climate and local environment), and create a *bird table* or nature area designed to attract birds. The next step is the collaborative creation of a *data collec-tion sheet,* a copy of which is then sent electronically to participating schools. For three months, students in all locations collect data about the birds they see in the school grounds, including a description of the weather conditions at the time of sighting, the birds sighted (English and Latin names, if possible), the numbers of birds sighted, a description of the birds' activities (feeding, flying, courting, etc.), and the dates of sighting. They send the data to a listserv for distribution to all sites once a week. Students examine the data they receive each week from each site, looking for similarities, differences, patterns, and other factors of interest. Teachers at participating sites exchange information on how they are using this project as a springboard for activities in language, math, science, and art classes.

Through this project and others, students at Manor Park Primary School have developed links with schools in the United States, Germany, New Zealand, Australia, and even a rather unusual connection with students in South Africa (http://www.ecosaurus.co.uk/coventry/educatn/primary/manorpk1.htm).

Many but not all of the collaborative projects have science as a focus. A project titled *K–12 Folks Tales from World Communities*, for example, uses the collaborative power of the Internet to focus students on English, reading and writing. The Fahan School, overlooking the Derwent River in Hobart, Tasmania, is the originator of this project, and its Web site (which can be found at http://www.tas.gov.au/fahan/). Children in year 4 at Fahan School have been studying traditional folktales from their local aboriginal community and comparing elements of the Dreamtime stories with those of European traditional folks tales, and now, with stories from around the world. Their Web site is a great launching pad to stories from Indonesia, East Java, Malang, the indigenous people of North America, the indigenous people of Mexico, Iran, the Dalriada Celtic Heritage Trust, Amsterdam, Australia, Romania, and more. When participants send in folktales, they send in paragraphs telling how they learned of the story, and are encouraged to include e-mail addresses to promote collaboration with the tale's readers.

Scrawl Walls.   There is another, less formal way to collect thoughts from the Internet. Through Common Gateway Interface (CGI), a language designed to enable programmers to pass data from one computer application to another, it becomes possible to write programs that allow World Wide Web users to fill out online forms and have the information they provide stored in a database and then used in a variety of ways. Some sites have used this capability to develop what have become known as *graffiti walls* or *scrawl walls* (Carvin 1996). When a user completes a form—say, adding comments about that Web page's topic—the CGI program automatically adds the new contribution message onto the page, where it will become available to other visitors. This is similar to the way that online *chatrooms* work, but the purpose is not to create an exchange between participants in almost real time, but to gather and display information. This might be useful to creative educators and students who went to collect and display opinions in an *online survey*, with the results made instantly available to participants.

Resolving Complex Social Problems.   Life is more complex than most books or lessons make it seem. Most authors and teachers seek to simplify topics for students in order to enhance their ability to understand them. The result is often a superficial understanding of a complex problems. Most social problems require multiple perspectives or viewpoints in order to understand them. To get students to wrestle with appropriately complex problems, teachers need to encourage exploration of those multiple perspectives. Sizer (1996) says we are focused on covering topics rather than developing a deep understanding of them. In the following excerpt, he uses the topic of immigration as an example:

> The function of secondary education is not so much to get students to understand the immigration question as to get them to understand how an issue such as immigration can be understood. That is, the subject matter is but an important foil for enduring intellectual habits. Sloppy work will lead to sloppy habits.
>
> Of course, even after giving major attention to the immigration issue, high school students will not become experts in this field. What they will gain, however, is a sense of the wide sweep of important influences on an issue of this sort

and humility about what they now can and cannot say about the matter. From such humility—an awareness of the complexity of things and of all that one does not yet know—comes deep understanding. (p. 87)

In *International Relations and Foreign Policy in a Post Cold War World* (http://www.nscds.pvt.k12.il.us/nscds/us/seniorseminar/project/main.html), students at North Shore Country Day School discuss foreign policy events and issues as they are reported in their own country, and contrast these reports with reports gathered from around the world. By exploring issues such as foreign policy, the United Nations, and terrorism with peers from around the world, it becomes obvious that these issues are even more complex than they appear when they are viewed from a single nation's perspective.

Another Internet project that promotes complex understanding is *Nuclear Power in Seaside* (http://204.102.137.135/PUSDRBHS/NUKEWEB.HTM), developed by students from Rancho Bernardo High School. This project is designed to help students understand the pros, cons, and complexity of the issue of nuclear power so they can answer the question, "Should a nuclear power plant be built in the town of Seaside?" Students conduct research on the Internet, develop and deliver PowerPoint presentations in a town meeting, and then try to reach consensus on this complex issue.

Another example of addressing complex social issues is North Hagerstown High School's *Prejudice Reduction Through Global Telecommunications* project (http://inet.ed.gov/Technology/Plan/NatTechPlan). Through this project, students from around the world exchanged biographies, essays, poetry, and graphical data via the World Wide Web and e-mail. The understandings they developed by reading submitted work and by communicating with people from other cultures helped them achieve the project's goal.

The Internet is a tremendous information resource for students with good questions. Rather than automatically seeking the wisdom of the teachers, students develop information-seeking skills and gain the satisfaction of answering their own questions. Whether the question is "Why is the sky blue?" or "Why do golf balls have dimples?" the answers and the people who wrote them are probably out there: check out http://www.spacecoast.net/users/dcampbell/chris/whyblue.htm, http://math.ucr.edu/ home/baez/physics/golf.html, or http://www. proqc.com.tw/~wilson/figure_e.html.

Collaborative Authorship. Another interesting Internet project is titled *The Pigman—Chapter Sixteen.* In this project, developed by Eileen Skarecki of Columbia Middle School in New Jersey, students read the popular adolescent novel, *The Pigman,* which, in Skarecki's words "leaves the reader hanging." Her response? Have students write a final chapter, and post the submissions on the Internet for others to read and respond. Collaborating with authors they are reading enhances the reading experience.

This simple activity will help students to think deeply about the book and about writing. It will also encourage them to write with a purpose, to think critically about what they write, to read what others have produced, and to compare their own work to the work of others.

This is but one example of a reflective use of the Internet. Others might include putting students in contact with professionals or hobbyists who will help them think about their work. The Internet also offers great opportunities for peer tutoring. Consider setting up mentoring programs that pair young students with older ones. Such programs have proven to help students at both ends of the mentoring relationship.

It is worth noting that the mere prospect of placing their work on the WWW for public access inspires many students to take their work more seriously and to engage in a level of reflection about their work that is otherwise rare. In addition to this new level of reflection inspired by Web publishing, it is possible to design activities that cause students to be more reflective—to think about their work and the work of others in ways that lead to academic growth.

Groupware Supports.   Responding largely to a global economy in which many corporations have offices distributed around the world, software developers are racing to meet a new market by providing a new line of software products known as *groupware*. These products, including Lotus Notes and First Class, are designed to make it easier for people in different locations to work, think, and learn together.

Groupware products will make it possible for people in different locations to share computer screens and documents, and increasingly audio transmissions as well. For example, suppose that you were helping us to write this chapter. It is now possible for us to make a connection through the Internet that carries our voices and lets us look at a single computer screen, leaving both our keyboards and mice active. We would be able to talk about changes, and take turns making edits—both working on the same document at the same time. All but the audio part of this scenario can be accomplished right now. If we were using a product called Timbuktu and talking on the telephone at the same time, we could do this today.

Today, exchanges between collaborators are usually *asynchronous* (separated in time). In the future, collaborators will work together in *real time*, despite distance, linked by the Internet and its offspring. This will change the nature of electronic collaboration. In some ways it will be for the best, but in other ways today's asynchronous collaborations are better. In synchronous collaboration, one strong partner (faster or more vocal) can overpower other quieter participants, who if given time to produce on their own can make important contributions. And, because time differences will always be a factor between distant locations, the availability of synchronous communications might tend to limit collaboration with partners in time zones that are not too different.

Learning Processes   Social co-construction of meaning through conversation is primarily constructive and cooperative. When joining in conversations, individuals are required to articulate their points of view and to reflect on the perspectives provided by other participants as well as their own. Collaborative discussions are primarily conversational and, of course, cooperative in nature, with individuals contributing to the discussion. What is most significant about this combination of learning processes is the level of ownership that students feel when they are in control of the discussion.

Student Roles   Students assume a variety of roles. They make arguments or provide perspectives, hopefully supporting those perspectives with coherent discussion and evidence. Students will often generate their own topics of discussion. The topics they provide will likely generate much more discussion than teacher-generated topics. Those topics might be voted on by the whole group or provide separate threads of discussion that different subgroups may participate in. The most effective discussion will be monitored and regulated by the students. Self-regulation shows a high level of responsibility and should be the goal of any discussion group.

Teacher Roles   You may begin the process by positing a question or problem, if students don't have one to begin with. Chances are that students will soon generate their own issues or topics to focus discussion on. So the primary role of teachers in this kind of activity is to monitor the discussion. Teachers should continuously monitor the contributions of students to make sure that they are tasteful and to the point. Students who "flame" or needlessly criticize another's perspectives should be censured. A policy that highlights appropriate behavior during a discussion may be appropriate. You may also use this activity to teach students about points of argumentation—that claims should be supported by principles or well- articulated beliefs that should be supported by evidence. Try not intervene in the conversation unless necessary.

Assessing Learning   The quality of any conversation is implicit in the level of interactivity and the nature of individual contributions. Assessing these two factors is the difficult part. To evaluate conversations, you might want to use some of these criteria:

- What were the affective goals of the project? Were they achieved?
- How many learners contributed to the project goals? What was the nature of their contribution—that is, how meaningful were student responses? Were the contributions evenly distributed among students?
- How many perspectives or views were represented? Did groups support their perspectives with evidence?
- Was there consensus provided—that is, did the collaborative project reach any conclusions?
- What information sources were used? Were those sources critically chosen? Did they contribute important evidence?
- How interactive was the collaboration? Did students seek information/ input from all members?

Cybermentoring: Communicating Through the Internet

The Internet provides many different forms of communication. E-mail, listservs, newsgroups, low-end videoconferencing, and even MUDs can be used effectively to get students talking about what they are learning, and to enrich their thinking with input from others (these are discussed in greater detail in Chapter 5). The projects that we describe in this chapter may be redundant to those in Chapter 5, but we hope to communicate the overlap in the ideas that we have tried to convey throughout this book: that technology (in this case, the Internet) can be used to create strong relationships that have the potential to change the learner's perception of the whole learning enterprise.

Al Rogers, a true pioneer in the educational uses of networked computers, has found startling differences in the way schools use the Internet. In *A Visit to Hillside School*, he wrote about how some schools use it simply as a publication medium, missing the major benefits of the conversational potential of the Internet, while others take advantage of this and their students and projects take on new life:

> As I talked to Mrs. Collins and her students, I was bowled over with the contrast with my previous day's visit: These students had stories . . . hundreds of stories . . . to tell about their learning and Web publishing. It was evident that they were excited about what they were doing, and they were eager to share their experiences with me. It soon became evident that their excitement resulted from their interaction with their readers: the conversations and dialogs which grew out of their Web presentations. Their Web server is really a magical door-opener, which brings into their classroom a world of peers and professionals and interesting people who become catalysts for motivating deeper understanding and learning for her students. (Rogers 1996)

All of this begins to make more sense when you start to understand the native medium of the Internet. The Internet is first and foremost a communications medium, not a publishing medium. It was designed to facilitate communications and the exchange of information among people. The new paradigm implicit in the World Wide Web is the ability of the Internet to foster conversations between writers and readers. Given the potential of this kind of interactive dialog, we now see an amalgamation of various strands of educational research of the past dozen or more years. Constructivist and cooperative learning, process writing, authentic assessment, and more are all logical and natural aspects of this new medium. They are built right into the medium. Much of what educational reformers have sought to do is happening as a matter of course in well-designed Internet and Web-based projects (http://www.gsn.org/web/tutorial/intro/visit.htm).

E-mail Mentoring Program: Creating Electronic Advocates for Students at Risk
In an article titled "Using the Internet as a Tool to Reconnect Students to the Educational Process," Kathy A. Kane describes a program at Pennsylvania's Montgomery County Intermediate Unit Youth Center, a detention center designed to return problem students to the normal classroom environment. The program's goal is broader than just correcting unacceptable behavior, however. Educators are working to "develop students committed to lifelong learning, students who are competent, responsible, respectful and contributing members of our society." The program "helps students to connect to their education through: a strong core curriculum that is developmentally appropriate; distance learning; use of the Inter-

net; and on-line mentoring." They understand that the special circumstances of the detention center magnifies the need to engage students in meaningful learning, and they find that technology can help them meet this challenge.

The center's Buddy Project uses the Internet to "bring the world into the classroom, accommodate varied learning styles and paces of learning within one classroom, encourage students to become lifelong learners, develop the students' proficiency in basic technological skills needed to take their places in society, and most importantly, pique the student's curiosity and motivate the learner to seek more knowledge through continued education, by staying in school." Their students perform a variety of Internet-based activities, including creating Web pages, conducting research, publishing their work, and talking via e-mail with professionals who have agreed to serve as mentors.

The mentoring program is extensive, with mentors identified from across the country, who report that they have long wanted to make a contribution, but the travel and the longer sessions required by traditional mentoring have prevented their participation. By eliminating the need to go to schools or homes on a regular basis, replacing that with a series of briefer (but more frequent) electronic contacts, a high-quality pool of mentors has emerged. Their mentors include: scientists working in the biotechnology field; chemists; an attorney for the appellate court of North Carolina; a medical doctor; a retired psychologist; a playwright/educator; a scientific advisor for a patent firm; Montgomery County Health Department directors; a university library conservator; a physicist; a sales representative for San Diego Zoo; an Australian woman who works in La Jolla, California; a scientist who works at Salk Institute in California; a Harvard Law School student; and two chemists who work for the U.S. government who correspond with Spanish-speaking students in Spanish. (The Spanish-speaking students correspond with their mentors in Spanish, so that they can communicate freely, and they translate all correspondence to share with their English-speaking teachers.)

The project reports that the mentoring relationship serves students by:

- Enriching children's lives and addressing the isolation of some students from adult contact
- Providing support and advocacy, personalized attention and care, affiliation for detained students
- Fostering a spirit of success and helping move students toward their education, career, and personal goals
- Providing assistance to define goals and implement a plan to meet goals
- Improving relationships, communication, and writing skills
- Providing the student motivation, knowledge, skills, and solutions to use resources available to succeed
- Providing security of a caring relationship with a responsible adult who will listen to and respect the student's opinion
- Increasing student's regard for people of other races and cultures
- Promoting access to people of different occupational and social worlds

Benefits to the mentor are reported to include:

- Satisfaction derived from helping others
- Personal growth
- Opportunity to make a difference in the future of a young person
- Pride of being selected as a mentor

Like many teachers who understand the power of the Internet, Kane and her team use a variety of Internet-based strategies to produce an engaging school day, and these activities, too, are valued:

> Internet activities improve a student's education by requiring the student to think critically, analyze information and write clearly. Using the Internet as a classroom resource instills problem-solving, discriminatory and organizational skills and teamwork while it improves computer skills and encourages a positive attitude toward learning. Exploring the Internet and contributing original work instills confidence in the student's own ability. When students prepare work for the world to see, they seem to be more careful about spelling, punctuation, grammar and content; be more willing to write, proofread and rewrite; enjoy writing more; be better organized and more fluent, and state their ideas more clearly and with more conviction. The Internet is an invaluable and comprehensive classroom resource. (Kane 1997)

Congratulations to this team of educators who have put technologies to work to create impressive learning environments for students who had been unsuccessful in traditional classrooms!

Learning Processes   Although cybermentoring engages most of the forms of meaning making, the most distinctive characteristics of learning are authentic and cooperative. Cybermentors are from real-world contexts with real-world experience—that is, they are more authentic. Because of that, they are more believable. Successful mentors are collaborators, rather than teachers, as they interact with their pupils.

Teacher Roles   Although student roles vary with the relationship, good mentors maintain an honest and productive conversation with their pupils. Their most important goal is to establish and maintain the student's trust. Having done that, they focus on how their experiences can relate to the students. They should function as coach and cheerleader for the student, rather than purveyor of wisdom.

Virtual Travel   When learning experiences are situated in real-world contexts, as is the case in problem-based or case-based scenarios, learning, retention, and transfer to other situations are enhanced. The Internet, once again, provides a rich set of opportunities for the creative educator to develop context-rich challenges for students to face. Although most of the projects already described in this chapter are context-rich, consider a few more examples.

BikeAbout the Mediterranean   An interesting organization known as Bike-About (http://www.ime.net/~ddg/BikeAbout) provides a context for learning

TECHNIQUE

- The educator who sets up an electronic mentoring program has a crucial role to play. As Kane reports, the relationship that is developed between the mentor and the student is the most important component in the success of a program like this. For this reason, she personally contacted each mentor and outlined the expected outcomes of the mentoring relationship. Kane required each mentor "to agree to give personalized attention and caring, to maintain a positive attitude and high expectations of the student, and to make a commitment to the student to be accessible and responsive in a timely manner."

- Student and mentor must get to know each other quickly. To achieve this purpose, Kane asked all of the Internet mentors to send a short biography through e-mail, and allowed students to read the biographies, select a mentor, and begin to correspond with the mentor. This selection process was, in itself, a valuable learning experience in disguise, because during this process students are engaged in thinking about careers, places, and the attributes of people that make them attractive and useful. Consider using student-generated home pages posted on the WWW as a way for mentors to get to know their students.

- Online mentoring can be a great strategy, but you must do your homework. Make sure that the mentors are good models for sustained contact with students, and make sure they are committed, since a mentor who takes the job lightly can be worse than none. Make sure students and mentors get to know each other quickly. Establish the understanding among students and mentors that they can contact you at any time with any type of information (good or bad). Consider requesting regular reporting, perhaps alternating this responsibility between the student and mentor. And then, step back and let the relationship grow.

about people and places by sending a team of well-equipped riders bicycling through a region sharing their experiences with schools around the world in a variety of forms. For example, their focus for 1997 was on the nations bordering the Mediterranean Sea. Here's how they describe the project:

A pre-selected team of four BikeAbout riders and their computers will set out eastward from the Spanish city of Ceuta located on the Moroccan coast and bicycle the full circumference of the Mediterranean basin, finishing six to ten months and more than 10,000 miles later in Gibraltar. The journey will take BikeAbout and an excited Internet network of schools and enterprises through Morocco, Algeria, Tunisia, Libya, Egypt, the Gaza Strip, Israel, Lebanon, Syria, Turkey, Greece, Albania, Yugoslavia (Montenegro), Bosnia, Croatia, Slovenia, Italy, Monaco, France, Spain, and Gibraltar. . . .

By example and through talks, lectures, presentations and class discussions, including demonstrations of basic on-line services, i.e. email, live on-line "chats" and World Wide Web discussion groups and forums, BikeAbout will highlight the growing importance of cooperative regionalism, international exchange and the use of technology in education, as well as environmentally sound travel and the safe practice of sport.

We're not sure what pedagogical value virtual tours have, except that they can provide personal interpretations of worldly experiences. That must have some value to learners.

CONCLUSIONS

The 1996 report "Getting America's Students Ready for the 21st Century" included a section titled "Characteristics of Successful Technology-rich Schools." That section summarizes a host of research on the effectiveness of technology in schools, and then describes the characteristics shared by the most impressive sites. Here's their summary of the research:

> We know that successful technology-rich schools generate impressive results for students, including improved achievement; higher test scores; improved student attitude, enthusiasm, and engagement; richer classroom content; and improved student retention and job placement rates. Of the hundreds of studies that show positive benefits from the use of technology, two are worth noting for their comprehensiveness. The first, a U.S. Department of Education–funded study of nine technology-rich schools, concluded that the use of technology resulted in educational gains for all students regardless of age, race, parental income, or other characteristics. The second, a 10-year study supported by Apple Computer, Inc., concluded that students provided with technology-rich learning environments "continued to perform well on standardized tests but were also developing a variety of competencies not usually measured. Students explored and represented information dynamically and in many forms; became socially aware and more confident; communicated effectively about complex processes; became independent learners and self-starters; knew their areas of expertise and shared that expertise spontaneously." Moreover, research that demonstrates the effective use of technology is borne out in many successful schools across the nation. (p. 22)

Pay close attention to the last few lines of that paragraph. Many of the major benefits reveal themselves in ways that are not generally measured. The real benefit of students learning with technologies are in higher-order skills and understanding of complex processes. This should come as no surprise if the technologies are used in the ways described in this chapter—to engage students in important, challenging work, and to cause them to discuss this work with others and to think deeply about it themselves.

The report identifies four "key features" these successful schools have in common:

- Concentrated, conscious, and explicit planning among school leaders, families, and students to create "learner-centered " environments
- Clearly articulated goals and challenging standards for student achievement
- School restructuring to support the learner-centered environment and achievement of standards (such as redesigned classrooms and buildings,

changes in the use of time, new methods of delivering curriculum, better partnerships among teachers, administrators, parents, and students)

- Near-universal access to computer technology—at least one computer for every five students (p. 22–23, 25)

There are real benefits to be harvested by putting today's networked computer technologies in the hands of students, especially when students are asked to use those technologies in ways that are active, constructive, collaborative, intentional, complex, contextual, conversational, and reflective. Do some active, reflective, complex, constructive, and perhaps even collaborative thinking *of your own*, and you'll see many opportunities to enhance the learning environment you create for your students.

THINGS TO THINK ABOUT

If you would like to reflect on the ideas that we presented in this chapter, then articulate your responses to the following questions and compare them with others' responses.

1. Why is the Internet far more than the "blackboard of the future?" What does the blackboard imply that limits our conception of the Internet?
2. Why is the concept of technology literacy so limiting? Should we study technologies? If so, how? Have you ever taken a course in washing machine literacy? Why is it unnecessary?
3. The Internet is the connection of thousands of networks. Can you think of an analogy for this agglomeration?
4. Is the Internet hardware, documents, or people? Is it the computers, the programs, and multimedia documents that people store and make available on them, or the people who contribute the ideas? Or is the Internet "only minds"?
5. With the evolution of the Global Schoolhouse, will physical schoolhouses disappear in the future? What evidence can you provide to support your prediction?
6. In the virtual school, students have classmates all over the world. What draws them together? How can that attraction be used to restructure the ways that physical schools operate?
7. Many educators worry about the effect of students' interactions with the world outside the school as they survey other students and the community at large. Are there dangers? What are the educators really worried about?
8. In Chapter 3, we suggest that students make videos about themselves. How are student home pages different from videos? Which is better able to convey the individual?
9. Research has shown that browsing without a purpose probably will not result in focused learning. Yet thousands of hobby-oriented sites exist.

Do individuals learn from exploring their hobbies? If so, what lessons are there for curriculum design?

10. What kinds of tools might be helpful to support student surveys using the Internet?

11. Groupware is becoming more powerful, enabling individuals to share and collaboratively work on text, graphics, sounds, video, or any other kind of file. How will software like this affect the educational process?

12. If you could select a mentor to teach you what you would like to know, who would it be? What would you like to know from him or her? How could the Internet be used to foster that relationship?

REFERENCES

Carvin, A. (1996). *EdWeb: Exploring technology and school reform* (http://edweb.cnidr.org:90/web.effects.html).

Classroom Connect (1996). *Educator's Internet companion.* Wentworth Worldwide Media, Inc., Lancaster, PA.

Gardner, H. (1991). The unschooled mind: How children think and how schools should teach. Basic Books: New York.

Hughes, K. (1994). *Entering the World Wide Web: A guide to cyberspace* (http://www.sr.net/srnet/enteringwww/guide.01.html).

Kane, K. A. (1997). Using the Internet as a tool to reconnect students to the educational process. *Interface* (monthly newsletter of the Montgomery County Intermediate Unit). Available: 1605 B West Main Street, Norristown, PA 19403.

Marsh, M. (1995). *Everything you need to know (but were afraid to ask kids) about the information highway.* Computer Learning Foundation: Palo Alto, CA.

Papert, S. (1990). Introduction by Seymour Papert. In I. Harel (ed.), *Constructionist learning.* Boston: MIT Laboratory.

Rogers, A. (1996). *A visit to Hillside School.* Available online: http://www.gsn.org/web/tutorial/intro/visit.htm.

Sizer, T. (1996). *Horace's hope: What works for the American high school.* Boston: Houghton Mifflin.

U.S. Department of Education (1996). *Getting America's students ready for the 21st century: Meeting the technology literacy challenge.* (http://www.fred.net/nhhs/nhhs.html).

CHAPTER 3

LEARNING BY VISUALIZING WITH TECHNOLOGY: RECORDING REALITIES WITH VIDEO

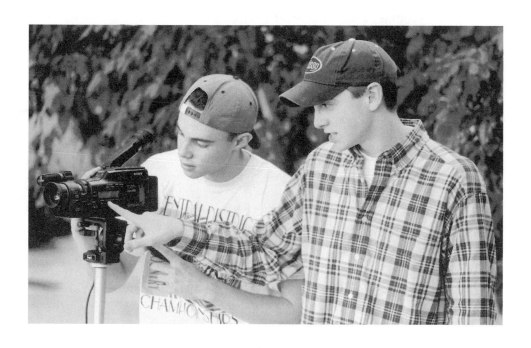

BROADCAST TV (LEARNING FROM) VERSUS VIDEOTAPING (LEARNING WITH)

Commercial television stations began broadcasting in the United States in the post–World War II years, quickly revolutionizing the ways that Americans entertained themselves. A country inured to attending movies in public theaters suddenly began to stay home and stare at their nine-inch television screens. As with every technological development in this century, educators immediately considered how this nascent technology could be used to teach. Commercial entertainment eclipsed educational programming, as with most technologies. [Interestingly, the Internet (see Chapter 2) emerged in the public sector and is predicted to become dominated by commercial interests. Stay tuned.]

Educational television (ETV) emerged in the early 1950s as several universities began offering telecourses. More often than not, these courses consisted of professors, supported with a variety of visual aids, lecturing at the cameras in much the same ways that they lectured in halls around campus. Many college courses began to be delivered exclusively by television. And for two decades, thousands of research studies compared the effectiveness of those televised courses with traditional courses. Most of the research was so poorly conducted that meaningful conclusions were impossible (Chu and Schramm 1967; Reid and MacLennan 1967). The remaining research showed generally that televised instruction was just about as effective as traditional—not a startling conclusion, since television teachers were teaching in front of cameras in the same ways they were normally taught in front of classes.

In the 1960s and 1970s, the scope of ETV expanded with the emergence of the public television network. Telecourses became miniseries, which began to exploit the capabilities of the medium, focusing less on college courses and more on public information, news, and cultural programming. The formation of the Public Broadcasting System ushered in many excellent programs and series that were hailed as cultural successes (e.g., *Civilization* and *Cosmos*) despite the fact they are rarely viewed by more than 5 percent of the population. Why has ETV, which had the potential of starting a cultural renaissance in the United States, been perceived as so successful, yet had so little effect on education? Why has television, which is the most universally common communication medium in the world (available in more than 95 percent of U.S. homes) had so little effect on the ways that we learn within the educational system, yet such a profound effect on the ways that we perceive the world?

The Case for Television

Although much of the content of commercial television is vapid, vulgar, and violent, television also supplies us with a rich collection of cultural, informational, and educational programming. Hundreds of instructional programs have been broadcast and thousands more are available on videocassette. Instructional and educational programming, such as *Sesame Street* and *3-2-1 Contact* from the Children's Television Workshop, employed teams of learning psychologists, educators, and television producers to design and produce the best educational programming possible. By 1980, thousands of high-quality, commercially prepared television programs were available, either broadcast via state networks or available on videocassette, to supplement classroom instruction. It was widely believed by producers and educators that these programs could not fail because they consisted of high-quality audiovisual messages that exposed students to experiences and cultures throughout the world that they could not be exposed to otherwise, brought multiple viewpoints into the classroom, and presented new content in the classroom that teachers could not possibly know. Television has provided a common ground for conversation and understanding internationally; it contributes to the fund of general knowledge; and provides the closest thing we have to a democratic information medium (Wagschal 1987). While all of these arguments for television are true, there exist implicit limitations to the effectiveness of television viewing for school learning. Two reasons for this lack of efficacy were examined in the 1970s: the way that television programs were integrated into the classroom and the ways that children viewed the television messages.

In order to foster meaningful learning from broadcast or videotaped instruction in classrooms, that instruction needs to be properly integrated into classroom instruction. Teachers were taught that they should preview and evaluate programs before using them; prepare students for learning from television by introducing new vocabulary, providing overviews and advance organizers; remain with students and encourage active viewing of the television program; and follow up the program by summarizing, reviewing, discussing, and evaluating the content learned by students (Jonassen 1982). The problem was that teachers seldom performed these integrative activities. Television became an electronic baby-sitter or substitute teacher in too many classrooms. When students realized that they would not be responsible for understanding any of the messages from the television shows, they usually did not attend actively to the shows, repeating their well-rehearsed home-viewing habits in school. In an attempt to change those habits, educators attempted to change the passive reception of television messages by teaching children to become critical viewers of television.

During the 1970s, many educational and children's advocacy groups, such as Action for Children's Television, developed and promoted critical viewing curricula to ensure that elementary and junior high school students (especially) did not just watch television, they monitored it. While watching TV, children should be aware that TV programs and their messages are created to achieve specific results, that each person interprets programs and messages differently, that TV violence may take many forms, and that TV programs have an underlying economic purpose (National Cable Television Association 1995). Most of these critical viewing curricula taught children how television and television production work, the components of entertainment television stories, the purpose of commercials and how to view their claims critically and become informed consumers, how their lives differed from television characters, that television violence should not be imitated, and how to get the most from television news programming—generally, how to be critical viewers of the medium (Hefzallah 1987). In order to take charge of TV viewing, it should become a conscious, planned-for activity, an interactive family event that should provide springboards to other learning experiences (National Cable Television Association 1995). Potter (1976) best articulated these springboards by describing how commercial television could support the development of reading, thinking, math, and social studies skills—especially from reading television scripts and books about television, thereby developing valuable language skills. The major purpose of these critical viewing efforts was to make sure that children became aware of television's persuasiveness in terms of how much and what kinds of television they viewed, and to teach children to view commercial advertising skeptically. However, only a small minority of children have ever been exposed to these critical viewing curricula, while a majority of children continue to spend 25–30 hours per week in front of the television (more than in classrooms, and six times more than working on homework). Very few children, it seems, view television critically.

The Case Against Television

Can students learn from viewing television programs? What are the effects of entertainment television viewing on learning and study habits, and does such viewing affect the abilities of students to think and learn? These have become important questions for teachers and parents in the past two decades.

The major reason that students do not successfully learn from watching televised instruction is that they are not mentally engaged by it. Salomon (1984) found that learners thought that learning from television was easier than learning from reading, so they did not try as hard when watching television programs. This differential investment of mental effort results in less learning from television because it is passive. Learning from television cannot be effective unless learners are helped to actively process television messages and think about them. We agree with this amount-of-invested-mental-effort argument and must conclude that the reason that television has failed to enlighten students is that viewing prerecorded television programming does not sufficiently engage learners in active, constructive, intentional, authentic, and cooperative learning (which, incidentally, is the goal of this book).

Salomon's research has been confirmed by a considerable amount of reading research. Beentjes and van der Vort (1988) reviewed a great deal of international research, concluding that television's negative effects had the greatest impact on advanced cognitive abilities needed for understanding, and that television:

- Displaces leisure reading
- Requires less mental effort than reading
- Reduces children's attention span and tenacity in solving problems

Ironically, these effects are greatest on socially advantaged and intelligent children, who are heavy viewers.

Why are children not engaged by watching television? Because watching TV does not fulfill any purpose. It is not intended to fulfill any cognitive objective. More often than not, the only reason for TV watching is to kill time. In order for television to foster learning, learners have to have a reason for watching it. They should be seeking answers or confirming hunches, either about themselves or about some problem that is presented on the television show.

Why is television programming not supportive of learning? Because most research and development, even with instructional television programming such as *Sesame Street*, has been conducted to make television programming more alluring. The small amount of quality research that has been conducted confirms that television viewing has three primary effects on children's learning abilities (Healy 1990).

First, children's attention to the fast-paced auditory and image changes is fragmented, which causes attention disorders when trying to perform complex cognitive tasks, especially those that require sustained attention. This has been referred to as a lack of vigilance, meaning that children maintain a low state of alertness. The inability to pay attention by those who watch a lot of television makes it more difficult for them to stay actively focused on complex learning tasks. If material is the least bit boring, they stop paying attention unless something alerting or salient happens, as it always seems to in most commercial and many educational television programs.

The second major effect of television viewing is a lack of persistence. Because of the fast-paced, ever-changing nature of the image, television requires little sustained effort. So, if materials being studied are not readily understandable, TV viewers tend to give up more readily.

Third, viewers become readily "glued" to the tube. That is, their brain activity slows down, causing a hypnotic, trance-like state while viewing. This form of addictive behavior is obviously not conducive to active learning. Wagscahl (1987) also cites the simplicity (lowest common denominator) of most television programming, trivializing everything so that it is impossible to distinguish fact from fiction. Other critics, like Marie Winn, have examined the social isolation that television viewing brings about, reducing interpersonal interactions among children, increasing irritability of children, and causing a disintegration of the family unit.

We must conclude that despite attempts to improve the ways that teachers use television and the ways that students view it, television viewing (watching television to learn lessons without a clear, cognitive purpose) is not sufficiently active or constructive enough for learners to engage in meaningful learning. Leisure television viewing habits appear to be impossible to discard when the content is educational. Also, and more perversely, heavy television viewing affects the ability of students to pay attention, stay on task, and make sense out of what they are viewing. Our solution is simple. If students are to view television, then give them a good reason for using television to find meaning (e.g., the *Jasper Woodbury* series, described later in this chapter). More effectively, let students produce video rather than watch television. The process can and will engage them in active, meaningful learning.

The Case for Video

The premise of this chapter, as reflective of the entire book, is that television is a powerful learning tool when students are critical users and producers of television, rather than consumers. Producing videos requires learners to be active, constructive, intentional, and cooperative. Video production requires the application of a variety of research, organization, visualization, and interpretation skills, similar to those engaged by producing multimedia, as enumerated in Chapter 4. Producing videos engages critical and creative thinking in order to plan and produce programs. Additionally, there are a variety of social values of producing videos in schools (Valmont, 1995):

- Improving students' self-confidence by planning, producing, and sharing video productions in class
- Producing feelings of self-satisfaction
- Providing valuable feedback to students about how others perceive them
- Fostering cooperative learning while sharing ideas, planning and producing programs, and evaluating outcomes
- Providing great public relations at open houses and other school functions

As mentioned earlier, there are thousands of research studies on learning *from* television. However, there are relatively few studies on learning *with* video. We argue in this chapter that students will learn more by creating videos than by watching TV. We hope that this belief and the assumptions that it rests on will be researched more in the future.

In this chapter, we will describe a number of learning activities where television can provide meaningful learning contexts that can engage learners when they identify a purpose for viewing the program in order to find information and solve problems. However, most of the activities described in this chapter make students television producers. As producers, teachers and students need to understand a little about video production hardware, which we describe next.

VIDEO HARDWARE FOR THE CLASSROOM

Using video to engage meaningful learning requires three things: imaginative students willing to take chances, ideas for how to engage them, and some equipment. The equipment may be the easiest part, so let's briefly describe some of the hardware that you will need first. Following that, we will provide numerous ideas for engaging learners. You will have to provide the students.

In the 1960s and 1970s, producing educational television programs required teams of directors, engineers, camera operators, lighting technicians, and a host of others to run the bulky and expensive production equipment. A studio would include large cameras, sets, and thousands of watts of lights, while the control room included floor-standing videotape recorders, engineering consoles for controlling the video image, audio mixing boards, and a director's console, all in a separate room from the studio. Since then, video equipment, like computers and most other hardware, has become incredibly smaller, cheaper, and more efficient. Today, an entire studio of equipment has been crammed into a single small box, the videocamera (otherwise known as a camcorder). We will briefly describe videocameras and some auxiliary equipment that you will need to use video in the classroom.

Videocameras.   Videocameras are small recording systems in a box. They include a lens for visually capturing images, a video pickup tube for converting the image into 525 lines of television image (the standard in the United States), a cassette transport system, a videotape recorder for encoding those lines of television images onto video-cassettes, and a small viewer or monitor for viewing the image as it is being recorded or during playback. Only a few years ago the capabilities of the videocamera required several pieces of "portable" equipment, including a 20-pound camera mounted on a tripod, a 50-pound recorder connected to the camera via a cable, and a special-effects keyboard and generator. All of this equipment had to be plugged into electrical outlets in order to operate. All of that is now compacted into a battery-powered recording system that can fit in the palm of your hand (see Figure 3.1). The standard recording unit uses 1/2-inch VHS videocassettes, although 8-millimeter units and the smaller VHS-C units are also popular now because of their even smaller size. Digital video-cameras are now available. These cameras record and digitize information at the same time, producing broadcast-quality video. Although they are expensive now ($3,000 or more), their costs should drop soon. Whichever format you choose, all of your recording, editing (described later), and playback equipment must be the same. We recommend VHS because it is the most reliable and commonly used format in schools, so student productions can be played back at home or just about anywhere.

Most videocameras feature the following (Figure 3.2):

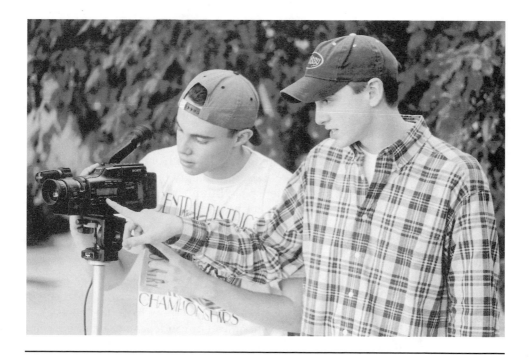

Figure 3.1   With a modern videocamera, students can film at remote locations.

Figure 3.2   Modern videocamera

- Zoom lens (often 12:1 ratio in focal length) with electronic zoom controls and automatic focusing
- Built-in viewfinder monitor
- Videocassette recorder with record, playback, fast forward, and rewind controls, and playback through the viewfinder
- Built-in microphone and jack for external microphone
- Battery (for shooting without electrical outlet) and AC adapter to electrical outlets
- Automatic and manual video controls for adjusting light levels, white balance [for different sources of light of light (daylight, incandescent, fluorescent], and shutter speed [number of images per second)]
- Separate jacks for inputting and outputting audio, video, or RF (for playing back through regular television)
- Character generator for adding titles, time, and/or dates to your video programs
- Special-effects generator (fades, wipes, dissolves)

The recording procedures will vary slightly from videocamera to videocamera, so we will not attempt to show you how to do these things. You should consult the manual that accompanies your videocamera and experiment extensively with your equipment before trying to use it for learning.

The backbone of student video productions is the videocamera, so we suggest that you purchase as many videocameras as possible, so that different student groups can work on projects simultaneously. For important or complex video productions, different students can record the same events from different angles or perspectives. Modern videocameras range from $500 to $1,000, based on their features. We also recommend that for every videocamera you acquire, you purchase a stable tripod to hold the videocamera steady while it is being used. The tripod also permits individuals to videotape themselves.

Monitors/Televisions.   Although most videocameras are capable of playing back recorded videos in the viewfinder, viewing through the viewfinder is limited to a single individual, and the quality is not very good. Learning through video is completed when students critique and reflect on their productions, so you will need to acquire a large television set or monitor for playing back student productions for the class. Monitors are preferable. They permit viewing of video and audio images directly from the tape. Normal television sets are able to play only "modulated" RF (radio frequency) broadcast TV signals (the kind that are transmitted from broadcast towers or received via cable). Most modern videocameras have modulators built in to enable playback on regular TV sets, which are cheaper than monitors. Monitors are more flexible. They can be used with editing equipment (discussed later), producing clearer images that are less susceptible to electrical interference, but are more expensive. Whichever you get, your televisions should have at least 20-inch screens, though larger is better for most classroom-viewing situations. You will probably want to purchase an audiovisual cart to move the monitor/television around, since they are bulky. The monitor is extremely valuable. Most of the social values of producing videos in schools rely on group viewing of the videos. You may also want to purchase a videocassette recorder (VCR) for playing back tapes in order to free up the videocameras for use elsewhere. The standard VCRs that populate most American homes are commonly available for less than $200 and are fine for replaying videotapes in the classroom.

Editors.   Most television productions these days, even professional productions, have moved out of the studio and onto location. Rather than building large, expensive, single-purpose studios and sets, television producers are shooting with portable equipment on location and editing the location tape into a television show. So, rather than re-creating a historical setting, for instance, they will go to the original setting to shoot. When they have finished shooting video in one setting, they will go to other scene location to shoot. When all of the shootings in the various locations have been completed, they end up with a large number of disconnected scenes on different videocassettes. In order to arrange those disconnected scenes into the coherent program envisioned in the script, the videotape sequences must be assembled into a program. When film was the most common visual medium, this assembling process was accomplished by cutting the piece of film on which scene 1 was shot and gluing it (literally) to the piece of film on which scene 2 was shot. The scenes were glued together into a sequence. With video, this process is done electronically using an editing suite. The most common kind of editing suite consists of a playback machine, an edit controller, and a videocassette recorder (see Figure 3.3). Scene 1 is played back on the playback

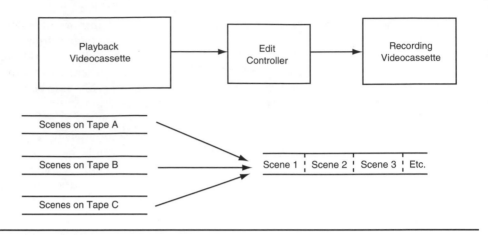

Figure 3.3   Common type of editing suite

machine, which is controlled by the edit controller, which copies the scene from the playback machine onto the recorder. Each scene is added to the end of the previous one. More expensive editing systems permit the producer to insert scenes in the middle and add special-effects transitions between scenes, so scenes can dissolve, fade, or wipe into the next scene. Editing suites are fairly expensive additions to your video-recording capabilities (from $1,000 to 10,000, depending on quality and capabilities).

These editing functions can also be accomplished on multimedia computers with movie-making software, such as Adobe Premiere. In order to edit on computers, the video scenes must be digitized into a computer file. A cable connects the Video Output from the videocamera to a Video Input on the computer (not all computers are equipped with video boards, although most multimedia computers are). As the video is played back on the videocamera, it is captured (digitized, i.e., converted into a digital computer file) on the computer where each scene can be assembled into a QuickTime movie using an amazing variety of transitions and visual embellishments. The video can be colorized, posterized, or visually manipulated in a variety of ways. Computer editing is fast and convenient. Our experiences have shown that kids readily learn how to perform sophisticated editing. The major disadvantages of computer editing are related to cost. In order to edit, you will need an expensive multimedia computer with a lot of memory, both random access memory and disk storage. Video files on the computer require large amounts of memory to store, so an external storage device will be needed. Additionally, computer software that allows you to edit video is fairly expensive. If this kind of equipment and software are available, then computer editing may be a desirable option. For long video programs (more than a few minutes), more traditional videocassette storage may be necessary (see Figure 3.4).

Figure 3.4 Students can quickly learn to edit videos.

Microphone. The only other piece of equipment that you may want to consider purchasing is a microphone or two. All videocameras have a built-in microphone, so that whenever you record video, you are automatically recording audio as well. These microphones tend to be very sensitive, omnidirectional mikes. That is, they record sounds coming from all directions. Although this is a convenient way to record ambient sounds, you may also record camera and operator sounds (breathing, talking, jiggling, walking), which can be distracting to the message you wish to record. An external, omnidirectional microphone can be plugged into all video-cameras, reducing the operator sounds (see Figure 3.5). Moving the microphone closer to the source of the sound improves the quality of the sound. In some cases, such as an interview, you may want to use an external, unidirectional microphone (sensitive to sound from only one direction—the direction in which the microphone is pointed). A good choice here would be a lapel mike, a tiny microphone that you clip to your lapel. Decent microphones can be purchased inexpensively (less than $50). Be sure to get one with a fairly long cord.

Summary. Most of the activities described in this chapter require only a video-camera and a television monitor. The more video production that you do, the more adventurous and demanding your students are likely to become, so the more equipment you will want. As money is collected from the school budgets, grants, car washes, activity fees, benefactors, or other sources, your video production facilities can be embellished.

Figure 3.5 An external microphone can improve sound quality.

VIDEO LEARNING ACTIVITIES

Video is, for the time being, the most familiar communication medium for students. Children are intimately familiar with the syntax and semantics of television, the ways that ideas are conceived, visualized, organized, and presented. Unfortunately, that experience is purely for entertainment and not for learning. With few exceptions, educational television is normally anathema to most students. Two of those exceptions are the *Jasper Woodbury* and *Scientists in Action* series, which are presented first. In these cases, video is used to convey an interesting problem that students are required to solve. Most of the remaining video learning activities in this chapter describe students-as-video-producers. When students become producers of video, rather than viewers, they naturally assume more active, constructive, intentional, authentic, and cooperative roles. Because of their familiarity with video, students are able to easily assume roles as directors, producers, camera operators, set designers, and actors, and they enjoy it. They construct their own understanding for ideas by representing them to others through this familiar medium. Most important, they have ownership of the product, so it naturally has more meaning to them. The final two learning activities engage teachers in the same kinds of constructive learning experiences as the students.

Jasper and Scientists: Anchoring Instruction

Learning Activity   The Cognition and Technology Group at Vanderbilt University (CTGV) has developed and tested video-based instruction that is designed to help students to reason, think, and solve problems. They engage students in these processes by creating what they call a macro-context, which is a reasonably complex everyday situation and story that contains a problem (CTGV 1992). In solving the problem, students are required to write persuasive essays, do informal reasoning, explain how data relate to their investigation, and solve complex problems that require mathematical reasoning. These problems are different from textbook problems, which apply only the skills covered in the chapter. These problems require learners to figure out necessary subproblems, generate solutions, develop arguments and explanations to support the solutions to those subproblems, and finally to assemble those subproblems in a sequence necessary to solve the overall problem.

Most students who are successful in solving textbook problems find it difficult to solve these complex problems. The problems are embedded in an adventure story that is represented with high-quality video. In one program, Jasper Woodbury, the hero, goes fishing in the wilderness, where he comes across a wounded eagle. He uses his radio to correspond with his friends, who decide to use an ultralight aircraft to rescue the eagle. However, calculating the route requires that they consider several variables (wind direction and speed, aircraft speed, fuel capacity, location of the veterinarian, the meadow, and the gas station, etc.). The final solution requires the identification and solution of more than 20 subproblems. All of the information needed to solve these various subproblems is embedded in the video. The students need to search the video in order to find the needed information after they have determined what they need to know.

In another series, *Scientists in Action*, science learning begins with a problem, such as the *Overturned Tanker* (Goldman et al. 1996). A tanker truck, containing an unknown but obviously toxic chemical, has overturned on a highway. The tank has ruptured and the chemical is spilling into the creek. The video portrays a day-in-the-life of a hydrologist and a chemist, who are called into action following the news story about the tanker. The video ends, and students are left with the tasks of figuring out what the chemical is, how it may affect the stream, and whether it is likely to flow toward the lake or the city. Using authentic materials (topographic maps, chemical test kits, and emergency guidebooks), they have to develop a plan of action. They check their responses against the experts' when the video resumes to present more information and more problems. The purpose of the program is for the students to solve problems similar to those that real scientists would solve—ergo, scientists in action. With both sets of materials, the research conducted by CTGV has shown that students, even special-education students, can successfully solve these contextualized problems because the problems are interesting and engaging, and students' problem-solving skills transfer positively to new problems. Scientists are problem solvers. Anchored instruction causes learning to happen by presenting students with real-world problems.

The important elements of these macro-contexts are that they are video-based, use a narrative format, require learners to generate the ending, embed the needed information in the story, and are complex and realistic enough to be challenging

(CTGV 1992). Video was chosen because it can convey the setting, characters, and actions in a more interesting way. Video also allows the portrayal of more complex and interconnected problems and helps learners to form their own mental models of the problem. The other very important characteristic is the story format. Stories are understood and remembered better than expository materials. Obviously, it is more engaging to the students than textbooks are. This model of instruction is known as anchored instruction, where the learning and thinking are anchored by a realistic, video-based problem. Anchoring learning in rich contexts is becoming an increasingly popular approach to learning in schools and universities.

Learning Processes   The primary characteristic of meaningful learning that is exemplified in anchored instruction is authentic. Learners who work on meaningful, real-world tasks or simulated tasks in complex, case-based or problem-based learning contexts better understand and transfer what they learn to new situations. Seeing ideas embedded in a real-world context makes them more understandable. For instance, showing students videos of native French speakers conversing in real-world contexts throughout the school year enhanced the listening comprehension of the students in a French class (Secules, Heron, and Tomasello 1992). Student modeling of complex performances is better than student regurgitation of ideas. Anchoring instruction in authentic contexts makes learning more real.

Needless to say, students engaged in solving complex problems are active learners. They must carefully observe the video, looking for important pieces of information that they use to construct a solution. Constructing the solution requires that they continuously articulate what they know about the problem and reflect on its sufficiency for solving the problem. Finally, anchored instruction problems are usually solved collaboratively in groups. Cooperation requires that the group share the goal of solving the problem and discuss what they need to do in order to solve it.

Student Roles   Students assume responsibility for solving the problem. If the problem is interesting enough, students see it as a challenge. The more that they strive to solve it, the more ownership they have. The more ownership that they have for the problem, the harder they will try to solve it.

Teacher Roles   In order to support solving anchored instruction problems, the teacher functions as a coach. When students inevitably encounter difficulties in solving these complex problems, the teacher needs to prompt students for the next step by asking questions or suggesting things to think about—not by giving them the answer. If students learn that every time they encounter problems the teacher gives them the answer, they will cease to be engaged by the problem. The teacher also needs to help students to set realistic goals for themselves—that is, to identify potential steps in the solution process and to assign time, effort, and responsibility for achieving those steps. Teachers may also model problem solving by accepting another problem and showing students how they would solve it. When modeling performance, it is important not only to model the solution process but also to reflect on the reasoning used to solve each step ("This is why I did this. . . "). Generally, the teacher's role in anchored instruction should not be a direct teaching role but rather a supportive, coaching role—prompting, encouraging, and providing feedback.

Assessing Learning: Creating Your Own Macro-Contexts and Stories
Anchored instruction is especially effective in the sciences, math, and social studies; however, there is a shortage of anchored instruction problems around. One way to alleviate that shortage and also to assess learners' understanding of the kinds of problems they are solving is to have students design and produce their own problems, and embedding them in their own video-based macro-contexts. Having students create their own problems is the clearest way to assess whether students can transfer their learning.

Understanding the concepts and principles well enough to generate a new problem is one of the most complex forms of thinking possible. In order to do this, students need to identify a problem and design a story that engages other students in solving them. In developing these stories, it is important for the students producing the macro-context to set up the problem, but not to solve it. The video should take learners to the point that they ask, "What do we do next?" Also it is important that all of the information needed to solve the problem is included somewhere in the video story, not as a litany of facts but rather as a part of the story. This is a difficult task—one that students should find challenging but very enjoyable. The problems that students create can be assessed using the following criteria:

- Is the problem representative of the kind of problem in the lesson objective?
- Is all of the information needed to solve the problem contained in the story?
- Is the story interesting enough for other students to accept?
- Can students articulate the steps needed to solve the problem?
- Can students help other students to solve the problem?

Students love to produce problems for their teachers and other students. That is a meaningful challenge that they readily become absorbed in. Anchored instruction provides a powerful model for engaging students in problem solving. Problem solving is necessarily more meaningful that memorizing information from textbooks and lectures.

Video Press Conference

In most classrooms, the teacher and the textbook are the intellectual authority. They represent the truth, and it is the students' responsibility to understand the world as they convey it. In this next video-based activity, students learn by becoming the authority for ideas being learned. What is most challenging is that they have to subject their authority to the queries of their peers.

Learning Activity   In most press conferences, an expert or a spokesperson makes an announcement, describes a new product or process, or explains some actions. Most of us are familiar with the press conference format through our viewing of news programs. If students are not familiar with this format, then videotape a couple of press conferences and show them to the class.

What should students conduct press conferences about? One way to make students responsible for understanding the discoveries, findings, or beliefs of experts or controversial topics is to play those experts or their representatives in a role-playing press conference. For example, in studying beginning genetics, let students play Crick and Watson, while the rest of the class asks questions about their DNA discovery. In social studies, let students assume the role of prominent people, such as presidential candidates, the secretary of state, governor, mayor, or any other prominent political figure who has to defend legislation, new regulations, or plans for a new project. A quick perusal of any newspaper will provide numerous topics. The more controversial the topic, the more animated the conference is likely to be. In English class, let students assume the role of important literary figures or writers who just published a new book. They have to learn enough about the person and the work of literature to be able to discuss it. There is no subject area where press conference cannot be used. It is especially effective in foreign language classes, since it provides another reason for students to think and communicate in the foreign language. Have students conduct the press conference in Spanish, French, German, or whatever language the students are studying. Have the student(s) being interviewed assume the role of prominent, social figures (such as an entertainment star) from that country.

Conducting a press conference is easy. You simply need to install a podium in front of any normal classroom, and you have a useful set for a press conference. Open the press conference with a prepared, two-minute statement from the expert in whatever language or style is appropriate (students need to study the people they are portraying intensively enough to render a meaningful portrayal). Following the opening statement, open up the conference for questions and answers.

Individual press members can identify themselves and the organization they represent, in order to add another layer of interest to the exercise. The press members need to be prompted to ask Who, What, Why, When, Where, and How questions. A good way to practice this questioning performance is to play "Five W's and H," where students write questions while watching a news story (Stempelski and Tomalin 1990). You may want to prompt students with specific issues to construct questions about. This scenario can be adapted by asking the real people to attend class and allow students to "grill" them.

VIDEO TECHNIQUE

Press conferences require limited set design and camera capabilities. The set consists of a podium, commonly available in most high schools. If not available, one can be simulated by propping up a piece of plywood on top of a table in front of the classroom. Try to position the podium opposite the classroom windows—certainly never in front of the windows. Additional scoop lights, available inexpensively at most hardware stores, or a line of fake microphones in front of the podium, can add realism to the set.

For this exercise, only a single camera is required. If you are operating with only one video camera, the camera operator should mount the camera on a tripod and posi-

---

(continued on next page)

tion it toward the back of the audience (classroom). Most of the time, the camera will be focused on the speaker, holding a medium shot or "waist shot" (from the waist up). Leave a little (but not too much) headroom at the top of the frame. As students from the audience ask questions, the operator can zoom out a little and pan the camera right or left to include the questioner, zooming back as the speaker begins to talk. If you are using two cameras, leave one focused on the speaker and position the other in the front corner of the classroom so that the operator can shoot the questioners from the front. Those shots should be a medium or bust shot (bust to the top of the head).

We would recommend using an external microphone connected to the video camera. There is a lot of ambient noise in a classroom (coughing, shuffling, etc.), so a microphone on a stand placed directly in front of the speaker will produce much better audio, as well as add some authenticity to the scene. A second mike should be taped to a broom handle so that it can be pointed at the questioner. You will need another crew member to serve as the boom operator if you do this. If you use two microphones, you can use a Y connector to plug both mikes into. Better yet, purchase a small, inexpensive (less than $50) audio mixer. Plug both mikes into it so you can control input levels for each one. See Utz (1989) for more detail.

Videotaping the press conference makes it seem more real and provides an opportunity for feedback on the accuracy of the expressions (see Figure 3.6). It is probably best to replay and evaluate the videotape during another class period. Delayed feedback will be more objective, and will also serve as a review of the

Figure 3.6 Videotaping a student presentation provides an opportunity for feedback.

ideas being questioned. A useful follow-up activity is to allow students to add questions after the videotape replay that they wished they would have asked during the press conference. Requiring students to think and act like someone else will require them to understand the ideas on a more intuitive level.

Learning Processes   The primary characteristic of meaningful learning through press conferences is constructive. The students being interviewed must study and reflect on the knowledge, beliefs, and perspectives of the person being portrayed. They must construct an identity and an understanding of the person. That construction is not only cognitive. Students should also focus on the affective and stylistic characteristics of the person.

In this exercise, not every student will be active. Certainly the students being interviewed are very actively engaged. The camera crew is also actively engaged. The audience may or may not be. In order to make every student a more active participant, require all of them to have two or more questions to ask the student being interviewed.

The press conference format adds some authenticity to the project. If students review press conferences before participating in their own, they may perceive the activity as even more authentic.

Student Roles   The students are the focus of this activity. The students being interviewed are the most active, as they research the characters they are portraying, write the scripts, rehearse their character's style and their opening remarks, and answer questions. Students not being interviewed must study the topic enough to be able to ask meaningful questions, just as a newspaper reporter would, while the video production students are actively engaged in producing quality video.

Teacher Roles.   The teacher has little responsibility for this activity other than suggesting and approving topics for the press conference. The teacher should help students select roles to play, ensuring that they experience the range. The teacher may also critique or provide feedback about the scripts, making sure that the student has included most of the salient points. The teacher may also critique students' questions to be asked of the interviewee. Providing general classroom management may be the most taxing role as the students express their enthusiasm. Perhaps most consistently, the teacher should be a cheerleader, keeping the students motivated to complete their tasks.

Assessing Learning   The products of this video-based learning activity are captured and available for assessment on videotape. The teacher may assess the video for the following:

- Did the interviewee's statement accurately convey the person's point of view? Were the important elements of their position conveyed?
- Were the student's answers to questions consistent with the person's beliefs? Where they clear, incisiveness, and adequate?

- Was the portrayal of the character appropriate; did they capture the person's personality?
- Were the other students' questions meaningful? Were they clear, incisiveness, and adequate? Did the questions require the interviewee to think? Could the interviewee understand and answer the questions?
- Was the quality of the video production adequate?

Newsroom

Related to the press conference activity is the newsroom, where students produce videotaped news programs. Producing a news program is an engaging and complex activity. Many schools have closed circuit broadcast systems built into them so that the entire school can watch the student-produced news program. In many schools, students produce a daily news program that is broadcast over the school's closed circuit television system. Showing the students' news program to the entire school increases the need for quality and certainly enhances the importance of the event for your students. The pressures of meeting daily deadlines can become intense, although they offer excellent object lessons about real-world performance.

A news program can also be produced on special topics being examined in nearly any classroom. The news program simply provides a familiar format for having students understand and represent, in their own way important ideas.

Learning Activity   Assembling a news program is a complex activity. Stories have to be identified, assigned, researched, written, and then produced. The teacher needs to work with the students to determine the scope of the stories that will be included in the program. The stories may include current events in the school or local community; local, regional, national, or international political issues and events; scientific developments, discoveries, or research conducted locally or anywhere in the world; literary or movie reviews (yes, even reviews of books of likely interest to students); health news or interest (e.g., inoculations during flu season or exercise programs); even mathematical riddles or puzzles that might interest other students. There is no reason why these stories should not be substantive; this is not a play activity. Decisions about assignments should be made by an editorial board of students, with the teacher as advisor. A useful twist on the newsroom activity is to produce the program in a foreign language being studied.

After being assigned stories, students must conduct research, preferably in teams, write the stories, locate pictures or video sequences about their stories to be included in the news program, and edit the stories. Prior to production, these stories need to be approved by the editorial board and edited to fit within time allotments. Finally, a video script is developed showing the sequence of the stories so the video producers know who the next newscaster will be.

During production of the news program, a crew of students videotapes the newscasters and their graphics. The news anchor introduces the program and the stories, with individual newscasters presenting the stories. A member of each team can assume the role of on-air talent, while the other members check the accuracy of their presentation. If the news program is broadcast live, the newscasters and

VIDEO TECHNIQUE

The simplest kind of set is a semicircular table or desk with a fairly neutral foreground. The anchor, of course, should sit in the middle. A mural can be drawn or painted to go behind the desk in order to add an air of authenticity.

You can produce a news show with only a single camera. If only a single camera is available, then place it in front of the semicircle. The semicircular shape allows the camera operator to pan from reporter to reporter.

Producing a news program like this can be accomplished live or delayed. A live broadcast would require a video switcher, recorder, and multiple cameras. The switcher allows the director to switch back and forth between the camera, focusing on the reporter and the graphics camera or videotape player. If a second camera and switcher are available, the second camera can focus on the pictures or graphics that student teams have produced to illustrate their stories. The director of the program must follow the script and switch to the graphics camera whenever there is a cue in the script. See Utz (1989) for more detail.

The other production option is to shoot all of the video and edit it together, dubbing in the voices of the reporters after the video is assembled. An editor will enable you to insert video clips recorded off-air or filmed by your students on location. This can also be accomplished if you have a switcher; however, that requires a great deal more planning.

camera crew must practice more extensively in order to ensure a smooth presentation. Regardless of whether the news program is live or recorded, daily or weekly, an incredible amount of thinking and learning will be invested in its production.

Learning Processes   The primary learning characteristics of the newsroom are constructive, intentional, and cooperative. Students have to research information in order to construct scripts. They combine and sequence the scripts to construct a program. In order to do all of this, they must intentionally look for information to substantiate their scripts, and must develop a carefully timed and sequenced program. That process requires a great deal of self-regulation—timing program sequences, evaluating the quality of the ideas being presented, and so on. All of these activities rely on cooperation within the teams to produce the best scripts and between the announcers and the television production crew to complete the program.

Student Roles   As with most of these activities, the students are in command. They select the topics, conduct the research, write the scripts, assemble the program, produce the program, and evaluate its effectiveness. The activities call on extensive writing and planning skills.

Teacher Roles   The primary roles for the teacher in the newsroom scenario are evaluator of the product and regulator of the process. The teacher should avoid directing the students but should intervene in the process if they begin to stray off course. The complexity of the process may be too much for some students, so they might need the regulation that a teacher can provide. Like the video press conference, teachers should help identify appropriate roles and function as cheerleader for the students.

Assessing Learning   We are sure that an English or journalism teacher could add meaningful criteria to our list, but these are some criteria that occur to us for assessing and evaluating the news programs that students construct:

- Is the information contained in the news stories accurate?
- Do the stories comply with standard forms for news stories: lead-in, issues, explication, and conclusion?
- How good is the writing? Is it grammatically and syntactically correct?
- Do the visuals used clarify the intent of the news stories?
- Are there meaningful connectives between the stories to tie them together?

Student Talk Shows

One of the most popular genres of commercial television, the talk show, can provide a powerful medium for student-produced videos. Daytime and late-night television present numerous hosts interviewing a variety of guests. It is such a common format that children naturally assume the roles of both interviewer and interviewee. Author Jerzy Kozinski experimented with videotaping children in talk-show settings and found that they naturally assumed the insouciant air of television personalities and that during interviews would divulge the most intimate secrets about their lives, even when they knew that their parents and teachers would likely see the video. We are not recommending that students be compromised or that they emulate the salacious nature of many daytime talk shows. Rather, the talk-show format is a natural medium for getting students to converse in meaningful ways. It is important to structure the talk show so that students are discussing meaningful ideas. The following learning activity is an example of one way of doing that.

Learning Activity   One of the most creative educational shows ever broadcast by the Public Broadcast System, in our opinion, was *A Meeting of Minds*, which was written and produced by Steve Allen. Each episode featured very improbable combinations of four guests (e.g., Ghengis Khan, Marie Antoinette, Socrates, and Charles Manson) from different historical eras in a talk-show setting, moderated by Steve Allen. He would provide the initial questions, and off they would go, usually culminating in passionate exchanges of ideas and beliefs. This is a rich idea for getting groups of students to reason beyond surface-level meaning about ideas. The individuals that your students portray would not have to be as diverse as Allen's in order to engage discussion. If they represented multiple perspectives on more focused historical issues, for instance, students could understand the multiple viewpoints that make up an issue. For example, students could take the role of the major players at the Pottsdam conference after World War II, or they could assume the role of popular scientists versus creationists in a discussion about evolution. Discussions could also deal with contemporary issues, and finding persona who represent divergent viewpoints (Democrats and Republicans, conservationists and developers) might make the experience more interesting. A related activity would be to construct home pages for each of the characters or pages describing the events (see Chapter 2). Issues are everywhere. Again, peruse and copy of *Time* or *Newsweek*, and issues will bubble out of the magazine.

It will also be necessary to select a narrator for each talk show. The narrator should be prepared to ask questions, resolve differences, and draw conclusions from the discussion. A separate team will be needed to write questions that provoke the participants and to prepare the narrator for his or her role.

Learning Processes   More than any other characteristic, the talk show is collaborative, primarily because it is founded on conversation. Forming teams to research characters, determine their responses to issues, and develop the characters will probably enhance the quality of the characters. The talk show is also very constructive, as students articulate the ideas, personality, and dialogue of the characters they are developing and reflect on the kinds of responses they would likely make on different issues. They have to know the characters much more deeply than the student writing a report on the character.

VIDEO TECHNIQUE

If only a single camera is available, position the actors close together in a V arrangement, with the moderator in the middle. Position the camera at the top of the V so that the operator can pan smoothly between the participants. A medium shot of individual participants or a two-shot (a medium shot including two people) is preferable. See Utz (1989) for more details.

Student Roles   Students putting together a talk show are researchers, talent directors, and actors in a complex interaction of the real and the pretend. What makes this activity challenging is the conjecturing and speculation that students must make about how their characters might respond to different issues. The reflection on their caricatures will require a great deal of hypothetical reasoning, which will be new for most students.

Teacher Roles   The teacher's most vital roles in this activity will be to provide encouragement and feedback to the participants when writing their scripts. The hypothetical reasoning will be new for most students who may well give up when they find there is no right or wrong answer to their constructions. Helping them to capture the character of the people they are portraying will require a delicate balance between suggestion and questioning the students about their characters.

Assessing Learning   Since the learning outcomes from this activity are speculative, the criteria for evaluating them will also be somewhat speculative. They will be difficult to evaluate, not because the better responses will not be obvious, but because the criteria are not objective.

- Were the questions appropriate for the participants being portrayed? Were they likely to be able to answer them?
- Did the students accurately represent the beliefs or perspectives of the persons they were portraying?
- Did the students understand the beliefs of their character, and were they able to convey those beliefs in impromptu comments?

Video Documentaries

Video is the tool of choice among modern ethnographers, those social scientists who study cultures using observation, interviews, and other qualitative methods. When ethnographers visit and observe sites and interview native peoples, they often videotape the experience. The video gives them a bimodal (auditory and visual) representation of the experience, which they can study later to better convey their findings. Students can become effective ethnographers as well, as described in Chapter 4. Ricki Goldman-Segall has developed a multimedia shell for students to collect their videos, stories, and interpretations. Her students have studied many of the First Nations cultures in British Columbia. Student ethnography can be focused on local issues, as well. Students can create video documentaries that examine local issues or controversies. In doing so, they become more concerned and productive members of society.

Learning Activities   A good way to get students warmed up to the process of creating documentaries is to create personal documentaries. That is, they produce a documentary about themselves. They decide the most appropriate setting, the perceptions about themselves that they want viewers to have, and the format of the personal description. Personal documentaries have taken many forms. Some students create a personal diary. Others have taken viewers on a tour of their room, while others have played musical instruments, recited poetry, or acted out different personae. The self is the most interesting topic for most kids, so this can be an engaging activity.

A twist of the personal documentary is to conduct it in a foreign language. Pelletier (1990) recommends sending students in foreign language classes out with a videocamera to tape a short tour of their room, home, classroom, library, or a video synopsis of some activity, such as a family supper, miniature golf, or bowling, or any other activity, requiring them to conduct the tour in the language they are studying. Personalizing the use of language, rather than treating it as an object to be studied, is an important component in language acquisition. So students combine new words with previously learned vocabulary in order to express more meaningful ideas. Have the students be as verbally expressive in their narrations as possible.

Pelletier also recommends that guidance be provided to students about the scope of the project. The tour should be short (3–5 minutes), focusing on a limited number of objects or phenomena. Imagine videotaping the basketball or football

VIDEO TECHNIQUE

Pelletier recommends that students should not attempt to record the narration or any dialogue while videotaping the scene. That would result in choppy audio and poor-quality video. The videocamera will probably be hand-held, so students should practice producing steady shots. Avoid excessive zooming in and out (a well-worn tendency among novice camera operators). Pans (side-to-side movements) should be slow and smooth. The operator should not pan while the camera is zoomed in (it accentuates the effects of the movements and will make the audience feel seasick). Shoot the scenes first, then log all of the shots, write the narration, and then dub in the audio while viewing the video in order to realize the best results. See Utz (1989) for more details.

game and having students do the play-by-play in Spanish. You are capitalizing on the natural interests of the students. We can guarantee that vocabulary learned in this activity will be better remembered and retained than that rehearsed from a textbook.

Video documentaries should migrate outside the school into the community. The local newspaper details many local issues or controversies that students can examine. Students need to research the problems, identify the stakeholders, interview them, and draw some conclusions. Video is normally used to describe the problem (e.g., showing the traffic congestion, dangerous crosswalk, ecological problem) and to interview stakeholders. Like the personal, foreign language documentaries, these documentaries need to be shot out of sequence and later edited together into a coherent program.

Record problems in search of solutions.   As a teacher, you can identify problems or work with students to identify problems at a local level or a national level. Local polluters, construction of a new highway through a state forest, alleviating traffic congestion on local streets, or solving the Middle Eastern crisis can be problems where video documentaries developed by students requires them to understand the issues and ideas better. Students in an English-as-a-second-language class who produced a documentary on eating establishments on campus not only acquired significant English skills, but also developed interviewing skills and gained more confidence in the use of English (Gardner 1994). Creating video documentaries requires students to use a complex combination of skills that leads to meaningful learning.

Learning Processes   Producing video documentaries is a meaningful learning activity, incorporating active, constructive, intentional, authentic, and cooperative learning. It is authentic because students examine personally relevant topics. It is very constructive, because they produce a complex video program. It is perhaps more intentional than other video activities, because students must declare a specific purpose and consistently regulate their performance in its completion. Most video documentaries, other than the personal ones, require a great deal of cooperation among teams of students. Responsibility for interviewing different people, researching documents, videotaping sites, and editing the video needs to be negotiated and monitored. These activities require extensive collaboration and discussion. More than anything, video documentaries have students actively engaged in representing the personal perspectives, so there is extensive ownership (and therefore meaning) of the final product.

Student Roles   Students, once again, are primarily responsible for most of the performance. They need to select meaningful and appropriate topics (with teacher feedback), research issues, identify stakeholders, research them, videotape sites and interviews, plan the treatment, and edit the video. In producing documentaries, planning becomes more important, as shooting will likely occur in different locations with different talent. The primary means for planning video productions is the storyboard (see Figure 3.7).

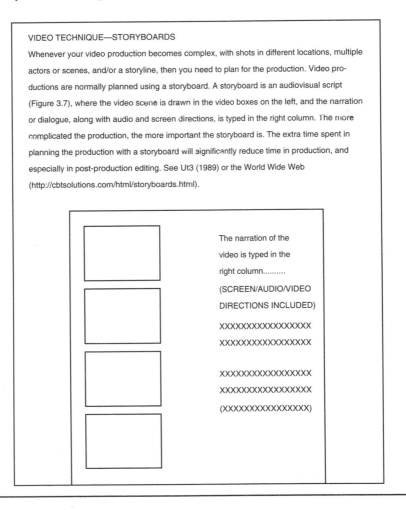

VIDEO TECHNIQUE—STORYBOARDS

Whenever your video production becomes complex, with shots in different locations, multiple actors or scenes, and/or a storyline, then you need to plan for the production. Video productions are normally planned using a storyboard. A storyboard is an audiovisual script (Figure 3.7), where the video scene is drawn in the video boxes on the left, and the narration or dialogue, along with audio and screen directions, is typed in the right column. The more complicated the production, the more important the storyboard is. The extra time spent in planning the production with a storyboard will significantly reduce time in production, and especially in post-production editing. See Ut3 (1989) or the World Wide Web (http://cbtsolutions.com/html/storyboards.html).

The narration of the
video is typed in the
right column..........
(SCREEN/AUDIO/VIDEO
DIRECTIONS INCLUDED)
XXXXXXXXXXXXXXXX
XXXXXXXXXXXXXXXX

XXXXXXXXXXXXXXXX
XXXXXXXXXXXXXXXX
(XXXXXXXXXXXXXXX)

Figure 3.7   Video storyboard

Teacher Roles   The teacher's role is primarily regulatory, making sure that topics are acceptable, stakeholders are appropriate, coverage is tasteful, and the project is not overly controversial. They will also oversee the planning stage, to make sure that students are prepared when they begin shooting.

Assessing Learning.   Assessing the effectiveness of video documentaries will require some research and understanding by the teacher of the issues that the students are examining in order to make these assessments:

- Was the issue or controversy clearly identified and explained?
- Were all stakeholders identified and interviewed?
- Did the video clarify the issues?
- Was the treatment biased?
- Did the sequence of the program represent a coherent argument?

Video Theater: One-Act Dramas

Learning Activity   Creating video sketches requires analyzing dialogue. An interesting learning activity prior to writing their own plays is to provide many recipes for having students analyze both verbal and nonverbal cues and reason from short video clips (Stempelski and Tomalin 1990). In language arts lessons, such as "Speech Bubble," students view narrative sequences and supply their own dialogue. Students are constructing meaning for what might have been said, using TV sequences as the stimulus. Students can also construct their own video sequences, rather than interpreting existing sequences.

After students become familiar with analyzing dialogues, they can produce their own. Students in any class can develop short dramatic sketches to represent ideas being studied. In history, students could write and play the roles of serfs or noblemen in medieval Europe. In science, they could create a skit reviewing the events leading up to an important discovery. In literature, performing scenes from plays would make them come alive. Have students rewrite plays using modern dialogue to help them to interpret meaning. These skits could be translated and performed in another language for foreign language classes.

VIDEO TECHNIQUE

A skit such as this should be carefully scripted, with the camera shots determined before you begin shooting. Multiple cameras and editing will produce much better results. If only a single camera is available, position it so that when it is zoomed all the way out, the shot will include a wide, long shot of the entire set. Start with it as an establishing shot. Know what action will occur next, so that your camera is not zoomed all the way in just as an actor takes off. If an actor is leaving the scene, do not follow him or her off stage. Let the actor walk out of the shot.

Learning Processes   Producing video skits requires interpretive work, translating ideas and events into dialogue. This activity requires a very creative form of knowledge construction. Staging and producing plays also require a lot of cooperation. Cooperative learners use conversation as a means to seek out opinions and ideas from others in order to produce more creative performances.

Student Roles   Dramatic sketches require students to write or think in dramatic form, check the accuracy of the parts and rules being conveyed, stage the skits, videotape the performance, perhaps edit the video, and then evaluate their performances.

Teacher Roles   The teacher may assist students by initially acting as the director, helping to organize students' activities and providing feedback about the dialogue, the nature of the characters, and the sets. Teachers should fade out their involvement as soon as students are able and willing to assume responsibility.

Assessing Learning   Evaluating plays is a subjective process. What pleases one person may offend another. Appreciating plays is a very personal process. We recommend checking with your drama teacher for more criteria, but here are some criteria that may be used for evaluating student-produced video skits:

- Did the play address all of the events, issues, or phenomena it was trying to depict?
- Are the characters in the performance believable, time-appropriate, and consistent with their position within the play?
- Did the setting enhance the dramatic character of the performance?
- Did the play make use of dramatic conventions?

Video Modeling and Feedback

In these final two activities, teachers can become involved in the video productions as well as, or instead of, the students. Just as video production is engaging for learners, it can also be a very engaging learning experience for teachers. The teaching materials that result can be very useful.

Learning Activity   Perhaps the most obvious way to use video for teaching is to model specific performances. Video models are used frequently in teaching athletics, where skilled performers show you how to improve your golf or tennis swing. However, video modeling is useful, not just for psychomotor tasks. Any kind of performance can be modeled by the teacher or other skilled performer, such as public speaking or acting for theatrical performers, empathic behavior for counselors or social workers, interpersonal communication skills for personnel workers or librarians, even thinking and research behaviors.

Teachers and students together might think about developing a study strategies video by acting out what a skilled learner would do in order to write a term paper or study for a test. Shoot the video from the point of view of the student—

reading a book, looking in a catalog, searching the library stacks, turning off the television. After shooting the video, dub in the voice, using an echo chamber to make it seem like the person in the video is talking to himself or herself. Find out what skills students possess, and videotape them performing what they do best. Not only will you have a series of useful videos, but students will gain self-confidence, as well. Getting students to articulate what they should be doing is usually a good idea.

When modeling performances for students, it is important to model not only the actual performance but also the mental processes (decision making, questioning, resolving) involved with the performance. This think-aloud process can be very informative for the learners while watching the video performance, especially if the teacher conveys his or her uncertainties as well as solutions while thinking aloud.

Although providing video models of any desired performance is one of the most powerful video teaching methods available, it is maximally successful if used in conjunction with video feedback (described later). Essentially, providing video models and then videotaping the learners' performances and using those tapes as feedback is probably the most powerful use of video possible.

Students may also produce video models. When they do, they have to learn the performance to be modeled, practice it until they are skilled, and then perform it in front of a camera. That is, they need to become model performers. Another version would be to have students model some performance that they do well—playing an instrument, caring for pets, solving logic puzzles, nearly any skill.

VIDEO TECHNIQUE
Generally only a single camera is needed for this application. The preferred shot will depend on the kind of action being modeled. If you are demonstrating how to do something, then try to get an over-the-shoulder shot of the performer doing the task, Even better is to shoot the action from the point of view of the performer with only hands included in the shot (if they are appropriate). This will add realism and show the viewer just how to perform the activity.

Learning Processes Regardless of who the performer is, the process of modeling performance is very constructive. The performer needs to articulate the performance in the clearest possible way, which requires a great deal of reflection about the nature of their performance while they are modeling it.

Assessing Learning Through Video Feedback The most powerful use of video, we believe, is to provide feedback on an individual's performance. Select virtually any meaningful performance task in schools (theatrics, foreign language usage, public speaking, performing a chemistry experiment, anything but test-taking) and assess the learners' performance by videotaping them while performing the activity. That performance can then be evaluated, and feedback about their performance can be provided to the student. Video feedback is one of the deepest, most incisive learning experiences possible. Having learners watch themselves perform provides them with an unfiltered, unbiased view of themselves. This method is often (though not often enough) used to help prepare preservice teachers for teaching. Teachers are videotaped teaching lessons to students. Reviewing the videotape, with or without a supervisory teacher to provide feedback, teaches new teachers more about teaching than all of the textbooks they have read.

In addition to providing performance feedback, video feedback affects self-perceptions (Jonassen 1978, 1979). Viewers become more evaluative and less role-oriented in their perceptions of themselves. This experience is very powerful and should not be used with troubled individuals without proper care.

Video can help learners reflect on their own performance primarily through video feedback—videotaping a performance and then viewing that performance, with or without a teacher or expert accompanying you. For instance, Orban and McLean (1990) use videocameras for self-evaluations and teacher evaluations of French-speaking ability. "Video is like a mirror in which a magician practices his tricks, a way to evaluate his performance over and over" (Taylor 1979, p. 28). You can use video to engage constructive (articulative/reflective) learning with the following activities.

A related technique for assessing individual understanding of processes and systems is the teach-back. The idea is simple. After teaching something to students, require them individually to teach back the ideas or processes. Students may teach the ideas back to the teacher or teach it to other novice students. Either way, it is a useful method for identifying student misconceptions or unclear mental models. These teach-backs can be videotaped and replayed later by the teacher as a form of assessment or simply as a learning activity for the students. This method capitalizes on the time-worn adage that the best way to learn something is to have to teach it. So you may want to allow students the opportunity to collect models, visuals, or conduct additional research before teaching the ideas to others. Videotaping the teach-back provides an easily assessable record of the students' understanding.

VIDEO TECHNIQUE
This application requires only a single camera, which maintains a medium shot of the student teacher, occasionally zooming out to include students' reactions to their teaching.

Teachers as Videographers: Creating Contexts for Learning

Students shouldn't have all of the fun. The following learning activity describes how teachers can enhance learning by producing their own instructional videos. We have argued throughout this book that learning that occurs in the context of some real-world activity is usually better understood and more readily transferred to new situations. Teachers can create those problem contexts, just like the macro-contexts described earlier in this chapter, for their students.

Learning Activity   Authentic contexts for engaging learners in problem solving can be created for any class. In mathematics, identify mathematical problems in the real world, such as the calculations and problem solving for building a house, erecting a bridge across a creek, predicting the vote from various precinct votes in the past, and so on. Science problems are everywhere. Chapter 7 describes project-based science activities where students and teachers monitor the creek next to their school.

For language classes, teachers can take their videocameras along on vacation when visiting foreign countries. Record everyday scenes (ordering in restaurants, buying a newspaper from a newsstand, asking a policeman for directions, buying a ticket to a tourist spot). The best scenes are those in which the student has to answer the question that was posed on the tape or pose the question that was answered on the tape. These scenes can also be assembled into macro-contexts so that students have to think and act in the foreign language in order to get across the city on the Paris Metro or find a museum in Barcelona.

Science teachers can also record video experiments for use in class. Show the process of setting up the experiment and stop just before the outcome. Require the students to predict the outcome of the experiment. If these experiments can be set in real-world settings, rather than school labs, they will be much more meaningful for learners (for instance, estimating the height of a tree in the forest for a lumbering company, disposing of wastes from a local film lab, designing a lightning rod for the local courthouse).

Lawrence (1994) used video contexts for evaluating his students in physics. He shows experiments or demonstrations and asked his students to predict the outcome of the experiments and to explain any discrepancies between their predictions and the actual outcomes, which he showed after students made their predictions. "When students make their prediction, then watch what actually occurs, then make a revision, they are modeling the scientific method" (p. 17).

Social studies teachers may want to videotape a city council meeting where a controversial topic is being debated. Show students all of the perspectives and even go on location to videotape the object of discussion (e.g., expanding the waste-water treatment plant). Then allow the students to debate and resolve the issue in class and see how their solutions compare with those of the city council. The student debates may also be videotaped.

The world outside of schools is full of meaningful learning experiences. Videotaping those experiences and bringing them into the classroom connects in-class learning with the real world and makes it so much more meaningful for learners. Videocameras are an easy and flexible way of bringing those experiences into the classroom.

The learning processes, students' and teachers' roles, and assessment methods will vary so much with the nature of the problem that is videotaped that it is impossible to specify them.

VIDEO TECHNIQUE
All of these kinds of productions will have to be shot on location and edited together later using a video editor (described earlier). A tripod might be the last thing that you want to haul along on vacation, but it will always yield better videos. If it is too cumbersome, then practice holding the camera steady. Plan your shots to highlight the desired action. You should generally get an establishing shot—that is, a long shot of the scene establishing the context for the action. If you are asking a police officer for directions in French, then a medium or close-up shot of the asker and the officer would be appropriate. Experiments should generally include close-up shots of the apparatus. Again, avoid camera movement while zoomed in.

Videoconferencing: Communicating Through Video

What was science fiction a couple of decades ago—full-screen viewing of people while conversing over the telephone—is now common practice in many educational institutions. Holding face-to-face conferences over high-capacity ISDN telephone lines (special, high-capacity phone lines that cost several times as much per month to rent as a regular telephone line) is afforded by different technologies. PictureTel systems provide cameras for sending pictures of people, graphics, or video, microphones, and computers to decode and compress the video images so they fit the limited capacity of telephone lines. PictureTel systems allow up to three groups to meet and simultaneously share graphics and video images as if they were in the same room. These systems can simulate face-to-face teaching situations. There are some downsides. These systems are expensive ($20,000–$50,000), require up to four or more dedicated ISDN telephone lines, and do not provide full-motion video (the compressed images are choppy because half the images are dropped out). In the long run, however, the systems are cheaper than flying people all over the country to train them. These systems are used to provide specialized classes (e.g., advanced sciences, Latin, calculus) to rural school districts in Iowa that cannot afford specialized teachers. These more expensive PictureTel systems are being replaced by smaller, cheaper desktop computer videoconferencing systems that cost about $5,000. They provide most of the functionality of the larger systems at a greatly reduced price.

Videoconferencing systems have revolutionized the way that corporations conduct meetings and provide training. IBM, for instance, maintains studios in France and Germany, from which they provide training to their employees all over Europe. Videoconferencing is also revolutionizing the way that universities provide courses. It is no longer necessary for students to reside in a university town in order to attain a university degree. Distance learning programs are being offered by most colleges and universities around the country. We regularly teach our classes to learners located in other cities or countries using PictureTel.

Although videoconferencing sounds like the answer to many educational problems, we must report that it often is not. Videoconferencing often elicits the worst kind of education—teachers lecturing at an audience in another location. There may be some logistical advantages to videoconferenced classrooms, but there are not always learning advantages. Learners in these settings are assuming the same passive role that they always have. Can videoconferencing support meaningful learning? We think so.

Videoconferencing best supports meaningful learning by helping diverse learners to collaborate and converse with each other in order to solve problems and construct meaning. There are several ways that videoconferencing can support meaningful learning. Mainly, it can connect communities of learners.

Form Discourse Communities. Videoconferencing can support the formation of discourse communities (see Chapter 5), where students with common interests can talk about, illustrate, model, or teach those interests. Most schools sponsor after-school clubs to enable students to pursue their own intellectual interests (e.g., chess, farming, photography, etc.). In schools where only a few students share a particular interest, they may be able to videoconference with students at other schools in order to share activities.

Supporting Communities of Practice. Videoconferencing can also support discussions among communities of practice (see Chapter 5 for more on this). Lave (1991) sees learning not as a process of socially sharing ideas that result in internalization of knowledge by individuals, but rather as a process of becoming a member and developing an identity as a member of a sustained community of practice. As teaching and learning become less school-building–based and more distributed throughout society, people who work in the same businesses will be able to learn from each other though videoconferencing. For instance, when new hairstyles emerge, haircutters can show others how to cut hair in that particular way.

Again, the learning processes, students' and teachers' roles, and assessment methods will vary so much with the nature of the videotaped problem that it is impossible to specify them.

CONCLUSIONS

In this chapter, we have shown how video can be used to create macro-contexts for engaging learners in complex problem solving. These videos are not used to teach, but rather are used to hook students into authentic situations for learning. Most of the chapter focused on the use of video as a medium for student constructions, engaging them in planning, writing, visualizing, organizing, creating, and a host of other meaningful learning activities. These video applications are but a sampling of the numerous ways that you can use video in the classroom. As you begin to use video in your teaching area, more creative ideas should occur to you. Whenever students produce their own videos, it is important that they each:

- Participate in all of the activities that are involved in shooting and producing videos
- Receive encouragement to be as creative as possible in their productions
- Use video to provide feedback on their performance
- Reflect on and analyze the ideas and skills that they have learned

THINGS TO THINK ABOUT

If you would like to reflect on the ideas that we presented in this chapter, then articulate your responses to the following questions and compare them with others' responses.

1. Is it ever possible to learn from television alone—that is, learn how to do something merely from watching television instruction? What meaning will it have after only watching the show? What meaning will it have after you try it yourself?

2. "Public television exists to enrich people's lives." What does that mean? In order to be enriched, what does the individual viewer have to contribute?

3. What does it mean to be a critical viewer of commercial television? What are critical viewing skills? How could you teach your students to be critical viewers?

4. Why do students think that television is easier than reading? How can you get students to invest more effort in viewing television for learning?

5. Video production is a constructionist activity; that is, students are learning by constructing an artifact. What other kinds of constructionist activities can you think of (using technologies or not)?

6. In the 1950s, the comic cop Dick Tracy wore a watch that was a picture telephone. How soon will that be reality?

7. The *Jasper Woodbury* series believed that by providing a rich, video-based story with a problem in it, learners will understand the problem better. Can you think of other ways that stories have been used to set up problems? How are they the same? How are they different?

8. After the Watergate investigation that brought down Nixon's presidency, investigative journalism increased dramatically. What kinds of issues (personal, local, regional, national) would be most likely to attract students to investigative reporting? How can you support that in your school?

9. Think of characters that your students would like to become if they were producing their own version of *Meeting of the Minds*. Why did you select them?

10. In 1997, a modern version of *Romeo and Juliet* was released as a motion-picture film. The film was a hit with youngsters, because the theme was universal but the setting was current. Can you think of other plays, stories, or books with universal themes that students would like to adapt into a modern interpretation?

11. Video feedback has been called a "mirror with a memory." Why is seeing yourself on television such a compelling and incisive experience? How do you see yourself? Why is that so powerful?

12. Do you think that technologies such as videoconferencing, which make instruction available anytime, anywhere, will eliminate the need for schools and classrooms? Why or why not?

REFERENCES

Beentjes, J., and T. van der Vort (1988). Television's impact on children's reading skills: A review of the research. *Reading Research Quarterly*, 23(4): 389–413.

Chu, W. G., and W. Schramm (1967). *Learning from television: What the research says.* Stanford, CA: Stanford University Institute for Communication Research (ERIC ED 014 900).

Cognition and Technology Group at Vanderbilt (1992). Technology and the design of generative learning environments. In T. M. Duffy and D. H. Jonassen (eds.), *Constructivism and the technology of instruction: A conversation.* Hillsdale, NJ: Lawrence Erlbaum Associates.

Gardner, D. (1994). Student-produced video-documentary: Hong Kong as a self-access resource. *Hong Kong Papers in Linguistics and Language Teaching*, 17: 44–53.

Goldman, S. R., A. J. Petrisino, R. D. Sherwood, S. Garrison, D. Hiskey, J. D. Bransford, and J. W. Pelligrino (1996). Anchoring science instruction in multimedia learning environments. In S. Vosniadu, E. deCorte, R. Glaser, and H. Mandl (eds.), *International perspectives on the design of technology-supported learning environments.* Mahwah, NJ: Lawrence Erlbaum Associates.

Healy, J. M. (1990). Chaos on Sesame Street: Does this carnival of images help students read? *American Educator: The Professional Journal of the American Federation of Teachers*, 14 (4): 22–27, #39.

Hefzallah, I. M. (1987). *Critical viewing of television: A book for parents and teachers.* Lanham, MI: University Press of America.

Jonassen, D. H. (1978). Video as a mediator of human behavior. *Media Message*, 7 (2): 5–6.

Jonassen, D. H. (1979). Video-mediated objective self-awareness, Self-perception, and locus of control. *Perceptual and Motor Skills*, 48,: 255-265.

Jonassen, D. H. (1982). *Nonbook media: A self-paced instructional handbook for teachers and library media personnel.* Hamden, CT: Library Professional Publications.

Lave, J. (1991). Situating learning in communities of practice. In L. B. Resnick, J. M. Levine, and S. D. Teasley (eds.), *Perspectives on socially shared cognition.* Washington, DC: American Psychological Association.

Lawrence, M. (1994). The use of video technology in science teaching: A vehicle for alternative assessment. *Teaching and Change*, 2 (1): 14–30.

National Cable Television Association (1995). *Taking charge of your TV: A guide to critical viewing for parents and children.* National Cable Television Association.

Orban, C., and A. M. McLean (1990). A working model for videocamera use in the foreign language classroom. *The French Review*, 63 (4): 652–63.

Pelletier, R. J. (1990). Prompting spontaneity by means of the video camera in the beginning foreign language class. *Foreign Language Annals*, 22(3): 227–32.

Potter, R. L. (1976). *New seasons: The positive use of commercial television with children.* Columbus, OH: Charles Merrill.

Reid, J. C., and D. W. MacLennan (1967). *Research in instructional television and film.* Washington, DC: U.S. Government Printing Office.

Salomon, G. (1984). Television is "easy" and print is "tough": The differential investment of mental effort in learning as a function of perceptions and attributions. *Journal of Educational Psychology*, 76: 647–58.

Secules, T., C. Herron, and M. Tomasello (1992). The effects of video context on foreign language learning. *The Modern Language Journal*, 76: 480–87.

Stempelski, S., and B. Tomalin (1990). *Video in action: Recipes for using video in language teaching.* New York: Prentice-Hall.

Taylor, C. B. (1979, January). Video to teach poetry writing. *Audiovisual Instruction*, 27–9.

Utz, P. (1989). *Video user's handbook: The complete illustrated guide to operating and maintaining video equipment.* New York: Prentice-Hall.

Valmont, William J. (1994) Making videos with reluctant learners. *Reading and Writing Quarterly: Overcoming Learning Difficulties*, 10 (4): 369–677.

Wagschal, P. H. (1987). Literacy on the electronic age. *Educational Technology*, 27 (6): 5–9.

CHAPTER 4

LEARNING BY CONSTRUCTING
REALITIES WITH HYPERMEDIA

MULTIMEDIA IN EDUCATION

Multimedia have a rich history in education. Instructional media, such as slide/tape and multi-image presentations, interactive video, and video productions, have used multimedia representations to convey instructional messages for decades. With the advent of inexpensive, high-resolution monitors, sound and video compression technology, and massive memory (random access and fixed storage) for personal computers, multimedia have become standard modes of representation in software. The multimedia desktop computer (see Figure 4.1) is now able to capture, synthesize, and manipulate sounds, video, and special effects such as animations, and integrate them all into a single multimedia presentation. They are relatively common in schools.

As with most technological innovations, multimedia's first successes were in the commercial sector. Touch-screen videodisk technologies combined graphics, audio, and video in point-of-sale and point-of-use kiosks in shopping malls, museums, corporate headquarters, and retail outlets to provide sales information to potential customers. Some were even connected directly to catalog sales operations to enable customers to do some virtual shopping.

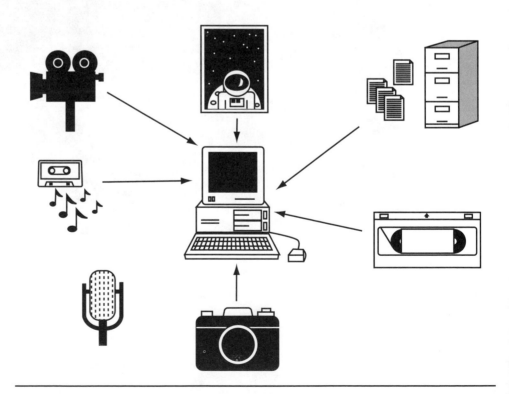

Figure 4.1   Multimedia in a computer

Multimedia have been used in corporations to deliver employee training. The advent of multimedia was largely responsible for a whole new approach to corporate training, called *electronic performance support systems* (EPSS). Rather than providing training to employees, whether they need it or not, EPSS provide just-in-time training using multimedia resources to provide individual employee training at the time they need it, which is the most teachable moment. Andersen Consulting, for instance, developed a business practices multimedia course for all new employees that could be completed at their work site when they need the information. Most commercially viable software packages now provide point-of-use, just-in-time, on-line training on how to use their software.

In addition to training, multimedia are becoming an essential component of corporate and educational communications. Multimedia enhance group lecture presentations. Most presentation software, such as PowerPoint, integrates multimedia resources and links into their packages to allow presenters to dazzle their audiences. In order to support internal communications, most videoconferencing systems (see Chapter 3 for more discussion) allow users to share and interactively manipulate graphics, text, audio, and animation while seeing and talking with each other in real time. Most corporate communications have gone multimedia. Schools will likely follow.

In education, multimedia evolved, as most technologies have, as a technology in search of a problem. In the early 1990s, it seemed that the multimedia computer was the answer to whatever educational question was being asked. After all, this is the MTV generation, so students need to be entertained by continuously changing, multimodal, multimedia learning shows. Providing information in multiple modes would surely make it more interesting and therefore more understandable to students. Educators, enamored of the multisensory representations afforded by the new multimedia technologies, claimed, as Edison did about motion-picture film, that students could and would eventually learn everything they needed to know from multimedia. That zealous prediction failed, in part, because commercial multimedia producers were more committed to producing adventure games than educational programs. In the past few years, numerous multimedia reference titles (databases, encyclopedias, and other information programs) and some quality educational software titles have been produced that can support educational objectives; however, multimedia have not substantially affected K–12 schools. Why not?

Multimedia, when used to deliver instruction, too often lack a clear goal or objective or adequate instructional strategies to support any educational goal, because most commercial multimedia producers do not know how to be educators and because multimedia technologies have no implicit or explicit structure for teaching. Although a number of educational multimedia producers have developed fine examples of educational software, using multimedia merely because they provide multisensory representations of ideas is not enough to support meaningful learning. How should multiple media be combined?

Multiple channel research from the past implied that when the channels provide complementary information, learning should increase, but when the information in different channels is redundant, no improvement in learning normally occurs. And when the information in different channels is inconsistent or distracting, decrements in learning will likely occur. When stories were presented verbally, with and without video, and with voice, video, and text, no differences in recall, recognition, or visualization occurred (Ottavianio 1993). Stamper (1991) showed that even intensive studying from multimedia materials for a two-year period produced no changes in critical thinking skills or attitudes toward school or attendance in sixth and seventh grades. Although little, if any, research exists to support the predicted effects of multimedia on learning, multimedia have become an accepted teaching device, nonetheless.

WHAT ARE MULTIMEDIA?

Multimedia represent the integration of more than one medium into some form of communication. The media represent different modes of experience, including visual, auditory, olfactory (smell), tactile (feeling), and even gustatory (taste). For instance, consuming a sizzling plate of fajitas or quaffing a complex beer involves all of the senses—observing the color, feeling the texture, tasting the piquancy, smelling the aromas, and hearing the sizzles or bubbles. These are multimodal, multimedia experiences—stimulating all of the sensory modalities. Instructional multimedia, however, typically involve only the auditory and visual modalities in the integration of media such as text, sound, graphics, animation, video, imaging, and spatial modeling into a computer system (von Wodtke 1993). Multimedia can also include record-based data, numeric data, animations, and just about any other form of communication that can be digitized (Figure 4.1).

Today multimedia representations in software are taken for granted. Nearly all information, including that on the World Wide Web, has multimedia representations. Why are multimedia so popular? Multimedia presentations are engaging because they overstimulate the senses with a barrage of sounds and images. For today's video generation, they are attention-getting and attention-holding. But is that enough for meaningful learning? Attention is a necessary condition for learning, but we believe it is not sufficient. Meaningful learning, as we have argued throughout this book, requires much more than attention.

Multimedia Technologies

Just as the contents of multimedia vary a lot, so do the ways that multimedia are stored, retrieved, and delivered. The major disadvantage of multimedia, when compared with text, is the enormous amount of memory required to store multimodal information, especially video. A number of multimedia formats have been developed over the years for storing ever larger computer files.

Videodisk.   Multimedia received a major boost from the development of videodisk technologies in the 1980s. Designed initially as a replacement for videotape, it was quickly adopted as a popular medium for instruction because of its random access and still-frame capabilities. Videodisks hold continuous motion, analog video (at 30 pictures or frames per second), just like videotapes do. However, rather than encoding information magnetically, as on audio- and videotape, tiny pits corresponding to the strength of the video signal are engraved on videodisks by a high-power laser in a spiral pattern on the disk from the inside out. A low-power laser is used to reflect light off these pits. This reflected signal is converted back into an analog video signal, which is reproduced on a television monitor. This signal-encoding method enables the user to access and play up to 54,000 individual pictures on the disk, which may hold audio, motion video, or still images.

Videodisks can be used in standalone mode to replay audio, video, or images, or they may be connected to a computer as a peripheral, visual storage device. The computer program organizes and presents information, calling on the videodisk to supply instructional video in stereo (or bilingual), still slides, computer-generated images, or animation on demand. In these interactive programs, the computer output is typically seen on one screen while the videodisk output is replayed on another screen. By adding a video overlay card to the computer, both the computer output and videodisk output may be seen in combination on the same screen, allowing computer-generated graphics, arrows, or other cues to be overlaid on video images.

The digital revolution has rendered videodisks nearly obsolete, because audio and video are now normally digitized and stored in the computer's memory, just like text or other forms of information. Although a number of educational programs produced on videodisks are still being used, very few, if any, educational videodisk programs are now being produced.

Compact Discs.   Compact discs have emerged, for now, as the dominant multimedia storage device. The tremendous growth of compact discs (CDs) resulted from the replacement of analog audio on phonographs and audiotapes to digital audio on CDs. Music is digitized by sampling the sound up to 44,000 times per second and encoding it as a number that is burned on the disk. Music is re-created by converting those numbers back into the range of sounds that are amplified and replayed through speakers in analog form. These sound bits are recorded onto a CD in much the same way as video was encoded onto videodisks.

Visual information is encoded onto CDs as individual screen pixels. The color and light characteristics of each pixel (dot) on the computer screen (512 pixels by 480 pixels for normal video) are encoded as a number. The number is read off the CD and displayed on the computer screen 30 times per second. One second of normal resolution video at 24 computer bits per pixel requires more than 20 megabytes of storage space, while a full minute would require more than a gigabyte (1 billion bytes). Such massive storage requirements would seem to make digital video impossible to store and replay on any normal computer. However, by reducing the resolution and size of the image or the number of bits per pixel, these massive requirements can be reduced.

More significantly, a number of video compression technologies have emerged. One of the standard compression routines, MPEG (Motion Picture Experts Group), looks at similarities across pixels and frames and stores only the changes, rather than discrete numbers for each pixel for each frame of video. These compression routines have reduced the storage requirements by factors of 100. Most require the addition of special software and/or hardware (video boards) to be added to computers to compress and decompress video images. Coupled with ever-larger storage devices (hard drives and CDs), digital video has joined digital audio as the standard. Two software standards, QuickTime and Video for Windows, enable reduced frame (size and motion) video to be played on most Macintosh and Windows computers. These operating system extensions provide a standard format for adding movies to any kind of document. Quick-Time, for instance, provides an industry standard for creating or recording video input and playing back that video as movies on any Macintosh.

CD-ROMs became popular multimedia storage devices because they could hold 650 megabytes of computer files, which in the early 1990s was significantly larger than any mass storage devices commonly available for personal computers. They became even more popular when inexpensive (less than $1,000) CD recorders became available for most computers, allowing users to record multimedia programs onto a CD. However, as of 1997, with most personal computers sporting multi-gigabyte hard drives, the CD-ROM is being replaced by other disk options (e.g., Jazz drives).

A new generation of digital video disks (DVDs), capable of holding 4.7 gigabytes on a standard CD, emerged in 1997. DVDs are being developed to deliver extremely high-resolution movies with multiple audio channels and information bases about the film and the actors, but they will also be used as DVD-ROMs to store computer files. Inexpensive drives, including an MPEG card to play DVD movies, are available for most computers. These drives can also play standard CDs, as well. Writable DVD-ROMs are in the works, and engineers are already working on 8.5- and even 17-gigabyte models. Change is a way of life in computer peripherals. What is certain is that future storage devices will become ever larger and faster.

Desktop Publishing. Desktop publishing programs emerged in the 1980s as sophisticated and special-purpose word-processing programs for formatting and producing print communications, such as newspapers, brochures, and announcements. They provide designers with tools for laying out print publications, using multiple fonts, and embedding pictures. Like word processors, desktop publishing programs have grown increasingly sophisticated, with capabilities for embedding graphics, sounds, and movies in documents. Although desktop programs lack the complexity of multimedia development programs, they do represent a common and important form of visual communication.

World Wide Web. The World Wide Web (WWW) emerged in the mid-1990s as a distributed computing option to the standalone multimedia computer. In the early stages, the WWW was used to store largely text-based documents on computers all over the world and to allow users anywhere to access those documents (much more information on the WWW is included in Chapter 2). With the evolution of more powerful servers and desktop computers, the WWW is rapidly becoming a giant, distributed multimedia knowledge base. Most Internet browsers, such as Netscape or Internet Explorer, can be enhanced with plug-in extensions, such as Shockwave, QuickTime, and QuickTime VR, that allow multimedia programs to be accessed, recorded, and replayed on any powerful desktop computer.

Although the WWW appears to be replacing current CD technologies for education, it is certain that new technologies will once again shift the balance of power in computer storage technology.

Multimedia Production Software

Mirroring the exponential growth in computational power and data storage in modern desktop computers, sophisticated software that exploits that computing power has emerged to support the design and development of multimedia programs. There is a continuum of tools for producing multimedia and hypermedia, from commercial, high-end multimedia production packages to special-purpose, educational multimedia authoring systems. They vary in power and price.

Commercial multimedia production packages tend to be expensive, powerful packages for producing multimedia programs. Programs like Macromedia Director and Authorware Professional provide sophisticated graphics tools, full animation, video production, and higher levels of interactivity, all at a cost of up to $5,000.

The most commonly used packages for producing hypermedia are a midrange class of tools like HyperCard, SuperCard, and Oracle Media Objects for the Mac and Toolbook, Guide, Linkway Live, and Oracle Media Objects for Windows machines. Producer versions cost up to $500 but afford a great deal of flexibility in programming more complicated, instructional hypermedia programs. In most cases, this flexibility has the cost of learning an object-oriented scripting language in order to produce advanced interactivity. These programs import graphics and movies, but have limited production capabilities themselves. They produce card-oriented presentations. Many school-based projects rely on Toolbook and Hyper-Card because of their flexibility, although they are not as easy to learn to use as the next class of multimedia/hypermedia tools.

Special-purpose authoring systems make the product of multimedia and hypermedia easier for younger students. Products like Mediatext, HyperStudio, Digital Chisel, and StorySpace are not as flexible or powerful as other authoring tools, but they are more friendly and easy-to-use environments for kids, and they are inexpensive (usually less than $100). We recommend using this type of software because they are easy to learn and, more importantly, because they are able to produce hypermedia—a special form of multimedia.

Hypermedia is simply the marriage of multimedia and hypertext. Hypertext is an open, user-selectable form of text where readers can move instantly from where they are reading to any other part of the text simply by pointing and clicking on a hot spot or hot button (maybe a highlighted word or set of words or a separate visual button on the screen). This is accomplished by breaking the text into nodes of text and interconnecting the nodes with each other In hypermedia, nodes may consist of different media forms—text, graphic images, sounds, animation sequences, video clips, or any other form of media. For example, rather than having users point to a hot button to retrieve a textual description of the presidential election, ABC created a hypermedia review of the 1988 election that mixed audio and video clips of speeches, pictures of the candidates, the text of their platforms, and so on.

The organization of hypermedia is open. The same set of nodes can be organized and accessed in many different ways to reflect many different conceptual orientations or perspectives (Jonassen 1991). The hypermedia author may create a very tight structure, restricting access to information in ways that make it most easily understood. Or the structure may be completely open, with immediate access to any node in the knowledge base. Large hypertext knowledge bases, like the knowledge base on British literature developed by the Intermedia project, consists of more than 5,000 nodes of poems, graphics, and recitations. The learners can access any of those nodes at any time or follow theme-oriented links to related information.

Hypermedia possess some or all of these characteristics (Jonassen 1989):

- Nodes or chunks of information of varying sizes and various media
- Associative links between the nodes that enable the user to travel from one node to another
- Network of ideas formed by the link structure
- Organizational structure that describes the network of ideas (may reflect different models or conceptual structures)
- Ability to represent explicitly the structure of information in the structure of the hypertext
- Dynamic control of information by the user—that is, a high level of inter-activity with the user so the user decides where to go
- Multi-user access to the information—many hypertexts are available to many users simultaneously

Although hypermedia, like multimedia, are normally used to convey instructional messages to learners, in this chapter, we argue that educators should think of hypermedia primarily as an environment to construct personal knowledge and learn *with*, not a form of instruction to learn *from*. Rather than trying to learn from instructor-designed hypermedia, students should be creating and constructing their own hypermedia knowledge bases. We believe that when they do, they learn more than they do from merely studying them. But first, let's look at how multimedia and hypermedia have been traditionally used.

LEARNING IN MULTIMEDIA ENVIRONMENTS

Although we primarily advocate multimedia and hypermedia as student construction tools, there are a number of powerful hypermedia environments that have been developed to engage learners in constructive learning. These learning environments (discussed in greater depth in Chapter 7) present interesting problems or challenges to students, using the multimedia to provide resources to help the learners solve the problem. Although the learning environments described in this section are similar to those we describe in Chapter 7, we focus here less on the design and more on how multimedia have been used to support meaningful learning.

Anchoring Instruction in Hypermedia Learning Environments

What makes these multimedia learning environments powerful is that they present a problem that is embedded in a real-world context. The multimedia are used to represent a macro-context, as described in Chapter 3 using video. Next, we examine three uses of multimedia for anchoring instruction. The macro-context for the first environment is a NASA observatory, the second a river basin, and the third a ship. These environments are presented as examples of how good multimedia learning environments can be. There are many others being developed on CD-ROM and for the World Wide Web. We encourage you to seek them out and engage your students with them.

Learning Activity: *The Astronomy Village* Developed by the National Aeronautics and Space Administration (NASA), the Astronomy Village provides rich multimedia resources and exploration tools in a virtual observatory community (Figure 4.2) to support exploration and scientific inquiry, analyzing data and images, and learning important concepts and methods of astronomy. In teams of three, students select and carry out up to ten stellar investigations (each lasting approximately four weeks). To help the students conduct their investigations, the village provides

Figure 4.2 *The Astronomy Village*

multimedia resources including more than 100 articles on astronomy, 335 images of stellar phenomena, video interviews with astronomers. Students also learn to use a powerful suite of tools, including electronic mail, a replica browser, an image browser, simulations, image processing software, a calculator, and a World Wide Web browser. The *Village* contains an Orientation Center, Conference Center, Library, computer lab, auditorium, cafeteria (for informal conversations), and of course the observatory on the hill (Figure 4.3).

Like all NASA multimedia products, *The Astronomy Village* requires student to select an investigation, develop a plan, and carry it out. *The Astronomy Village* supports ten different investigations, including:

- *Search for a Supernova*—uses neutrino data to locate a supernova
- *Looking for a Stellar Nursery*—views Omega nebula using different wave-lengths
- *Variable Stars*—identifying a Cepheid variable star in another galaxy
- *Search for Nearby Stars*—movement of stars' positions as Earth circles sun
- *Extragalatic Zoo*—different galaxies and clusters
- *Wedges of the Universe*—viewing depths of space in two wedges of sky

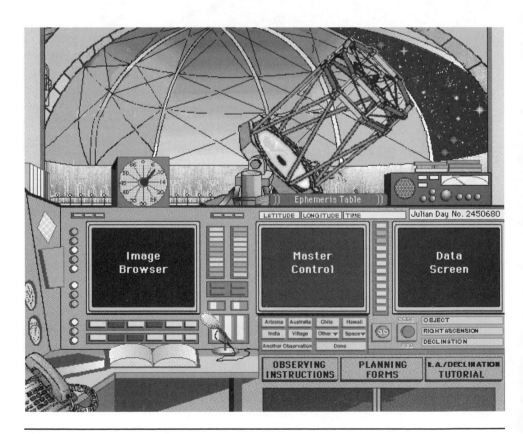

Figure 4.3   Observatory

- *Search for a "Wobbler"*—looking for stars that wobble in their motion
- *Search for Planetary Building Blocks*—examines Orion nebula for proplanetary disks
- *Search for Earth-Crossing Objects*—looking for asteroids that cross Earth's path
- *Observatory Site Selection*—selects a site for an observatory

Selecting an investigation begins in the Conference Center, which contains text and video descriptions of each investigation, or in the Auditorium to listen to lectures on each investigation. Having selected an interesting investigation, students develop a plan using the Research Path Diagram, which provides a path to guide them through their investigation, including background research that is needed, data collection, data analysis, data interpretation, and presentation. Students use the Auditorium, Library, and Replica Viewer to gather background research and then go to the Observatory to collect data. In the Observatory (Figure 4.3), they can use an image browser (Figure 4.4) or select a particular observatory from which to view the sky. Observations must be carefully planned in order to provide the best data.

At the completion of an investigation, students must make a presentation to their class and other astronomers about their findings. The presentation summarizes all of the data that they have collected and analyzed. Scoring rubrics and evaluation sheets are provided to help guide the evaluation of these presentations and all other student activities.

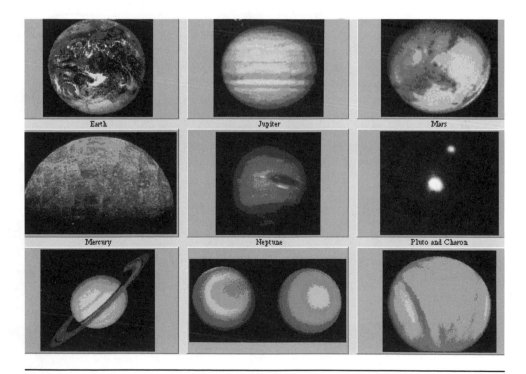

Figure 4.4 Image browser

Conducting scientific investigations, guided by the program but under control of groups of students, is the most compelling attribute of *The Astronomy Village*. Students learn to conduct scientific investigations by conducting scientific investigations. They are acting like scientists in a realistic simulation of a scientific environment. The environment and the activities they pursue are authentic. In order to conduct investigations, they must collaborate with one another in small groups. Students actively pursue a plan, which requires intentional learning. *The Astronomy Village* is an example of a complete, multimedia-based learning environment.

Exploring the Nardoo The Nardoo is an imaginary river in Australia that provides a rich context for ecological investigations to support biology, geography, social science, and language and media studies. While it is focused on ecology, the Nardoo's more general purpose is to engage skills in problem solving, measuring, collating, and communicating. While exploring the Nardoo, students study the interactions between living organisms and the physical and chemical environment in which they operate, with particular emphasis on the role and impact of the human species at both a macro and micro level. It is an active learning environment in which students participate in teams, investigate issues (take measurements, interpret maps and graphs, analyze data) and communicate their results.

Students begin their investigation of the Nardoo River in the Water Research Centre (Figure 4.5), where three different specialists describe the investigations

Figure 4.5 Water Research Centre

and provide help when requested. Items in the Center are hot buttons providing access to investigations (clicking on the River Investigation board takes students to a visual identification of the different investigations (Figure 4.6), a file cabinet full of information, video and radio clipboards, computer catalog, Plant and Animal book, text tablet, and a clippings folder.

Each investigation focuses on a different problem with different issues. They include flood problems, dams and catchment basins, algae blooms, coal mining, wildlife changes, logging, overgrown water plants and weeds, wetlands degradation, and farming impacts. One of the investigations focuses on how chemical pollution has affected the Nardoo River ecosystem:

> *Many of the children of Pilliga Crossing enjoyed fishing from the banks of the Nardoo River during their spare time. They noticed an increasing number of dead fish floating around their favorite fishing holes. Local media carried news reports dealing with this and other incidents which may be related.*
>
> *Your task: Find possible reasons for the fish kill. Prepare a report that details your findings, as well as any procedures that the community might adopt to fix the problem.*

In this investigation, students may access a rich variety of information sources about the investigation, including television reports (e.g., *Fish found dead in river, Chemical dumping to be fined, Chemical dumping witnessed*), radio reports (e.g., *Chemical disposal policy outlined, Tip poisons nearby river*), newspaper articles (e.g., *Keep out of river, Acid burns school boys at local tip, Industry suspected of dumping acid*). Students also have access to a Plant and Animal book to see how changes to the wetlands will affect the flora and fauna of the region. Students can sample the

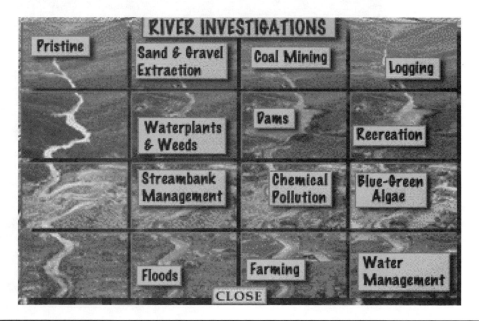

Figure 4.6   River Investigations

river at any point (see Figure 4.7) for a variety of pollutants (phosphorus, nitrogen, pesticides, oil), as well as for indicators of the stream's health (pH, water temperature, flow rate, turbidity, algae, oxygen). Their task is to identify the sources of pollution along the river, as well as to predict the effects of those pollutants on the river animals and plants. It is hoped that the students will form an opinion about the need for environmental controls of pollution.

To navigate and manipulate the multimedia environment, students use their PDA (personal digital assistant). The PDA (see Figure 4.7) provides access to information, navigation, and exploration tools, permitting students to take measurements, manipulate data and text, research multimedia information, and plan activities.

To support various investigations, the Nardoo program provides a number of simulators. For example, in order to learn about water usage, students can access the simulator in Figure 4.8. In this simulator, students identify the number of baths, showers, toilet flushes, dish washings, car washings, lawn waterings, and so on, their family uses per day. The simulator calculates the volume of water usage and compares it with national averages. Students can then implement various

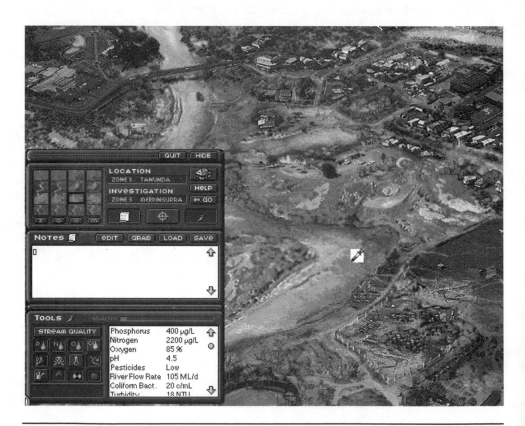

Figure 4.7   Chemical Pollution Investigation with PDA

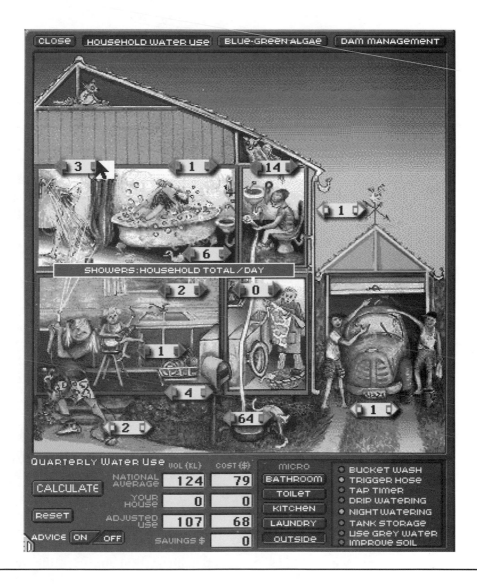

Figure 4.8 Water usage simulator

water-saving features in each of the rooms (bathroom, kitchen, laundry), rerun the simulation, and determine the level of savings attributable to these devices.

The Nardoo River multimedia program provides a problem-solving environment that enables students to actively manipulate a complex environment, seek information, and conduct investigations in order to construct their own knowledge about ecological issues. The teacher's guide provides a number of activities for both individual and collaborative use. This environment is another excellent example of a multimedia-based learning environment that can be used to engage learners in meaning making. It possesses most of the attributes of the learning environments described in Chapter 7.

Learning Activity: Sailing on the *Mimi*   One of the best known and most revered of educational multimedia programs, *The Voyages of the Mimi* (*Voyage* and *Second Voyage of the Mimi*), combine video, software, and print materials, along with a real sailboat, into an interdisciplinary science and math curriculum for the middle grades (4–8). Developed at the Bank Street College of Education, the Voyages, like anchored instruction described in Chapter 3, contextualizes and anchors learning in a series of video adventures. In the first series of the *Mimi* adventures, a video tells a series of adventure stories about a scientific expedition to study whales. The second series of stories tells of archaeologists in search of a lost Mayan city.

The adventures encountered by the *Mimi* on the videos include (among others):

Whalewatch—Provides a firsthand look at whale researchers at work and explores the variety of whale species.

On the Shoals—An electrical failure leaves the *Mimi* in danger of running aground in the shallow waters of George's Shoals.

Mapping the Blue Part—Scientists map the ocean floor using data collected by ship and by satellite.

Counting Whales—The crew conducts a whale census, using the computer to help analyze the data.

Whale Bones—Fossil records, evolution, field research methods, and the natural history of whales are the focus of work at the Smithsonian Institution.

Going Fishing—The crew observes humpback whale feeding behavior, and students get a glimpse of day-to-day life on a seagoing research expedition.

Songs in the Sea—An expedition to the studio of Katy Payne, whose work is the study of whale songs.

The *Second Voyage of the Mimi* continues the adventure with a group of archaeologists wintering off Mexico's Yucatan peninsula in order to study the Mayan civilization. Like the first series, it combines dramatic episodes and documentary expeditions to develop mathematical and scientific concepts in grades 4 through 8.

Replete with information about whales, ships, the sea, marine science, and survival techniques, the adventures in *The Voyage of the Mimi* provoke students' interest in scientific and mathematical concepts by observing their use in real-life situations. The adventures take place aboard the sailboat *Mimi* in the North Atlantic. Like the *Scientists in Action* series described in Chapter 3, the voyages introduce scientists who use science and math in their work. A series of documentaries explain the science and math themes from the adventure, such as global weather patterns, sampling techniques, and navigation.

Each adventure is supplemented with a wealth of print materials (lesson plans, activities, and projects) that help to integrate the video programs into science, math, social studies, language arts, music, and art classrooms. Additionally, software provides students with problem-solving games and simulations to enable them to practice the skills and concepts explored in the video material. For instance, Pirate's Gold challenges you, as the captain of a ship searching for treasure, to locate sunken treasure so that your diver can recover it (*Note:* you have only three tanks of air to dive with). Using chart books that show the latitude and longitude of the treasure, the students must navigate the ship most efficiently among hazards to locate the treasure.

Additionally, many students have the opportunity to experience the *Mimi* firsthand. The *Mimi*, a 70-foot ketch, docks in ports up and down the Atlantic coast. Over the past six years more than 150,000 school children have attended dockside learning festivals that included hands-on demonstrations of *Mimi*-related science and technology. The students get to visit the *Mimi* and ask Captain Granville questions. Some classes share their firsthand experiences via the Internet with other land-locked classrooms unable to attend the *Mimi* Fest. They ask students from around the country to e-mail their questions for the class to ask the experts at the *Mimi* Fest about the *Mimi*. The host class students ask the questions for their partner guest class and, after the *Mimi* Fest, formulate the answers and send all the questions and answers to each participating classroom. They also transport banners from the guest class to the *Mimi* Fest and display them.

The *Voyage of the Mimi* is one of three sets of prepackaged multimedia materials that students cannot manipulate and change that are described in this chapter. Most of the other applications described in this chapter engage learners as authors and producers of multimedia, rather than users of preprogrammed materials. However, there are many excellent examples of multimedia learning environments, because they include experiences that engage students in active learning. That activity stimulates curiosity and motivates students to dig deeper into content. The activity, a feeling of co-participation in the research process causes students to assume some ownership of the process, which is a key component of meaningful learning.

Learning Processes and Roles   The learning processes engaged by students in each of these three environments are complete: students are active, constructive, intentional, and cooperative as they conduct authentic investigations. It is impossible to describe all of the activities of every program. For this information, you are referred to the teacher's guides that normally accompany these programs. The point is: multimedia can be a powerful teaching tool, when it engages learners in student-controlled investigations. The multimedia are used to provide resources to support the investigations. The multimedia are requested by the students as needed, so they support intentional learning. This use of multimedia is distinctly different from multimedia lecture, where the multimedia are used (often ineffectively) to make verbal lectures more interesting.

Teacher roles in support of learning in these multimedia environments are, like the other activities described in this book, passive and regulatory, while the learner roles are active and intentional. Permitting students to regulate their learning in safe, scientific environments like these will enable them to better use those skills in the real world when they need them.

Learning by Constructing Hypermedia

Meaningful learning involves solving complex and ill-structured problems. Multimedia and hypermedia can be used to engage and support learners in solving complex problems. For example, high school students in an environmental science course produced interactive video programs on biomes in HyperCard using webbed or linear hypermedia models. Some of their hypermedia knowledge bases contained a conceptual model of the biome; others did not (Chuckran 1992). He found that the use of a webbed hypertext design strategy, indicating more complexity, improved content acquisition more than the linear strategy. When students explicitly linked content in their designs in order to show the interrelatedness or complexity of ideas, they were more likely to develop meaningful content structures. If you want students to understand complex ideas, then you need to allow them to represent the complexity of the real world in their own products. And, as with virtually every other study, this one showed that producing multimedia is a more powerful way of learning than studying already-produced materials.

Hypermedia construction has been shown to engage intentional learning with children as young as eight years old. Eight- and ten-year-old children used KidPix and demonstrated to adults hour to produce science-fiction stories (Gouzouasis 1994). Not only did they quickly become skilled producers, but they also were very comfortable in demonstrating their products to a group of adults. Their productions emulated the multimedia production techniques that they were exposed to on television and video games. Gouzouasis concluded that they had more fun producing multimedia than from learning about the computer.

Learning Activity: Students as Hypermedia Authors   We recently participated in a study with seventh-grade English and social studies students to discover what rhetorical constructions, cognitive strategies, and social negotiations students engage in when constructing their own hypermedia documents (McKillop 1996). We used ethnography, grounded theory, and phenomenology (including questionnaires, student learning logs, interviews, document analysis, videotaping, and observation as data sources) to study the process of composing hypermedia. This included the composing process, construction of hyperpathways, use of media, utilization of potentials and constraints of the technology, and the social construction of the knowledge. We asked: how will students compose; how will they collaborate; how will they approach and deal with the new environment; how will they work through links and spaces; how will they use media; and how will they utilize the constraints and potentials of the technology?

During the course of the study, eight students worked on the poetry unit, and eight worked on a biography unit. They collected multimedia artifacts— sounds, images, videos, and texts—which they digitized for use in constructing a StorySpace (from Eastgate Systems) multimedia document. In addition to this hypermedia tool, each student developed skills in using SoundEdit Pro for digitizing voice-overs and music; Adobe Premiere for digitizing video and creating original QuickTime movies; Adobe Photoshop linked to DeskScan for digitizing images; and ClarisWorks for word processing. In response to a teacher-generated scenario (see Figure 4.9), the poetry groups defined a series of terms and wrote

You live in State College. The year is 2021, two years after a nuclear holocaust has decimated your community, your country, life as it was. Although many aspects of your life are still disrupted, your community feels the need for some sort of continuity and beauty. Your computer-consulting firm (a few computers still work) has been assigned the task of bringing the knowledge of poetry to school-age children. Areas that you will need to concentrate on include the following: how a poem looks; how a poem sounds; how a poem expresses an idea; how a poem uses language in a special way. Although some poetry still exists from before the attack, you may need to write new poems of different types to provide students with the foundation they need. You may need to integrate or create film, sound, images, or original movies to complete your task. You will be working as a group for some sections of the project and as individuals for other sections. Good luck.

Figure 4.9   Teacher-generated poetry scenario

and edited their own poetry—incorporating sounds, images, original QuickTime movies, and video—to serve as examples in a StorySpace multimedia document that was to serve as a learning tool for younger students.

The students divided the topics among themselves, and they shared their poetry so that they could become familiar with what each member was doing. Each group composed its introduction collaboratively, trying to include navigational information, even though they were themselves a bit unclear at that point about how to navigate through StorySpace. One group decided to follow through on the scenario with a picture and an original poem by one of the members of the group. The other group addressed the scenario with an explanation of the purpose for their presentation.

The students concentrated on their poetry, which they wrote at night. One of the groups had decided that all of the poems would be nature poems, so any poem that did not fit that theme was eliminated from the project. This meant that more poems had to be written to serve as examples for each of the different types. The other group decided not to pursue a theme; in fact, they eventually included all the poems written by the group members.

Although the poetry was written by individuals, the groups were very careful about helping each other. For instance, since only one person could work at the computer at a time, the other group members would assist with scanning, digitizing, and locating pictures, sounds, and video for their group to use for their poetry. At this point, there was a lot of activity in the resource room, and the students accumulated great stacks of resources to assist them. Individuals also began to come in to work on their study-hall time.

In one group, the students were eager to include video, still images, and graphics right from the outset. Each day saw an increase to the resource pile. The students very carefully planned and executed original QuickTime movies. One young man even got the inspiration for a poem from several computed graphics on his home computer; he combined these to create a picture for which he wrote an engaging poem, "A Pig and His Marshmallow" (title inspired by the book *A Boy and His Dog*). One girl searched for and, with the teacher's help, found a video clip of bears eating fish in a spring. Not only did she use the clip, but she also, on the suggestion of her group members, changed the title of the poem because the clip focused more on the bears eating the fish—which she had already discussed in the poem. The video clip helped her to focus on the aspect of the poem that she liked the best, thus, the renaming of the poem.

In the other group, only one student started bringing in pictures right from the start. She scanned the picture and then used StorySpace's ability to open a card with the sound playing to recite her poem. In the end, she did not include a written text of the poem, just the picture and the audio reading. She also constructed an original QuickTime movie using still images and her voice-over reading a poem. It wasn't until she created these two pieces that the members of her group got excited about utilizing the capabilities of the computer. After a while, all the members of this group added pictures to their poems, although no one added any more movies.

Known as the "web view" because it graphically presents links between spaces, Figure 4.10 shows the topical organization of the project. Each space in this web view has two features: (1) the title of the space, which when clicked on, reveals a window for writing text and media called the writing space; and (2) the organizational space, in which subordinate spaces are represented by identical miniature boxes. The strings between boxes indicate author-generated hyperlinks between text/media contained in each of the writing spaces. Not all of the links in a document are visible at one time because each space can contain more spaces inside spaces inside spaces, and so on. When the reader double-clicks in the organizational space, a new web view of the next hierarchical level of spaces and links is displayed. A single click on the title of the space *Language* in Figure 4.11 reveals the writing space in which words, graphics, or video clips can be placed. Music can be included in a video clip or can be programmed to play automatically when the writing space is opened. A single group of words or a graphic area can be highlighted to make multiple links going to different destinations. When the author does this, a dialogue box appears with choices for the reader to follow. Figure 4.11 illustrates this navigational dialogue box because the students linked the word *simile* to two writing spaces: *Language* and *Beluga*. Figure 4.12 shows the result of the reader having chosen to follow the *Beluga* link. As the space opens, the computer highlights the words the students linked to *simile* in the previous window. In this case, the entire poem is highlighted as an example of a simile.

The biography groups were given the task of researching a famous person's life and composing a monologue to be presented in front of their classes. To mirror what their classmates were constructing without the aid of the computer, the students were instructed to write the monologue in first person. They began by brainstorming ways to present the projects, such as dressing up as Martin Luther—homemade monk suit and all—sitting Paul Revere atop a horse and filming part of the famous ride, capturing part of the J.F.K. assassination video from the movie *J.F.K.* One group decided to focus on a family tree to introduce their

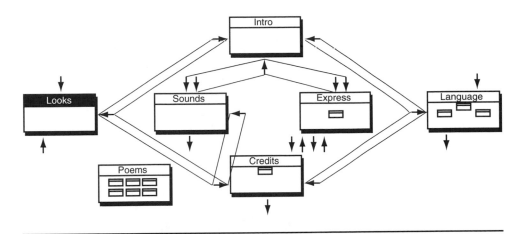

Figure 4.10   Web view of StorySpace document

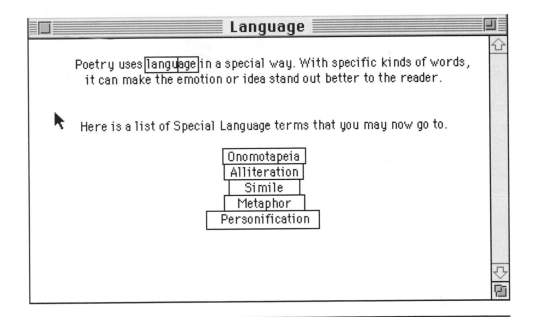

Figure 4.11   Highlighted links in StorySpace

subjects. While two members of this group decided to introduce their own sections in this fashion, the group as a whole opted for a movie introduction, which included all five students speaking while a picture of their person was shown. The other group also adopted this introductory movie idea, and one of this group's members even created his own introductory first-person movie for his person, Martin Luther.

Beluga

Like a fluffy marshmallow,
soft as a pillow.
Like a white cloud,
floating in a blue sky.
With two chubby flippers,
And a twinkle in its eye.
by
Allison Crnic

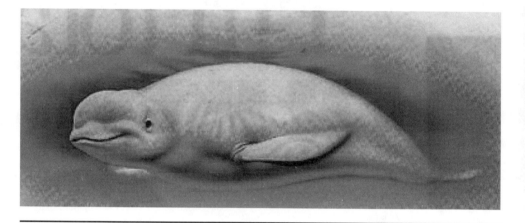

Figure 4.12　Student poem as example of simile

The students spent the rest of the time writing scripts, scanning images, recording and digitizing sound, creating movies, and planning and executing spaces. Most of the linking that these students did was implicit in the narrative structures that their projects were presented in, and they planned almost no other linking.

Storytelling in Shared Spaces　Learners sometimes work in learning and knowledge-building communities, exploiting each others' skills while providing social support, and modeling and observing the contributions of each member. One of the most interesting examples of the intellectual effects of collaborative multimedia production was demonstrated by Smith (1992), where Navajo school children in a reading improvement program collaborated to produce hypermedia programs. The students produced a multimedia version of a familiar, traditional Navajo story, "How Spider Woman Taught Changing Woman to Weave." Third- and sixth-grade students (Figure 4.13) used paint and text editors and picture-capture utilities to develop multimedia interpretations of this important part of their oral tradition.

Figure 4.13   Navajo children working on multimedia

Smith concluded from the experience that "simply inserting computers and other media into the curriculum without integrating programs and activities into the fabric of the curriculum probably will do little to effect meaningful change" (pp. 292–93). Navajo children lack apparent reasons to learn in traditional learning modes. Producing multimedia materials can help. The key to constructive learning is ownership. Navajo children have no ownership in traditional transmissive approaches to learning, because the context has little meaning in their cultural context. When they use technology to represent their own cultural beliefs, they own the productions and they believe in the products. Perhaps the most interesting conclusion from this study was that collaborative multimedia production was so effective in this situation because the Navajo culture is a cooperative, noncompetitive culture.

Designing an Information Kiosk for the Zoo   Contextual learning involves work on meaningful, real-world tasks or simulated tasks in problem-based learning contexts. That is, the students attempt to solve real problems. When this occurs, they understand what they are learning and transfer it more successfully to new situations. Multimedia and hypermedia are powerful tools for engaging learners in meaningful, real-life tasks. For instance, Beichner (1994) reported a project in which highly motivated junior high school students created a touch-sensitive kiosk to be installed in the local zoo. They were commissioned by the zoo to provide an information kiosk to complement the traditional displays of animals.

To prepare the multimedia kiosk, students talked to zoo visitors and staff. They had to work cooperatively to search out content materials from a wide variety of resources and convey that information in a hypermedia program for the kiosk using an on-screen audio recorder, a video tool to operate the videodisk player, color painting and text tools, and a data-linking tool for connecting pieces of information. The multimedia production tools enabled them to grab pictures, video sequences, or audio sequences from the videodisk and place them onto the screen. The students also wrote text and produced colorful drawings by capturing images using a scanner and electronic camera.

They quickly gained independence. Within a few weeks they demonstrated a strong desire to work on their own. Once the students had mastered the editor, roles rapidly changed. Students not only picked out what information and layout designs they would use, they also began showing other students and even their teachers how to best use the equipment and software. The students began skipping study halls and lunch periods in order to work on their screens. They used these tools to create buttons on the kiosk screen. By touching these buttons, zoo visitors could see and hear animals, look for more information, or even print out an information sheet, complete with a map of the zoo and student-generated questions and comments about the animal on the screen.

The students' enthusiasm did not diminish throughout the project. Often the computer coordinator would arrive in the morning to find students who had come in early and were waiting for her to open the door. The students were enthusiastic because they saw that their work had importance because it was a real-world problem. It was worthwhile for them to learn new material and uncover additional resources. By establishing an environment where creative thinking about the content material is combined with real-world assignments, students will learn content, enjoy the learning process, and recognize that they have created something worthwhile that serves the community.

Learning Activity: Students as Multimedia Ethnographers Conversational learners naturally seek out opinions and ideas from others in order to become part of knowledge-building and discourse communities. Reflective learners articulate what they are doing, the decisions they are making, the strategies they are using, and the answers that they are finding, while reflecting on the meaningfulness of it all. Multimedia environments may be used to engage both conversational and reflective learning—in this case, through multimedia ethnography.

Ethnographers are persons who investigate the customs, habits, and social behaviors of races and peoples. Ethnography has traditionally been used to research native, indigenous populations. Ricki Goldman-Segall (1992, 1995), at the University of British Columbia, has developed a multimedia platform, called *Learning Constellations,* for supporting ethnographic investigations and interpretations by students. *Learning Constellations* allows students to construct multimedia programs, including videos, pictures, and narratives written by them, about the topic of investigation. Her students have used *Learning Constellations,* for instance, to investigate the effects of clear-cutting in the British Columbia rain forests and examining the lives and histories of the First Nations of the Northwest.

Learning Constellations also allows readers to contribute their own interpretations of original stories as well as creating their own stories. These stories come from multiple authors (what Goldman-Segall calls multiloguing, rather than dia-

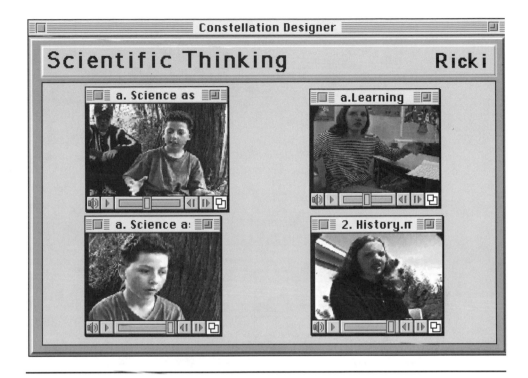

Figure 4.14   Perspectives available from *Constellations* knowledge base

loguing) and are linked together in clusters or constellations of perspectives. These multilogues produce what Clifford Geertz (1973) calls *thick descriptions* of phenomena. The constellations of video and stories that students produce represent larger and different patterns of meaning about the topics being studied (Figure 4.14). "Layers build; stories change; patterns emerge; and inquiry becomes reflexive practice" (Goldman-Segall 1995). It is that kind of refection that makes *Learning Constellations* a powerful multimedia experience.

The student storytelling afforded by *Learning Constellations* leads to the social construction of knowledge. Students work together to investigate issues in multiple levels of conversation. Students go out into the real world and investigate socially relevant problems. They collect evidence about those problems, usually in the form of video interviews and documentaries (see Figure 4.15). They analyze, digitize, and assemble those videos into multivocal story chunks, called *stars*, which include the videos and the student annotations of them. These stars, produced and told by different people to represent their unique points of view, are assembled into larger groupings called *constellations*. As other students or the public examine the students' multimedia database, they add their own views and annotations. Why? Because "the process of making discoveries and the process of recursive reaction, within the data and among the users, that meaning of an event,

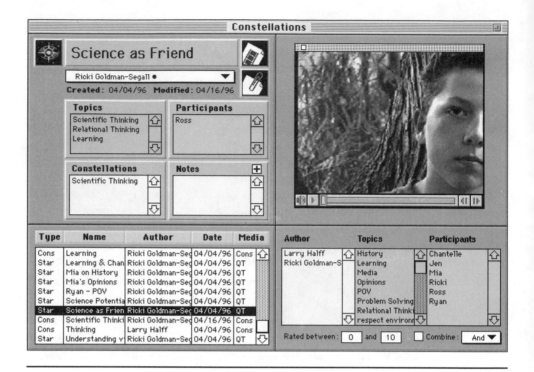

Figure 4.15   Available perspectives

action, or situation can be negotiated" (Goldman-Segall 1992, p. 258). Having students design and film their own video narratives creates a video culture in the classroom—not a passive culture of viewing video, but rather, a culture of constructing videos to tell a complex and important story. In becoming video ethnographers, students become friends with the camera; become a participant recorder by training fellow researchers, teachers, and students how to use video for observation; become a storyteller by selecting video chunks and writing narratives; and become a navigator by exploring using video in new situations (Goldman-Segall 1992).

Learning Processes   First and foremost, constructing hypermedia knowledge bases is constructive—literally and pedagogically. In the process of constructing hypermedia knowledge bases, students must construct knowledge to represent. The process of constructing knowledge bases is very active and very intentional. It is active, because students are manipulating the various modalities and representations afforded by multimedia programs. And, as evidenced by the students' roles (described next), the process is very intentional, requiring careful planning. Evaluating the fruits of those plans (assessing the effectiveness of the hypermedia knowledge base) requires very incisive reflection and self-regulation. Constructing hypermedia knowledge bases is among students' most complete intellectual activities.

Student Roles   Lehrer (1993) carefully described the intellectual activities that students must complete in order to build hypermedia knowledge bases. These activities include four major processes:

1. Planning requires that students make decisions about:
   - major goals of the knowledge base (who is the audience, what should they learn)
   - topics and content to be included in the knowledge base
   - relationships among the topics (how will they be linked)
   - interface design (what functions should be provided to the learner)
   - how the design will collaborate to complete the task
2. Accessing, transforming, and translating information into knowledge includes:
   - searching for and collecting relevant information
   - selecting and interpreting information sources
   - developing new interpretations and perspectives
   - allocating information to nodes and deciding how it will be represented, that is, which medium (text, graphic, pictures, video, audio)
   - deciding on the nature of the links necessary to interconnect content and create links
3. Evaluating the knowledge base includes:
   - assessing compromises in what was represented and how
   - assessing the information coverage and their organization
   - testing the browser
   - trying it out with users and soliciting their feedback
4. Revising the knowledge base from the feedback includes:
   - reorganizing and restructuring the knowledge base to make it more accessible or meaningful

Teacher Roles   The role of the teacher should be to coach students in these different processes. Coaching is a less directive method of teaching, usually involving prompting or provoking the students with questions about the content and treatment they are using. You may suggest issues but should not recommend answers or treatments. Those are the students' responsibility. Lehrer (1993) suggests questions such as:

- How are you going to organize your presentation, and why?
- How are you going to decide on what to include and what to leave out?
- Can you draw a map of the flow of your program? Does it seem logical?
- Which stories do you want to include, and what do they represent?
- Which are the most important themes in describing your content? How did you determine that they were the most important?

Lehrer also suggests modeling certain processes, such as using notecards to represent nodes and connecting them with pieces of string.

Assessing Learning   Hypermedia knowledge bases are rich indicators of students' understanding. They can be evaluated by asking questions such as:

- How is the presentation organized? How complex is that organization? How appropriate is that organization for describing the content?
- What auditory and visual resources were used? How did those resources complement/explain/or illustrate the ideas being conveyed?
- How many links were provided to interconnect the material? How descriptive were these links? How did they describe the information?
- How was the content conveyed in each of the nodes (expository, stories, questions)?
- How accurate is the information represented?
- Are all important information sources represented in the presentation?

Many more questions should occur to you as you begin to view and evaluate student productions. Student presentation of their programs will usually evince a level of pride seldom seen in classrooms.

CONCLUSIONS

Throughout this book, we have promoted our belief that students-as-producers-of-technologies engage in much more meaningful learning than students-as-receivers-from-instructional-technologies. With no technology is this belief more obvious than with multimedia. In this chapter, we have described a number of projects that use multimedia programs to engage meaningful learning and, more importantly, use multimedia as an authoring platform for students to represent their own meaning. For each of the projects that have been reported in the literature, there are surely many more that have not been reported. We are not suggesting that any particular project represents a model for how multimedia should engage learners. Rather, we have included these descriptions as indicators of how powerful the effects of producing multimedia and hypermedia can be in order to motivate you to consider trying it yourself. We do not suggest that it will be effortless. It is difficult for teachers at all levels to relinquish authority (control over the classroom and control of the meaning that is constructed by students). The level of activity that results from student construction of hypermedia and multimedia can seem frenetic (it is!), and the meaning that is being constructed may not be obvious while the process is going on. The benefits may require reflection by both students and the teacher. They should become obvious, however.

We recommend that these projects incorporate large chunks of time and curriculum. That is, the products need to be complex. More complex representations of students' knowledge yield better learning. These should not be small projects focusing on a single idea. Rather, they should attempt to integrate ideas throughout the curriculum and preferably from different disciplines. Hypermedia construction is an ideal medium for engaging and supporting interdisciplinary learning. The links in the knowledge base can represent different perspectives from different disciplines. In order to help students handle that complexity, we also recommend the use of an explicit hypermedia authoring tool that supports and emphasizes different link structures. Many multimedia authoring platforms emphasize only the presentation aspects, with no explicit linking available. There are many good products out there that foster student linking as an important component of the software. This is a difficult process that will require a good deal of practice. We have successfully used Post-It notes on a whiteboard with a marker to draw the connections. Students pick up the skill readily. And then they run with it. And run and run and run . . . .

THINGS TO THINK ABOUT

If you would like to reflect on the ideas that we presented in this chapter, then articulate your responses to the following questions and compare them with others' responses.

1. Is multimedia singular or plural—does it describe many things or a singular phenomenon?
2. Multimedia, like most technologies, achieved its initial success in the commercial sector. Has there ever been a technology that was developed exclusively for education that emerged first and prospered in the educational sector?
3. Is MTV multimedia? Why or why not? How could MTV be used for teaching?
4. Stories are powerful forms of communication. How would you use multimedia to tell about yourself? Suppose you had every multimedia resource available, how would you produce your life story?
5. How would you produce an ethnographic study about your school (or your town) using a multimedia program like *Constellations*?

REFERENCES

Beichner, R. J. (1994). Multimedia editing to promote science learning. *Journal of Educational Multimedia and Hypermedia,* 3 (1): 55–70.

Chuckran, D. A. (1992). *Effect of student-produced interactive multimedia models on student learning.* Doctoral dissertation, Boston University.

Geertz, C. (1973). *The interpretation of cultures.* New York: Basic Books.

Goldman-Segall, R. (1992). Collaborative virtual communities: Using *Learning Constellations,* a multimedia ethnographic research tool. In E. Barrett (ed.), *Sociomedia: Multimedia, hypermedia, and the social construction of knowledge.* Cambridge, MA: MIT Press.

Goldman-Segall, R. (1995). Configurational validity: A proposal for analyzing ethnographic multimedia narratives. *Journal of Educational Multimedia and Hypermedia,* 4 (2).

Gouzouasis, P. (1994). Multimedia constructions of children: An exploratory study. *Journal of Computing in Childhood Education,* 5 (3/4): 273–84.

Jeffcoate, J. (1995). *Multimedia in practice: Technology and applications.* New York: Prentice-Hall.

Jonassen, D. H. (1989). *Hypertext/hypermedia.* Englewood Cliffs, NJ: Educational Technology Publications.

Jonassen, D. H. (1991). Hypertext as instructional design. *Educational Technology: Research and Development,* 39 (1), 83–92.

Lehrer, R. (1993). Authors of knowledge: Patterns of hypermedia design. In S. P. LaJoie & S. J. Derry (Eds.), *Computers as cognitive tools.* Hillsdale, NJ: Lawrence Erlbaum

McKillop, A. M. (1996). Doctoral dissertation, Pennsylvania State University.

Nelson, T. H. (1981). *Literary machines.* Swarthmore. PA: The Author.

Ottavianio, B. F. (1993). *The effects of multimedia presentation formats on the memory of a narrative.* Doctoral dissertation, Columbia University.

Smith, K. J. (1992). Using multimedia with Navajo children: An effort to alleviate problems of cultural learning style, background of experience, and motivation. *Reading and Writing Quarterly,* 8(3): 287–94.

Stamper, K. N. (1991). *The effects of the use of multimedia on the higher-level thinking skills of seventh-grade students.* Doctoral dissertation, East Texas State University.

von Wodtke, M. (1993). *Mind over media: Creative thinking skills for electronic media.* New York: McGraw-Hill.

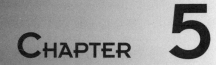

CHAPTER 5

CREATING TECHNOLOGY-SUPPORTED
LEARNING COMMUNITIES

FORMING COMMUNITIES

Margaret Riel (1991) tells a story about a four-year-old in her mother's office.

> The mother, wanting to involve her daughter in her work, realizes the daughter has never heard modem noises, and begins explaining:
>
> "You see these words on the screen. Well, this little modem takes those words and turns them into sounds. They go on the telephone lines just like someone talking, and a computer on the other hand is going to get them. Then that computer will send them to other computers. So my message will be sent all over the world!"
>
> The child looked up from her coloring and said, "Oh, like a talking drum."
>
> The mother, dumbfounded, finally asked, "A talking drum?"
>
> "You know, like a talking drum" The mother thought some more, and then she remembered that not long ago, an African storyteller had visited her daughter's preschool and shown the class an African drum. When villagers wanted to get a message out to neighbors about a festival or a market, they would use the drum, and the message would be sent from village to village.

The point of the story is that modems and networks are new and exciting, but people have always found ways to communicate with each other in order to support community goals and activities; they have overcome obstacles and used considerable ingenuity in doing so. If working and learning together in communities is so natural, why do schools individualize learning and make its outcomes competitive among students?

Years ago, John Dewey commented on the dangers of a complex society that relies on schools and classrooms to convey essential knowledge and tools to its youth:

> As societies become more complex in structure and resources, the need for formal teaching and learning increases. As formal teaching and training grows, there's a danger of creating an undesirable split between the experience gained in direct association and what is acquired in school. This danger was never greater than at the present time on account of the rapid growth of the last few centuries, of course, and technical modes of skill. (cited in Riel 1991)

The schism between real-world experience and school learning is a serious concern. As we have tried to illustrate throughout this book, technologies of various kinds can serve as bridges between schools and students' outside experiences, if they are used in the right way within a supportive context. Technologies can support learning communities by providing communications vehicles to all learners.

The notion of community is used in a variety of ways. We will discuss several key variations on the concept of community.

Discourse Communities

People are social creatures who like to talk with each other. Generally, they talk about common interests—sports, gardening, cars, dancing, video games—whatever objects and activities engage them. Whenever they can, people talk face to face about their interests. When they must reach beyond their neighborhood to find others who share their interests, or to expand their discourse community, people talk to each other at a distance through newsletters, magazines, and television shows. If you examine the magazine counter in your supermarket, you will find discourse communities focused on everything from brides to monster trucks. Cable television supports discourse networks on sports, cooking, and shopping. Computer networks have evolved to support discourse communities through different forms of computer conferences. For instance, thousands of bulletin boards, UseNet, and NetNews services support special-interest discussion groups oriented to a wide range of topics, from computer games to sexual deviancies. More than 500 different organized UseNet groups discuss computer issues alone. More than 10,000 other groups support conversations on topics as diverse as baseball, poetry, model railroading, abortion, gun control, and religion. Thousands of chat rooms and multiuser dungeons (MUDs) connect millions of users who daily converse about their lives, their dreams, and their inadequacies. The number of active and interactive discourse communities has expanded exponentially with the growth of telecommunications. These communities can now stay in constant contact about their interests.

Communities of Practice

In the real world, when people need to learn something, they usually do not remove themselves from their normal situations and force themselves into sterile rooms to listen to lectures on formal principles about what they are doing. Rather, they tend to form work groups (practice communities), assign roles, teach and support each other, and develop identities that are defined by the roles they play in support of the group. Jean Lave (1991) sees learning "as a social phenomenon constituted in the experienced, lived-in world, through legitimate peripheral participation in ongoing social practice" (p. 64). In other words, learning results naturally from becoming a participating member of a community of practice. You cannot do your job without learning about the skills, the knowledge, and the social context that surrounds that job because the context, to a large degree, defines the nature of the job. How many times have you heard the phrase, "the way we do it here"? Knowledge of the context and its customs is not only acquired by the people, but it also becomes part of their identity, which is part of the social fabric of the community, so that "learning, thinking, and knowing are relations among people engaged in activity" (p. 67).

Knowledge-Building Communities

Scardamalia and Bereiter (1996) argue that schools inhibit, rather than support, knowledge-building by (1) focusing on individual student's abilities and learning; (2) requiring only demonstrable knowledge, activities, and skills as evidence of learning; and (3) teacher-hoarding wisdom and expertise. Students' knowledge tends to be devalued or ignored, except as evidence of their understanding of the curriculum. What students know and believe is unimportant.

Or is it? Should student knowledge not be the focus of schools, and should not schools support student knowledge-building? The goal of knowledge-building communities is to support students to "actively and strategically pursue learning as a goal"—that is, intentional learning (Scardamalia, Bereiter, and Lamon 1994, p. 201). Learning, especially intentional learning by students, is a byproduct of schoolwork. To support intentional learning among students, Scardamalia and Bereiter have developed a Computer-Supported Intentional Learning Environment (CSILEs, described later in the chapter), where students produce their own knowledge databases in their own knowledge-building community. Thus, student knowledge can be "objectified, represented in an overt form so that it [can] be evaluated, examined for gaps and inadequacies, added to, revised, and reformulated" (p. 201).

When students own the knowledge, rather than the teacher or the textbook, they become committed to building knowledge, rather than merely receiving and reprocessing it. Knowledge building becomes a social activity, not a solitary one of retention and regurgitation. Technology plays a key role in knowledge-building communities by providing a medium for storing, organizing, and reformulating the ideas that are contributed by each community member. Although these knowledge-building technology environments treat knowledge as a commodity, to the community of students it represents the synthesis of their thinking, something they own and for which they can be proud. In this sense, we believe, the goal of schools should be to foster knowledge-building communities.

Learning Communities

Classrooms and schools can be communities of learners, although they often are not. Why? A community is a social organization of people who share knowledge, values, and goals. Classrooms typically are not communities, because students are disconnected or are competing with one another. The students do not share common learning goals or interests. Within classrooms there are social communities or cliques, but their purpose is not to learn together or from one another. Rather, those cliques seek to socially reinforce their own identities by excluding others. Learning communities emerge when students share common interests. Telecommunications connect learners within the same class or around the world in order to pursue some common learning objectives. The *Voyage of the Mimi*, described in Chapter 4, represents a scientific learning agenda that kids around the country can share. The Internet supports NetNews and UseNet groups that share common goals and interests. Learning communities emerge when learners work together toward their common goals. Many of the projects in this chapter constitute learning communities. They can be fostered by having the participants conduct research (reading, studying, viewing, consulting experts) and share information in the pursuit of a meaningful, consequential task (Brown and Campione 1996). Many of these learning communities support reflection on the knowledge constructed and the processes used to construct it by the learners.

The concepts of discourse community, community of practice, knowledge-building community, and learning community overlap considerably. Their common belief is that rather than forcing students to conform to prepackaged instructional requirements, emphasis should be placed on the social and cognitive contributions of a group of learners to each other, with students collaborating and supporting each other toward commonly accepted learning goals. Like learning environments (described in Chapter 7), learning and knowledge-building communities depend heavily on both student and teacher buy-in, responsibility, and continuing motivation, as well as a rich collection of information and learning resources to support them. We believe that learning communities can be an important vehicle for reforming schools. In this chapter, we show how technology can support learning communities. We then develop and illustrate the concepts of discourse and knowledge-building communities and suggest ways of nurturing a sense of community within classrooms and beyond.

SUPPORTIVE TECHNOLOGIES

Chapter 2 introduced you to the various technologies available through the Internet. In this section, we review both the underlying technologies and related activities and programs that allow learning communities to take shape.

The technological breakthrough that has afforded these learning communities is the Internet and networking technologies. The Internet, particularly the World Wide Web, has become more than a source for retrieving archived information; it has become the medium that connects scattered people and resources together. Why? In many ways, the Internet's strength lies in its decentralized nature.

As we saw in Chapter 2, the Internet is the ultimate distributed network, linking users and institutions together, allowing interactions of all kinds to occur. The Internet can become the communications vehicle that both liberates and ties learners together, including students and teachers, into coherent learning communities. The Internet can be part of the glue that keeps people connected—talking with each other, noticing and appreciating differences, working out divergent views, serving as role models and audiences for one another. The education future portended by the Internet, therefore, is not isolated and targeted to individuals. Rather, it is a community-centered future that accommodates each person through the workings of the larger community of learners.

At the core of learning communities is the cultivation of a certain quality of relationship among teachers and students. Learning communities are united by a common cause of mutual support and by shared values and experiences. Communities may originate from assignment (e.g., typical K–12 classrooms) or through self-selection (NetNews groups or chat rooms on the Internet). Learning communities provide a means for learning within an atmosphere of trust, support, common goals, and respect for diversity. They make use of various technologies— machines, products, information sources, even language itself—to accomplish their goals. Learning communities existed long before networking technologies came into being, but the potential scale of adoption expands with the technologies available.

Modern network technologies hold a key advantage that early visionaries did not enjoy: Students and teachers can more easily escape the confines of the closed classroom and open things up to include elements of the outside world— other classes, students, teachers, and experts; other information, projects, and media. As Riel (1996) noted:

> We send children to school to give them the opportunity to move beyond the constraints of family and friends to open to them a vast range of possible futures. However the classroom in today's society, by its very nature, is constraining. It isolates both students and teachers from many experiences that will help them to understand the past, develop skills for building a future, and to prepare for their role as citizens. . . . If it once took the whole village to raise a child, then can we expect a succession of isolated teachers to give students all the skills they need to [be] productive members of society? (Riel 1996; text re-ordered)

Students can be introduced to much more of the "world out there" through communications and multimedia technologies.

The Cognition and Technology Group at Vanderbilt (1994) developed a list of core values and principles for learning communities, presented in Table 5.1. The Peabody Perspective contributes to our discussion in two ways. First, it articulates in greater detail the instructional-design foundations upon which learning communities rest. Careful attention to the design of projects and curriculum is something inherited from the fields of instructional design and cognitive psychology. Second, the Peabody Perspective places learning communities within the school and community context, addressing issues such as assessment, support from the larger community, and management. This larger perspective further underscores the huge task of developing and maintaining learning communities, and the many systemic factors that must be incorporated into successful efforts.

On-line Communication (Telecommunications)

Communication in an on-line forum is different from, and in several important ways better than, face-to-face communication and other technology-based forms (like telephone conversations and videoconferencing). It is true that an on-line discussion doesn't have the richness or, to use a computer metaphor, the *bandwidth* of a face-to-face conversation. We lose important communication cues such as body language, tone of voice, accents, dialects, pace, pauses, and other important cues to meaning. Although this may be limiting, it may also be helpful, as authors must take more care to see that they are communicating clearly.

Paraphrasing a recent television commercial run by a major telecommunications vendor, on the Internet there is no race, no gender, no age, no infirmities— only minds: People talking to people.

On-line communications are often *asynchronous* (not in real time), making them different in important ways. Howard Gardner (1991) has proposed a Theory of Multiple Intelligences, which suggests that intelligence is not a single capacity,

Table 5.1   The Peabody Perspective on learning communities

---

1. Curriculum and Instruction

- Emphasizes active, problem-focused teaching and learning
- Integrates subject areas
- Emphasizes varied instructional strategies, depending on student needs
- Relies on heterogeneous, collaborative student groups/teams
- Focuses on project-based activities, while also giving attention to the development of key concepts and skills

2. Assessment

- Focuses on thinking and communicating as well as on concepts and skills
- Is authentic
- Informs instruction
- Gives schools the flexibility to respond to the uniqueness of the population they serve, while still being held accountable to state and national goals and standards

3. Professional Development and School Organization

- Provides meaningful opportunities for education to learn and improve
- Redefines "professionals as isolated experts" to "professionals as collaborators and facilitators of learning"
- Keeps decision making open and responsive to parent, student, and community input

4. Community Connections

- Keeps parents involved in their children's education
- Creates shared responsibility for children and cooperative efforts to provide resources and support for learning
- Ensures adequate and coordinated health and social services for children
- Fosters a concern for the common good

5. Technology

- Supports all areas of the learning community—learning, assessment, management, professional development, and community connectedness

---

Source: Cognition and Technology Group at Vanderbilt, 1994

but rather a series of distinct capabilities. He suggests that rather than asking "How smart are you?" we should ask, "How are you smart?" Some people, Gardner believes, are high in *verbal intelligence*. They are often verbally deft and capable of carrying out stimulating conversations. They tend to do well in traditional school environments. This does not mean they are the best thinkers or communicators. Other people want more time to consider an idea and formulate their responses. Rather than speaking extemporaneously, they are often minimal contributors to real-time conversations—the conversation is off to other topics before they have developed their ideas and ways to share them.

When given a chance to think and then speak, as is the case in several forms of on-line conversation, these people experience a new freedom and level of participation. They can be heard clearly, and the power of their responses is often impressive. When combined with the removal of biases, as already described, it becomes easy to imagine why a number of strong friendships (some crossing international borders and generations) and even romances have begun on the Internet.

Additional merits of on-line communication are described by Carvin (1996), who proposes:

> On-line discussions . . . are easier for some, since the form of communication changes from one that is interpersonal (live and in class) to one that is cyberpersonal (over e-mail, Web forms, etc.). And because conversation is on-line, it can be automatically catalogued and presented by the student as part of her processfolio. Granted, good old fashioned class discussion will not, and should not vanish with the advent of on-line class forums. But allowing students to work with each other and learn from each other will open the minds of many students who previously would not voluntarily open their mouths.

Table 5.2 shows how communication technologies—primarily e-mail, conferencing, and Web—facilitate a variety of learning activities, particularly those requiring collaboration and group effort. Moreover, technologies useful for individual or one-on-one interactions are subsumed and appropriated by collaborating groups, resulting in a fairly powerful set of tools available to groups and communities.

Forms of On-line Communication

Communication takes a variety of forms on-line, including simple browsing of Web pages, electronic mail, use of listservs, electronic bulletin boards and Net-News groups, on-line *chats*, low-end videoconferencing, and MUDs. After a quick overview of these forms of on-line communication, we'll see how they are used to promote meaningful learning.

Electronic Mail.   Electronic mail (e-mail) allows the sender to transmit a message, almost instantly, to an individual or a group of individuals. With modern e-mail programs, the transmitted message can include *attachments* that might include complex documents, images, sounds, or even brief videos. The receiver of a piece of electronic mail can easily respond, forward the message to other users, and efficiently save the message in electronic form.

The power of e-mail comes from its speed and its broadcasting capabilities. A print letter carried by postal services (*snail mail*) might take days to go in one direction, but electronic exchanges often complete two or three cycles in a matter of minutes. And sending e-mail to 20 people can be as easy as sending to one person. Another big difference is in cost. E-mail (when the computers and network connections are already in place) is virtually free.

Listservs.   Listservs are a variation of e-mail. When users interested in a particular topic *subscribe* to a listserv on some topic, they begin to receive messages from

Table 5.2. Learning activities facilitated by different levels of computer networking technologies (adapted from Paulson 1996).

Communication Level	Description	Enabling Technologies	Learning Activities
One-alone	Individuals can access information resources stored on the World Wide Web. These resources can also be used by groups.	On-line databases and journals Software libraries Tutorials and job aids Other Web resources	Independent inquiry Research and writing Browsing
One-to-one	Individuals can communicate to other individuals using e-mail, and can arrange for individual learning experiences such as internships or independent studies.	E-mail Chatting technologies using text, audio, and/or video	Apprenticeships and internships E-mail posts, private consultations One-on-one chats
One-to-many	Individuals can broadcast information to entire groups; information can also be "published" at Web sites to allow others access.	Distribution lists Web pages as a source of text and multimedia displays Web pages as links to outside resources	Lectures and symposiums Publishing results of research and inquiry activities Convenient access and dissemination of resources
Many-to-many	Groups of people can engage in open communication, through various discussion and activity forums, both real-time and asynchronously.	Listservs Chat and conferencing technologies MUD and MOO systems	Debates Discussion and support groups Group exercises and projects MUD and MOO learning activities

the other members of the list. To get a message to all of the list's subscribers, a user sends a single copy of the note to the list, and the computer that hosts the list sends a copy to all subscribers. The sender generally does not even know *how many* users there are, let alone who they are.

Lists often have hundreds of subscribers, and listserv participation sometimes results in e-mail in-boxes choked with messages. For this reason, some lists are "moderated," which means that one or more people read the message before it is copied to all members of the list, to determine whether it is worthy of distribution. For the same reason, membership on some lists is restricted.

Electronic Bulletin Boards.   Electronic bulletin boards, such as NetNews or UseNets, are similar in purpose to listservs. Instead of messages being sent to subscribers via e-mail, they are generally posted in a central location (on an electronic bulletin board) with a subject heading, date, time, and author's name. Users browse through the subject headings, read, and perhaps respond to messages of interest. Most responses are sent, via e-mail, directly to the person who posted the message, rather than being posted for all to see. It works sort of like a newspaper, in which you scan headlines, article titles, and classified ads, deciding whether to read them. If you respond, it may be to the paper itself (a letter to the editor), to an individual or organization mentioned in the article, or to the author. The software you use to look at NetNews generally keeps track of which articles you have read, and you can usually delete articles from your copy of the list of postings.

There are NetNews conversations on approximately 10,000 different topics, from trading baseball cards to discussing political science to destroying Barney the dinosaur. In fact, it is difficult to name a potentially interesting topic for which there is not an established conversation. However, teachers should be aware of two things: first, many of the conversations are not suitable for students (many are not really suitable for adults, either); and second, *flaming*, the practice of sending responses that are overly harsh, is relatively common. Students should be prepared for this before they encounter it.

Because of the storage demands created by thousands of conversations involving millions of people, Internet access providers make only a subset of the existing NetNews conversations available. If you or your students want to be involved in conversations on a particular topic, but it does not appear available, ask your Internet provider to investigate and provide it to you.

Chats.   Chats are real-time (synchronous) exchanges among individuals who are gathered in a *virtual location*, often set up as a house, with a lobby, library, kitchen, and dining room where people go to have private conversations. This is made possible by *Internet Relay Chat* or IRC software. IRC allows anyone to post a statement to the group by typing into a field and then clicking a button to submit the statement. The software adds each comment to a scrolling list. The list is sent out to participants' screens periodically, say every 20 seconds, keeping everyone informed about what has been said.

The conversations are often a bit confusing. It's rather like a cocktail party where there are several conversations going on at once. If the chat gets too busy, clusters of people can break off into another room to converse without the distraction of competing conversations. It is also possible to establish private chats, restricting entry to people who are registered to participate. Although some find this kind of communication confusing, others find it almost addictive.

Videoconferencing.   Low-end videoconferencing is also possible on the Internet. By connecting an inexpensive camera to your computer (less than $100 for black and white, less than $200 for color), you can turn your computer into a slow, but useful, videoconferencing tool. If you have a fast modem—or better yet, an Ethernet connection to the Internet—you can use it to conduct communicate with sound and rather jerky video.

New tools are becoming available each month that make this more and more practical. Internet users can connect via shareware software called CU-SeeME. They can see and hear each other. To cluster more than two sites, *reflector* software is used. People from different locations around the world contact the reflector, which displays their images for all to see. There is generally also a text-based option that resembles conversations described in the section on chats. These video-based chats are very stimulating to school-aged children, who love to see themselves on TV (or the computer) and who seem to get so much out of seeing the people with whom they are communicating.

Care should be taken, however, to keep the technology in a support role and not get romantically enamored of the tool itself. Riel (1996) observes:

> Building physical space should not be confused with building community. A [listserv], a conference or a Web page, in and of itself, does not define community. . . . It is the interactions and partnerships among and between the people who gather in these places that define a community. And these interactions will come to be perceived as "real" in the same way that we see talking on phones or listening to a president's address on television is real. These experiences do not replace face to face contacts, any more than phone conversation[s] replace meetings. They provide another form of social exchange that augment relationships and have real consequences.

Thus, the technologies (column 3 of Table 5.2) and the learning activities (column 4) serve an instrumental role in support of learning communities, and are not ends in themselves.

USING TELECOMMUNICATIONS TO FOSTER LEARNING COMMUNITIES

Classroom learning communities may look to members for their interactions, or they may venture out and create alliances with other classes and individuals. We believe that both kinds of interaction are important. Community begins with interactions among members, but can also be strengthened and defined by its outside encounters. In this section, we review a number of technologies designed to support learning communities, both within the classroom and beyond.

So far, we have focused on the Internet infrastructure—the e-mail, discussion, and chatting capabilities afforded by the networking hardware and software. These capabilities translate into a number of strategies for teaching and learning. Judi Harris (1994, 1995) has developed a list of *activity structures* suitable for the classroom, demonstrating the variety of activities that telecommunications enables:

1. **Interpersonal Exchanges.** These activities give students an opportunity to interact with others from a distance. By doing so, they come to appreciate how differently people see and make sense of their world. They also have opportunities to reinforce literacy skills through extended reading and writing activities. Harris (1995) cites several examples:

- Keypals
- Global classrooms
- Electronic appearances
- Electronic mentoring
- Impersonations

2. **Information Collections.** The focus of these activities is on collaborative, distributed collection, analysis, organization, and presentation of information. Students can participate in every step of this process. Information activities may help students internalize scientific methods. They may also strengthen students' information literacy skills. Examples include:
   - Information exchanges
   - Database creation
   - Electronic publishing
   - Electronic field trips
   - Pooled data analysis

3. **Problem-Solving Projects.** These projects focus on individual, small-group, or multigroup problems. They often require higher levels of collaboration and organization between sites. Students have opportunities to learn task-management skills in addition to content objectives. Examples include:
   - Information searches
   - Parallel problem solving
   - Electronic process writing
   - Serial creations
   - Simulations
   - Social action projects

SCAFFOLDING CONVERSATIONS IN STRUCTURED COMPUTER CONFERENCES

On-line communication presumes that students can communicate—that is, that they can meaningfully participate in conversations. In order to do that, they must be able to interpret messages, consider appropriate responses, and construct coherent replies. Most teachers realize that not all students can engage in cogent and coherent discourse. Why can't they? For one thing, most students have rarely been asked to contribute their opinions about topics. They have been too busy memorizing what the teachers tell them. So, it may be necessary to support students' attempts to converse. A number of on-line communication environments have been designed to support students' discourse skills. Three such environments are described next.

Collaboratory Notebook

Computer conferencing has been used effectively by the CoVis Project, described in Chapters 6 and 7, to connect learners from around the country in dialogues about science. Probably the most powerful part of the CoVis Project is the Collaboratory Notebook (O'Neill and Gomez 1994). The Collaboratory Notebook is a collaborative hypermedia composition system designed to support within- and cross-school science projects. What is unique about the Collaboratory is that it focuses on project investigations rather than curricular content. During a project, the teacher or any student can pose a question or a conjecture (Figure 5.1), which can be addressed by participants from around the country. Conversations may be public or private.

The Collaboratory provides a scaffolding structure for conversations by requiring specific kinds of responses to messages. For instance, in order to support the conjecture in Figure 5.1, a student may add evidence, such as that in Figure 5.2. When responding to a conjecture, learners can only "provide evidence" or "develop a plan" to support that conjecture. This form of scaffolded conversation results in more coherent and cogent conversations. In addition to scaffolding conversation, the Collaboratory also produces a notebook record of the conversation for review and reconsideration by the learners.

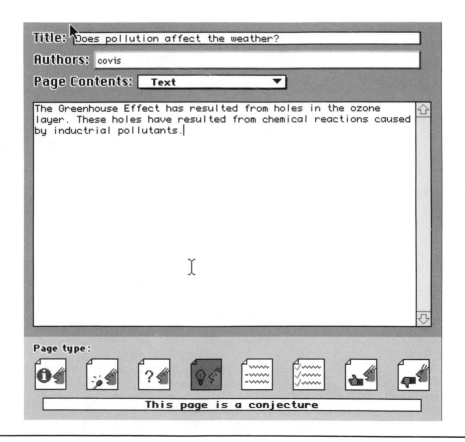

Figure 5.1   Conjecture made in the Collaboratory Notebook

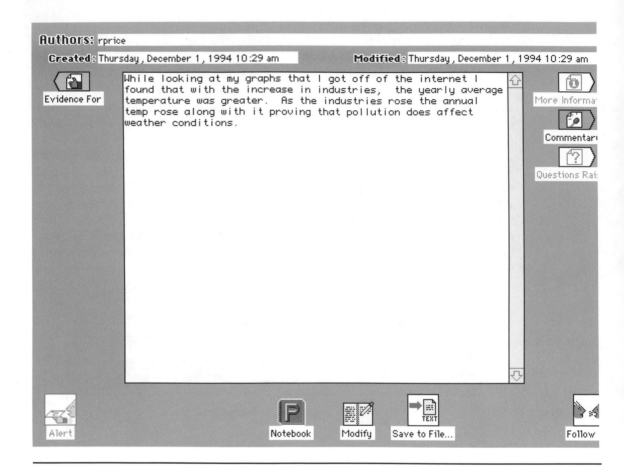

Figure 5.2   Evidence to support a conjecture in the Collaboratory Notebook

Computer-Supported Intentional Learning Environments (CSILEs)

Computer-Supported Intentional Learning Environments (CSILEs) incorporate a classroom model for student inquiry and knowledge generation, developed by Marlene Scardamalia and Carl Bereiter of the Ontario Institute for Studies in Education. The CSILE system has two important features:

- A special computer program for developing a common information base, typically installed on a local area network
- A systematic model of inquiry based upon the scientific method and informed by current research in cognitive psychology

CSILE includes "intentional learning" in the title because students are encouraged to make school more meaningful by being mindful and goal-directed in their pursuit of learning objectives. Learning is not a by-product of CSILE activities; it is a direct goal. Like scientists, CSILE participants approach a problem,

Table 5.3. Example of a CSILE discussion note. The various names (Problem, My Theory, etc.) are selected by students as they prepare messages. The topic is biology; keywords are biology and cell function. Adapted from Scardamalia and Bereiter (1996); used with permission.

Problem (Andrea):	How does a cell function?
My Theory (Andrea):	I think a cell functions by oxygen coming into the cell and the cell then can do its work by breathing.
My Theory (Jane):	I agree with your theory, but when the cell functions I don't think it is breathing. I think that the oxygen you're breathing in is doing it.
My Theory (Sue):	I think a cell functions by the "things" inside itself. (organelles)
I Need to Understand (Andrea):	How does the oxygen get into the cell, if the cell really does breathe oxygen?
My Theory (Sue):	I don't think that cells breathe oxygen, I just think that the cells need oxygen to do their work. But if the cells do breathe oxygen, I think there is some kind of a tube in the cell that helps the cell get the oxygen it needs.
New Information (Andrea):	I found out that the cell takes food and oxygen in through the membrane. This happens regularly. The cell then changes the food and oxygen into energy. It uses the energy to do its work.
I Need to Understand (Andrea):	How do the food and oxygen get to the cell's membrane?
My Theory (Andrea):	I think there are very small tubes that lead to each other and the food and oxygen go down those tubes and into the cell through the cell's membrane.
My Theory (Sue):	I disagree with your theory, Andrea. I think that the oxygen and food go into the cell automatically as a daily process.
I Need to Understand (Sue):	What does the oxygen do when it gets to the cell?
My Theory (Andrea):	This is what I think the oxygen does when it gets to the cell. I think that the oxygen goes into the cell through the membrane and then it goes to the nucleus where it is turned into energy.

develop hypotheses or theories about the problem, then seek to confirm, modify, or discard their theories through research, observation, and interpretation. Also like scientists, participants collaborate, review each other's work, and publish their confirmed results.

The theory behind CSILE is largely embodied in the software program used for entering, archiving, and retrieving student research. For example, students must select a label for each message they send, based on a simple set of categories. Examples are given in Table 5.3. To get a better feel for CSILE as a learning environment, you may wish to browse the CSILE Web site (http://csile.oise.on.ca/).

CSILE can be applied to various subjects, but it seems appropriate for science in particular. Unlike many on-line projects, which resemble electronic field trips or on-line databases, CSILE is a comprehensive model for inquiry designed to help students conceptualize and research a problem area. As such, it is more easily adopted within contained classrooms (relying less on outside Web access) and more demanding (requiring students to follow strict rules of reasoning and inquiry). Also in contrast to many on-line projects, considerable research has been conducted on CSILE, consistently demonstrating positive effects on learning (Scardamalia, Bereiter, and Lamon 1994). A World Wide Web version of CSILE is now available.

CaMILE

A third example of scaffolded conversations is provided by a program called CaMILE. Developed at the EduTech Institute at Georgia Tech, the basis of CaMILE is a collaborative NoteBase where students post notes associated with group discussions. Each added note is a response to a note that someone else has contributed to the discussion. Students enter a Comment note (bottom window of Figure 5.3) into an ongoing discussion (top window of Figure 5.3). In addition to the text, the student has included a QuickTime movie, as evidenced by the multimedia margin that shows links to pictures, sounds, spreadsheets, or any other kind of file. CaMILE also provides space for making suggestions (upper right) based on the Comment note. When a student reads through a discussion and wants to comment on a note, the student must specify the kind of response it is (a question, a comment, a rebuttal, an alternative—see Figure 5.4). Having to specify the response type scaffolds the development of discussion and argumentation skills.

Learning Processes   The three programs just described share a critical feature: Each provides an explicit structure for engaging in thoughtful, reasoned, written discourse. Students need to practice thinking and reasoning! Written papers require reasoning, but they tend to be one-way monologues without opportunities to respond to questions from an audience. In-class oral discussions also provide reasoning opportunities, but studies show that bright students tend to dominate class discussions, leaving many students in passive roles as observers. Programs like the Collaboratory, CSILE, and CaMILE seek to combine the best elements of writing assignments and live discussions. The communication medium is the written word, but the interactivity is similar to class discussions. But the programs provide more scaffolding and support for systematic reasoning than either writing assignments or class discussions: Their imposed structure directs students to provide support for claims, to consider competing evidence or hypotheses, and to carefully respond to counter arguments or queries from classmates. The structured discourse that results can help students learn the norms and rules of systematic reasoning, which, in turn, becomes valuable in other, less-structured settings.

Student Roles   Students play a number of roles in structured computer conferences. First, they, rather than the teacher, initiate conversations. Issues, ideas, or questions may be the starting point for a learning conversation. Once a problem is posed, students are asked to develop a framework to address the problem. There

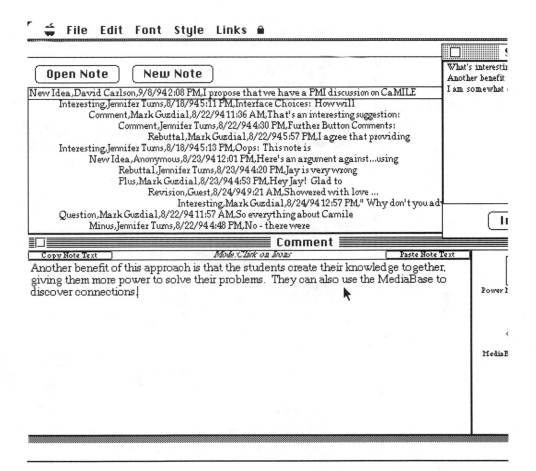

Figure 5.3 A Comment note added to CaMILE NoteBase

is room for both creative, playful search for possibilities, and for more disciplined, structured organization of evidence and problem solutions. As students engage in dialogue, they are asked to analyze the work of others, offering critiques or constructive suggestions for improving an explanation. Sometimes students are even asked to take on a teacher's role, helping each other come to understand how to frame a problem or follow a reasoning process.

Teacher Roles   As with so many constructivist methods, teachers are constantly observing student activities, with an eye for the individual student who is struggling or for the group that is stuck or engaged in dysfunctional processes. Teachers pay attention to content, reasoning, and outcomes, but also to attitudes, group chemistry, and the mutual support of team members. Teachers model both problem-solving processes as well as the kind of treatment of team members that is needed for successful team problem-solving.

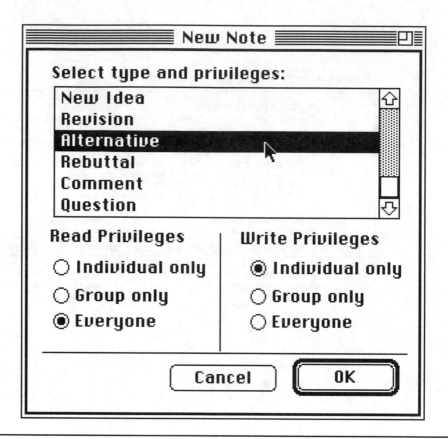

Figure 5.4   Specifying the response type in CaMILE

Assessing Learning   What constitutes a positive conversation? When are students learning, and when are they not? Teachers must monitor and evaluate a group's total activity, as well as the learning of individual students. This becomes a challenge in constructivist environments meant to accommodate multiple learning goals for different students.

Teachers continually make inferences about learning as they monitor and review student interactions. Teachers evaluate the total performance—not just the final outcome, but also the process students use in arriving at a conclusion. Structured computer conferences provide a rich, on-line record of student interaction; if needed, individual student contributions can be tracked from beginning to end. A huge amount of data is available to teachers—more than they can likely assimilate and fully use.

With such rich evaluative data available on demand, teachers must focus on the critical problems or obstacles faced by students. This is where teachers' professional judgment becomes crucial. Knowing where to focus one's attention—when demands on attention are being pulled in so many different directions—is a hallmark of the expert teacher.

To date, structured conferencing programs like CSILE have limited tools to aid learning assessment. Because of CSILE's explicitly documented nature, however, tools to aid student assessment should not be too difficult to develop. In future versions of these programs we would like to see a number of report capabilities, such as:

- Number and volume of contributions, reported by student
- Type of contributions, reported by student
- Certain kinds of response patterns (e.g., the number of comments made without a teammate's reply)

Such reports may be some help to teachers looking for evidence concerning student use of the system and may give an idea about the learning outcomes associated with the program. Use reports are no substitute, though, for the qualitative evaluation of student learning needs and outcomes.

The Buddy Project

Traditionally, the family has been the nuclear community that provided the strongest social foundation for children. Family involvement is seen as a key factor in children's educational success, particularly among disadvantaged families. Although technology has been partially responsible for the erosion of the family, it can also support family learning goals. In this innovative project described in "Getting America's Students Ready for the 21st Century" (p. 20), more than 7,000 fourth- through sixth-graders, at nearly 70 sites, are given computers and modems to take home. Students return the computers when they have "graduated" and moved on to another school. The program (sometimes called "Buddy Project" for short) is administered by the Corporation for Educational Technology, which receives funds from the state as well as from a variety of business interests. You may want to browse the Buddy Project home page at http://www.buddy.k12.in.us/.

Evaluations of the Buddy Project (Rockman and Sloan 1995) have documented a number of positive outcomes. Participating students increased the amount of time they spend on educational activities outside of school. Families became more involved in educational and learning activities. The students reported watching less television. There is some evidence that problem-solving and critical-thinking skills, writing and math skills, and computer skills all improved. Parents reportedly communicated more with their children and with their children's teachers, and appeared to be more aware of their children's assignments. The parents' own computer skills increased, because they used the computer for personal and business purposes. These parents are also reported to have spent more time with their families. The project also reported that students often taught their parents computer skills, and cited important consequences in enhanced student self-esteem and student/parent relationships.

Learning Processes Students and families connect to school and community resources, and use the Internet in a variety of ways. While in class, students receive homework activities that draw on intranet and Internet resources, and use e-mail for local and remote communications. The system also supports a number of outside activities, such as visits to the zoo, leadership camps, and visits to the state capitol.

Student Roles Students are given class and homework assignments that make use of computers and the Internet. Students are encouraged to share their learning with family members. A positive aspect of the program is the opportunity for family units to learn more about technology and accommodate computer activities into their lifestyles. Students have opportunities to be leaders in this change process.

Teacher Roles Teachers enrolled in the Buddy Project supervise the distribution of computers and modems to their students and families. These computer systems may be new or used. Teachers are supported in their administration of the program, but have considerable latitude in meeting the immediate needs of their students and families. Teachers are also encouraged to seek contact with family members and strengthen family support for their children's academic activities.

Assessing Learning Buddy Project activities are meant to be assimilated into the everyday learning activities of the classroom and the home. Teachers can assess student progress using a variety of in-class methods, and by reviewing student work completed at home. Program administrators have continued to seek evaluation data concerning the effectiveness of the program, and make corresponding refinements in resources and procedures.

Learning Circles

Learning Circles, sponsored by AT&T over the last several years, support constructive learning through collaboration. Developed by Margaret Riel and a team of collaborators, learning circles employ a "task force structure" (Riel 1991). Like a task force, learning circles have a heavy work or activity orientation. Groups of classrooms, usually about eight, sign on to communicate and collaborate from a distance, following a timeline to accomplish a defined task. The specific task may be any of a number of different activities, such as research, information sharing, compilation of a database, or publishing on a common subject. Riel (1996) also likens Learning Circles to local chapters of a larger organization, like scout troops affiliated with a larger council. Local troops "set their own goals and tasks but remain connected to those who work in other locations as part of a community with shared goals and values." She describes this cooperation between local and larger levels:

> In on-line Learning Circles, as in scout troops or in a Red Cross task force, the overall task and structure is clearly defined. There are enough examples for participants to use at every step. However, the members of the circle, troop or task force know that they can take control and develop the ideas that arise from the participants. (Riel 1996)

Learning Circles are often organized in support of a specific project or on-line activity. For example, the World Wide Web provides a number of interesting resources, such as:

- A tour of the White House
- A Web page describing and showing sacred lands of a Native American tribe
- A NASA project allowing access to space-shuttle pictures and data
- A virtual museum, with exhibits, artifacts, and descriptions

Individual students may choose to visit and browse these resources, or a teacher may incorporate them into a unit. Learning Circles may extend the usefulness of such resources by allowing collaboration and comparisons between classes on work related to the Web site. In this way, Learning Circles can augment an on-line resource into a deeper and more meaningful learning experience.

Learning Processes   Learning Circles require high levels of collaboration and teamwork within participating classes and, to some extent, between classes. Much of the learning takes place as students participate in the virtual world of Internet resources. Other times, students complete off-line activities, and report results to other members of their circle. The best Learning Circles have clear work activities specified that require planning, execution, and reporting of activities, followed by comparison and collaboration across sites.

Student Roles   Students collectively take most of the responsibility for Learning Circles. Within groups, student work assignments vary according to their interests and individual learning needs. One student may be asked to maintain a database or remind team members of scheduled responsibilities. Another student may enjoy artwork and volunteer to create graphics and page layouts. With such varied assignments, communication and sharing of accomplishments becomes especially important so that all team members can participate in the various aspects of project work.

Teacher Roles   The best teacher within Learning Circles keeps the project going, yet knows how to get out of the way when students are working well together. The teacher's critical role is one of attentive vigilance, with occasional support and intervention when obstacles threaten team progress. Teachers also need to maintain contact with other participating teachers, ensuring continuity and continuing attention to project goals.

Assessing Learning   Learning Circles are thought to be successful when projects continue through a defined schedule and reach some kind of closure by completion of a product or compiled report. Because individual student learning will vary widely, a number of self-assessment activities may be appropriate, such as group debriefing and reflection, written reflections of lessons learned from the Learning Circle, and before-and-after comparisons of student work.

SUPPORTING GLOBAL DISCOURSE THROUGH TELECOMMUNITIES

KIDLINK

KIDLINK is a grassroots project that is intended to interconnect as many kids, aged 10–15, as possible to participate in a global dialog. Running in annual cycles since 1990, more than 60,000 kids from 87 countries, from Antarctica to Finland, from Belarus to the Bahamas, have joined the conversation. Because of language constraints, KIDLINK provides several different dialogs. Some dialogs are individual and some are between classrooms.

Before joining a dialog, all new participants introduce themselves, answering the following questions:

Question #1: Who am I? What is your full name? How old are you? Are you a boy or a girl? Where do you live (city, country)? What is the name of your school? What are some of your interests, your hobbies, your concerns? What else do you want others to know about yourself?

Question #2: What do I want to be when I grow up? Share your vision of what you want to be when you grow up in terms of work, education, and in general.

Question #3: How do I want the world to be better when I grow up? How would you like to improve the way we treat each other and the environment we share? (see Figure 5.5).

Question #4: What can I do now to make this happen? What steps can you take now to realize your personal goals and your vision of the world?

KIDLINK supports different dialogs, with names such KIDCAFE (English and Spanish), KIDPROJECT, and KIDFORUM. In each discussion group, messages are indexed, so that when kids log on, they can review the index according to size (last 10, 50, 100, or 200 messages). For example, a recent list of messages included:

Brian Zimmer <lz61108@NAVIX.NET>
   Re: Survey-Fashion Express
Brian Zimmer <lz61108@NAVIX.NET>
   Survey-Football
Little 5th grade Class <little5c@PEN.K12.VA.US>
   Visited The Faberge' Exhibit Touring The USA?
NSRCMMS@AOL.COM
   Re: Query about Australia from Austria
Tommy Korsell <tommy.korsell@SKOLA.MARK.SE>
   Query about Australia from Austria
Lars-Erik <len@svenshog.burlov.se>
   How many hours in front of T.V?
SMS Irnerio - Bologna <irnerio@ARCI01.BO.CNR.IT>
   How many hours in front of TV
SMS Irnerio - Bologna <irnerio@ARCI01.BO.CNR.IT>
   How many hours in front of TV?
SMS Irnerio - Bologna <irnerio@ARCI01.BO.CNR.IT>

How many hours in front of TV? To Richard Salin and Mats Nyman
SMS Irnerio - Bologna <irnerio@ARCI01.BO.CNR.IT>
Re: survey request to ALL nationalities
"SMS A. Manzoni" <mediglia@IMIUCCA.CSI.UNIMI.IT>
Christmas in Peru
Diane Smith <dianes@HALCYON.COM>
Re: How many hours in front of the TV?
Yo, everybody in GB, USA and Australia -Reply
MELISSA COLE <2001508@MAIL.OLATHE.K12.KS.US>
Immigration -Reply
LISA RUECKERT <2000462@MAIL.OLATHE.K12.KS.US>
Yo, everybody in GB, USA and Australia -Reply
LISA RUECKERT <2000462@MAIL.OLATHE.K12.KS.US>
Re: music survey

It is obvious from the country codes in these messages that the dialog that day was indeed global (Australia, Italy Sweden, and the United States) and covered a wide variety of topics. Some dialogs are constrained by topic and language. For that reason, there are special dialogs, such as the Nordic dialog (shown in Figure 5.6).

```
I wish...

Date: Fri, 10 Jan 1997 20:17:00 -0500
From: Greg Novick <gnovick@CAPACCESS.ORG>
Subject: I wish...

Hey Liz!

I would wish for:

1. For the world to understand the power of Macintosh, the best computer
on the planet.

2. No final exams for a semester.

3. Worldwide understanding of all peoples in the world.

I think those were pretty self explanatory, right?

Happy New Year everyone!

Greg Novick
CAFETEAM
```

Figure 5.5   Personal introduction in KIDLINK

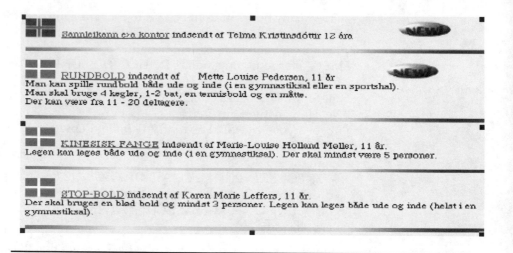

Figure 5.6   Nordic Cafe list

Global SchoolHouse

Another major project supporting global learning communities is the Global SchoolHouse (GSH) project. GSH seeks to create *telecommunities* to unite students from around the world and teach them to work cooperatively. Andres (1995) believes that the best collaborative projects require students to "measure, collect, evaluate, write, read, publish, simulate, hypothesize, compare, debate, examine, investigate, organize, share, and report." To accomplish this, teachers are encouraged to break up classes into small, collaborative teams. The teams access Internet databases relevant to their project and then relate their findings to other students through the Internet. GSH encourages students to serve as "student ambassadors" by training other students and teachers and acting as reporters.

Schools often collaborate on curriculum-focused projects, such as *Abdi & Mary's Hakuna Mata Adventure,* a field trip around the world via the Internet. Mary and her husband, Abdi, are traveling around the world and recording their experiences in an electronic journal, which they are sharing with kids all over the world. Starting in Oregon, their trip will take them through Europe to Turkey and then to Jordan, Bahrain, Kuwait, United Arab Emirates, through Africa, and then across Southeast Asia and its tropical forests, ancient ruins, and crowded cities. As their Web site describes, the *Hakuna Mata Adventure* provides students around the world the opportunity to explore other cultures, local people, geography, culture, the foods, sights, and sounds of the places they visit. Students will also communicate with each other on-line from schools that Mary visits. This virtual world tour is to "expose students to a global society, in which different cultures can be explored on a first-hand basis" and promotes "distance collaborative learning projects between students from various cultures."

Why should classrooms join telecommunities? Andres (1995) argues that students:

- Enjoy writing more when they are able to write for a distant audience of their peers
- Enjoy communicating with schools from different geographical locations
- Are given opportunities to understand different cultures and so begin to consider global issues, in addition to local issues

Clearly, telecommunities open up vast new horizons to students, engendering a broader, more tolerant world view for those involved. That should be an important goal of schools.

Learning Processes   Global telecommunities bear a strong resemblance to the Learning Circles just described. Global groups capitalize on cultural differences as a means of broadening students' perspectives and motivating learning. Studies in language, geography, current events, and culture can be augmented through these groups.

Student Roles   Students enter into social relationships with students like themselves, only in very different settings. The social relationships then become the grounding for a variety of academic learning activities. This is one more way to make school subjects seem relevant and interesting to students, who often see text-based learning as dull and monotonous.

Teacher Roles   Teachers are challenged to ensure that global communications go beyond chatting and socializing, but have a specific direction. This is done as the project is negotiated and defined. Teachers may need to monitor interactions to help students stay on task; however, students need a certain amount of slack to explore and become acquainted with different cultures and lifestyles.

Assessing Learning   A key learning outcome of global interactions has to be increased knowledge of foreign cultures, lifestyles, and languages. This can be assessed by examining products and interactions, or more directly through separate objective assessment. Other learning outcomes may be assessed using methods discussed in the cases provided.

MUDs and MOOs

New forms of Internet-based multi-user environments known as MUDs and MOOs are engaging learners in high-level conversations that support personal reflection. According to a MUD users group (http://webnet.mednet.gu.se/computer/internet-services.txt):

> [T]hese are multi-user, text based, virtual reality games. . . . A MUD (Multi-User Dungeon) is a computer program that users can log into and explore. Each user takes control of a computerized persona/avatar/incarnation/character. You can walk around, chat with other characters, explore dangerous monster-infested areas, solve puzzles, and even create your very own rooms, descriptions and items. There are an astounding number of variations on the MUD theme.

MUDs (multi-user domains) and MOOs (object-oriented MUDs) are virtual environments that you enter and participate in. Originally derived from on-line "Dungeons and Dragon" environments, some MUDs have an educational focus, such as MIT's MicroMUSE. Users can enter the virtual environment and travel between locations—for example, homes, museums, coffee shops, or science labs. Visitors not only interact, but, depending on their level of experience, can participate in the design and construction of the environment itself.

Currently, MUDs are text-based, but advances in virtual-reality and multimedia technologies will soon result in graphic depictions of these virtual environments. A simple search of the Internet will reveal several of these environments. Some welcome newcomers, but most are a bit difficult to understand and navigate. (Documenting their accomplishments and the interface is apparently not as stimulating as creating and using MUDs.)

To date, most of the MUDs and their offspring are primarily adventure games, with debatable educational value. Some projects, however, are specifically educational in nature. Hughes and Walters (1995; Walters and Hughes 1995) report their work with MariMUSE and Pueblo. Their initial findings are very promising and suggest that MUDs warrant continued attention from educational researchers and developers.

Learning Processes   Ironically, the low-tech nature of MUDs has become a learning asset. MUDs' text-only interface means that children must use words to communicate. Motivation is maintained by the game-like atmosphere. The practice and reinforcement of literacy skills can yield educational benefits for children participating in MUD environments. Another interesting aspect of MUDs is the ownership that students can assert over their virtual worlds. MUDs are not like game CDs; they can be co-designed and co-constructed by the users themselves, depending entirely on the users' investment in the program. The sense that worlds depend on our own construction is an important lesson for children.

Student Roles   The role-playing aspects of MUDs can have strong effects on children's confidence and sense of self. This fourth-grade teacher reports the dramatic effect of MUD participation on a young Native American child participating in the Pueblo project:

> This child is a young girl, who before MariMUSE, was very timid and shy. She went through a period this year, where she was afraid to enter the classroom, for fear of the other children. We had a hard time getting her to come to school, either she decided she was sick in the mornings, or her mother would put her on the city bus to come to school, and she would get off along the way at a library or something. Now this same girl will get on MariMUSE, look at the who list, and if there is someone on whom she doesn't know, she will page them to introduce herself, and get to know them. As well as carrying on many other conversations or e-mail correspondence with others she has met through

MariMUSE. This girl, who as I have mentioned didn't want to come to school, started staying at school until 6:00 every night. (Hughes and Walters 1995)

Teacher Roles   MUDs have primary appeal to individual users, and are not particularly well suited to whole-class participation. Dykes and Waldorf (1995) report the activities of an independent, after-school club whose members participated in MicroMUSE. MicroMUSE activities are set in a twenty-fourth century world, in a space station called Cyberion City II, which hovers above the earth (p. 3). Students enter the environment and encounter a variety of adventures and problems to solve, depending on their level of advancement.

Dykes and Waldorf's exploratory study yielded a number of findings, including:

- Boys seemed to show more interest than girls in the activity, although more boys than girls belonged to the club.
- Older children (11–14) participated more than younger children.
- Role-playing opened up interesting possibilities for exploration. Children can assume a virtual persona different from their real-world persona. One young boy, for example, wanted to assume a female identity, while another wanted to play a child from the eighteenth century.
- Children enjoyed opportunities to choose their own paths through the environment, with some eventually learning to construct their own rooms and environments.

Teachers making use of MUDs in the classroom will want to take steps to ensure equitable, responsible access.

Assessing Learning   Assessing the learning from MUDs could present a challenge to teachers. In current systems, students enter MUDs individually, without having to collaborate with other classmates. Teachers might be able to gauge student learning by tracking conversation, choices, or constructions. On the other hand, students may engage in game-playing without clear learning goals. This is clearly an area in need of continuing attention. As MUDs become more commonly utilized for learning purposes, improved methods of assessment are likely to be developed.

Right now MUDs have very little presence in K–12 schools. It is easy, though, to imagine a future in which MUDs evolve to become a low-end version of "virtual reality" with significant educational potential. Imagine, for instance, a MUD in which a student is placed on the main street in a small community in colonial America, with the option of entering stores, blacksmith shops, pubs, jails, homes, and other buildings of the period. Inside each building would be descriptions of the people and artifacts it contained. Students would make decisions and express their choices, to which the MUD's characters and objects (and other students) would react. Imagine, too, that teachers and their classes could work together to *develop* new buildings. This option (which is often provided in MUDs) could be a great incentive for research, collaboration, problem-solving, and other high-level activities.

Fostering Community

Learning communities can be fostered through communication, attention to differences, shared culture, adaptation, dialogue, and access to information resources. Each of these facilitating features is discussed here.

Communication   Imagine a classroom—perhaps a televised lecture—where the teacher sends out signals but has no means of receiving feedback from students. In such a scenario, the teacher's activities can spin wildly out of control, becoming less and less appropriate to students' needs. Students may be completely lost or completely bored, and the teacher has no way of knowing an adjustment is needed.

Communication is the key that allows people to make adjustments to each other. Feedback is given not just for correctness of answers, but in all sorts of subtle, informal ways, resulting in a feeling of inclusion and accommodation. Students come to feel, "I am being listened to, understood, and respected." Teachers can feel, "I am having some kind of effect." Effective communication among members allows the group to acquire a personality and sense of direction, while communicating the views and needs of individuals.

Attention to Differences   Like all complex adaptive systems, learning communities thrive on differences. Every group member shares some things in common with the group and holds other things unique. Most differences among group members go no further than the individual learner; however, every so often a different perspective or strategy will be found to have utility within the group as a whole. As different perspectives and strategies are routinely shared throughout the group, the powerful results of some innovations are noticed and diffused, eventually changing the practice of the entire group. Thus, differences between community members are a key to growth, leading sometimes to innovations that benefit everyone. The risk-taking, creative attitude that leads to innovation is important to the group's success.

Shared Culture   Appreciation of diversity is, however, only half the story. To move from "group" to real community, people need to feel bound together by something strong and enduring. This could be a shared goal or objective, such as passing a critical exam or producing a new product. Beyond outcomes, though, communities are fostered by a shared set of values, reflected in a local culture. "Culture" is like water to a fish. It's everything that's all around, but not noticed—how we talk, walk, listen, and participate; all the unspoken, unwritten rules that govern our behavior toward each other. Every learning community develops a local mini-culture, complete with accepted norms, practices, rituals, and language.

Teachers, as classroom leaders, are critical in setting a tone, creating expectations, and negotiating acceptable values. The teacher's influence comes through both precept and example. If a teacher occasionally belittles, ignores, or dismisses the needs of a student, then class members feel license to act that way toward each other. If a teacher is judgmental or arbitrary in asserting certain facts or knowledge to the group, then where are students to learn the rules of reasoning and support for claims? A successful conveyance of certain values—tolerance, respect, willingness to take risks, openness to change, commitment to hard work, and so on—make building communities much more feasible.

On-line communities in some ways mirror classroom communities; in other ways, they have greater latitude at defining themselves. Riel (1996) noted:

> There will always be a sense of adventure and excitement associated with frontiers—they are wild and free. We can design "places," within technical and social constraints, in ways that allow us to experiment with social reality. Freedom from time and space does not automatically lead to rewarding patterns of social discourse. On-line communities face the same issues of freedom of speech vs. censorship, of security and control, of private and public spaces, of inclusion and exclusion, of unity and diversity, that exist in all social organizations. It takes intense and continual social negotiation to find the best balance between absolute freedom for citizens and collective control.

As on-line collaboration increases, teachers will need to address these same issues over and over. But that's good, because that's the way the world really is!

Adaptation   A good teacher enters a classroom with an agenda—learning goals, planned activities, methods for assessing progress, and so on. At the same time, that teacher will be sensitive to the needs of the group. Within the first day of a new school year, a teacher may throw out the window certain planned goals and activities, realizing that the particular mix of students dictates adjustments in the plan. The teacher will adapt to the needs of the group. Similarly, students quickly learn to adapt to the style of the instructor and the norms of the group. Adaptation is the result of the change process, which we have seen is synonymous with learning—which is what education is all about.

Dialogue   What's the difference between argument and dialogue? In an argument, your job is to define a position and support it, to the point of convincing your advocate or a third party of the superiority of your position. A true conversation or dialogue is something different. You actually listen to the person across from you with the hope of learning something new. Dialogue, in the best sense, is not oppositional or confrontational; rather, it is just the opposite. Dialogue involves a willingness to *suspend* one's beliefs in favor of listening to another, to surrender and *give up* one's position if doing so serves the needs of the group. Within a community that values dialogue, reasoned arguments still have a place, but they should be conducted with mutual respect and trust toward all participants.

As you can imagine, cultivating an atmosphere of dialogue is not easily accomplished. In our culture, a willingness to surrender one's position and defer to the group seems almost un-American! Powerful forces push all of us toward a style of jousting competitiveness, flexing of muscles, posturing, and pretense. Yet these behaviors that are so easily the norm need to be tempered by the cultivated and taught values of dialogue, conversation, and commitment to the interests of the whole group.

Access to Information   Open, unrestricted access to information is the lifeblood of a democracy. In a similar way, access to multiple sources of information becomes critical for the success of a learning community. Students look to teachers as role models for reasoning more than as information dispensers; thus, students can come to respect the teacher's opinion without depending exclusively on it. Finding ways to triangulate and cross-compare evidence only serves to strengthen one's position and perspective. In many ways, the vitality of a learning community depends on the quality of the information available to it.

Some Internet critics are concerned about all the "garbage" available out there—not just the pornography, but the unreliable, unsubstantiated information. How can students be expected to weigh, evaluate, and determine the usefulness of information on the Web, much of it conflicting and inaccurate? To these critics, we respond, "Welcome to the real world!" Amid the conflicting perceptions and worldviews, our students can learn only by jumping in and participating. Rather than be shielded from complexity, students need to be guided through it and taught methods and tools for managing it. Formally trained librarians, who may be tempted to eschew Web resources in favor of more respectable published outlets, need to support students in their acquiring the "information literacy" skills needed to help them evaluate information from a variety of sources, Web as well as non-Web (Walster 1996).

Membership

Who participates in learning communities? Participants must be learners, willing to change and grow according to the goals and activities of the group. Certainly students are learners, but so are teachers. Teachers read and critique papers and projects, learning as they do so. They listen to students and learn from their interests and research. Teachers, for example, who lack technical skills with the Internet, can often be taught by the gurus in class who seem to know the answer to every question. The community thus is strengthened by its interdependencies—the teacher needs the class "techno-geeks," just as the students need the direction and support of the teacher. As St. Paul noted, "members," like hands and feet to the body, are needed parts, contributing to the healthy functioning of the whole community (1 Cor. 12). Thus, moving toward learning communities becomes a powerful staff-development exercise for teachers. Teachers should prepare to go into "high learning mode" and stay there for a while!

Outside experts can serve the role of "visiting scholar" within the learning community. While the experts' role is primarily to provide consultation and advice, the learning circle extends to include them as well. Experts should not be shocked when students ask questions that leave them at a loss; the normal flow includes having to go back to resources for answers. Experts unprepared to engage in the dialectical process of learning and teaching will prove to be of limited utility to the learning community.

Learning communities can also establish relationships with outside groups, at times forming a larger collaborating community. This is all to say that learning communities are not defined in fixed, immutable terms. Members may drift in and out, alliances may be formed with outside individuals and communities. Although they enjoy a degree of coherence, communities typically have "soft" boundaries.

Motivation

A continuing thread in the discussion is this: Learning communities depend on autonomous, responsible, motivated learners. But pull on that thread, and the fabric becomes unraveled. What can we say to the teacher who says, "My students just aren't motivated for this"?

Here is a catch-22 about any activities that empower students: *Doing* it can be incredibly motivating for students, but *helping* students get to the point of doing it can be a struggle. That is to say, how can students decide that they like something when they haven't seen it? And how can they come to see the advantages of an activity unless they cooperate?

This problem calls for a systemic perspective. Just as students can devolve into a loop of negative outcomes—working less at school, liking school less because they're not working, leading to even less engagement—so they can begin a loop of rewards and reinforcement—getting a taste of empowerment and ownership, leading to more engagement, which, in turn, allows further empowerment, and so on. Classes *become* communities by learning a step at a time. Granted, motivation is a key component to the success of learning communities, but striving toward learning communities is a key to motivation.

Advice to Teachers   Here are some responses to the teacher looking for ways to convert these ideas into some concrete actions in the classroom:

1. **Remember, the concept of learning communities is an ideal.** Nobody ever attains it completely. So relax; don't worry about perfection. Movement is the thing. Which way are you and your students moving? Are you approaching community, or moving away from it?
2. **Technology, resources, and models can help**. There is nothing magic about the technology, but certain activities and expectations are feasible with access to the Internet that would have been unthinkable without it. Just as you may require that a paper be typed or word-processed, with access to appropriate tools and resources, you can raise the bar and heighten your students' expectations for what can reasonably be done.
3. **It's not all or nothing.** Many of the models and technologies discussed here can be used in a variety of ways. Yes, each innovation takes work to integrate into the curriculum, but take it in small steps, observing effects and making adjustments as you go. Just as you ask your students to be thoughtful and innovative, your integration of new technologies is like a perpetual action research project of your own.
4. **Respect your own knowledge and situation.** Let's say you decide to engage in a Global SchoolHouse project. Al Rogers (1994) has a helpful

Table 5.4. Steps for successful design and completion of Global SchoolNet projects, adapted from Rogers (1994).

How to Design a Successful Project

1. Design a project with specific goals, tasks, and outcomes. The more closely aligned with traditional instructional objectives, the better.

2. Create a timeline. Set specific beginning and ending dates with deadlines for participant responses. Make a timeline that allows for lots of lead time for announcements and recruiting.

3. If possible, do a small-scale tryout with a close colleague.

4. Announce your project. Create a "call for collaboration" following a standard template, available on-line. Post your first call for collaboration six to eight weeks before the starting date. Repeat your call again two weeks before the starting date. Include in your call:
   —Goals and objectives
   —Grade levels desired
   —How many responses you would like
   —Contact person
   —Timeline and deadlines
   —Your location and complete contact information
   —Examples of the kinds of writing or data students will submit
   —What you will do with student and team submissions (teams will need some interaction or other incentives to collaborate)

5. Find and train students. You will need a cohort of responsible and trained students to help you with the project. This step becomes an essential time-saver when using technology in the classroom.

6. At the project's conclusion, follow through on sharing project results with all participants, including a hard copy of all publications, a Web-published, class-written project summary, and student-written thank-you notes. Also send the summary to your principal, PTA president, superintendent, and school board president.

model and checklist for embarking on such a project, and a Web site with links to accompanying literature and support (Table 5.4). Nonetheless, your classroom is unique. Your own learning community goes beyond whatever model used in its inception or design. Moreover, your success in adopting any particular framework or model depends as much on local factors as on the details of the model itself. The mix of students and teachers, the available technology and facilities, the expectations of the school and the surrounding community, your insights and energy as project leader—these will account for the success of the project at least as much as the quality of the thinking that went into the model in the first place. Another way of saying this is, "The community is not its model." Some theorists may forget this sometimes, but you never should lose sight of the primacy of your own experience and expertise.

5. **Your leadership as teacher is critical.** Riel (1991) stressed that networking technologies and Learning Circles are not magic. In a talk several years ago, she reflected:

> I have probably had as many network failures behind me as I do successes. It isn't easy . . . In fact the progressive education of the sixties failed, to a large extent, because people misunderstood the role of the teacher . . . as well as the problem of the technical support . . . .
>
> [T]eachers were told that they were supposed to be facilitators and that kids would learn on their own, teachers stood back and waited for things to happen . . . . People again and again think that you can put the technology in place and if you give people the communication potential, that suddenly, education is going to happen all by itself. (Riel 1991)

We suspect that Riel's success rate has improved over the years, but her remarks remind us to contain our expectations about our students and about the innovation. Indeed, students *can* learn to work on their own, but teacher support and guidance along the way is critical to success.

Our central goal has been to present some key ideas, then let you as a teacher find ways to incorporate those ideas into your daily practice. With years of experience, you are smarter than we are. You know your students, your school, your community. You can adapt concepts to your own situation; in that respect, you are much smarter than any technology or textbook ever devised!

CONCLUSIONS

Are learning communities just another educational fad? We think not. Seen as complex systems, networks become the mechanism that allows adaptation and change. And adaptation and change equates to learning. Thus, while a business organization "learns" by adapting to its environment, teachers and students learn when they respond and adapt to each other and to information resources. As we see in a variety of settings, adaptive change goes hand in hand with a certain kind of structure—not hierarchical, static, or centrally controlled, but decentralized, complex, dynamic, Web-like networks of collaborating contributors. When classes or groups of students function together like that, they become more capable of learning.

Individual community members—students and teachers—work independently as well as collaboratively. In doing so, innovations, insights, and solutions to problems are developed that are shared with community at large. As students and teachers continue their work, the community takes on common attributes that shape its overall character and behavior.

What advantages does computer conferencing have over a good old-fashioned discussion? Why not just converse face-to-face, rather than talking through computers? There are several reasons one might want to participate in a computer-mediated conference. First, computer conferencing can support discussions, debates, and collaborative efforts among groups of people who are co-located or at a distance. Students do not have to be in the same place in order to converse and learn. Many classrooms are becoming virtual—communications and learning spaces located within a networked system connecting learners all over the country. Why it is necessary for students to share the same physical space with a teacher in order to listen to the teacher, ask questions, get assignments, or otherwise communicate with the teacher? The obvious answer is that computer conferencing supports long-distance collaboration among learners.

A second advantage is that computer conferencing enables learners to reflect on their ideas or responses before making them. In addition to providing opportunities to research topics and to develop arguments (which can also be supported by using other Mindtools described in Chapter 6), conferences allow the students the opportunity to adequately present the group's position on the conference. That requires reflecting on your argument before carefully presenting it. Thinking about what you are going to say before saying it is fostered by computer conferences.

Third, and perhaps most important, different kinds of thinking can be scaffolded in computer conferences. Although in-class conversation is a powerful learning method, learners do not necessarily know how to constructively converse. Computer conferences can guide and scaffold students as they make comments, reminding them of needed support and development, and archiving past conversations for future use.

Computer conferences are not meant to replace face-to-face interactions. We have tried to show, however, that computer conferencing can support learners in unique ways as they engage in reasoned dialogue, collaborate with remote and diverse audiences, and learn to express themselves in writing. In learning communities, learners judge people by what they say, not by how they look.

THINGS TO THINK ABOUT

If you would like to reflect on the ideas that we presented in this chapter, then articulate your responses to the following questions and compare them with responses of others.

1. What responsibilities do teacher and students share in cultivating a learning community in the classroom? How can technology serve the goals of a learning community—and how might technology get in the way?
2. With technology-supported learning communities, students learn different things at different speeds. How can a teacher keep track of students' various learning needs and make sure everyone is progressing well?
3. Every community has outliers—people on the margins who don't seem to fit or who struggle to participate fully. How can a teacher draw all students into the community circle? What steps can be taken to motivate students who may be reluctant to participate?
4. Do you believe that learning by conversing in learning communities can be more effective than traditional instruction? What evidence would we need to confirm (or reject) that belief?
5. With the advent of virtual reality and enhanced graphical interfaces, language may become less important in communication, especially among learners of different languages. What would a virtual language look like? How would students use it to communicate?

6. Most scaffolded computer conferences support argumentation and collaborative problem solving. Would it be useful to develop a scaffolded conference to help students memorize stuff? If so, what would it look like?

REFERENCES

Andres, Y. M. (1991). *Advantages to telecomputing: Reasons to use the Internet in your classroom.* http://www.gsn.org/gsn/articles/article. advan.html.

Andres, Y. M. (1995). *Collaboration in the classroom and over the Internet.* http://www.gsn.org/ gsn/articles/article.collaboration.html.

Brown, A. L., and J. C. Campione (1996). Psychological theory and the design of innovative learning environments: On procedures, principles, and systems. In L. Schauble and R. Glaser (eds.), *Innovations in learning: New environments for education* (pp. 289–325). Mahwah, NJ: Lawrence Erlbaum Associates.

Carvin, (1996). *A new tool in the arsenal: The role of the Web in curricular reform* (http://edweb.gsn.org/web.forum.html/.

Cognition and Technology Group at Vanderbilt (1994). From visual word problems to learning communities: Changing conceptions of cognitive research. In K. McGilly (ed.), *Classroom lessons: Integrating cognitive theory and classroom practice* (pp. 157–200). Cambridge, MA: MIT Press.

Edelson, D. C., R. D. Pea, and L. Gomez (1996). Constructivism in the Collaboratory. In B. G. Wilson (ed.), *Constructivist learning environments: Case studies in instructional design* (pp. 151–64). Englewood Cliffs, NJ: Educational Technology Publications.

Farnham-Diggory, S. (1992). *Cognitive processes in education* (2nd ed.). New York: HarperCollins.

Gardner, H., and D. C. Lazear (1991). *Seven ways of knowing, teaching for multiple intelligencies: A handbook of the techniques for expanding intelligence.* Victoria, BC: Hawker Brownlow Education.

Harris, J. (1994). *Way of the ferret: Finding educational resources on the Internet.* Eugene, OR: International Society for Technology in Education.

Harris, J. (1995, February). Organizing and facilitating telecollaborative projects. *The Computing Teacher*, 22(5): 66–9. [Online document: http://www.ed.uiuc.edu/Mining/February95-TCT.html]

Hughes, B., and J. Walters (1995, April). *Children, MUDs, and learning.* Paper presented at the meeting of the American Educational Research Association, San Francisco, CA. [Online document: http://pcacad.pc.maricopa.edu/Pueblo/ writings/bib/AERA-paper-1995.html]

Lave, J. (1991). Situating learning in communities of practice. In L. B. Resnick, J. M. Levine, and S. D. Teasley (eds.), *Perspectives on socially shared cognition.* Washington, DC: American Psychological Association.

O'Neill, D. K., and L. M. Gomez (1994). The Collaboratory Notebook: A distributed knowledge building environment for project learning. Proceedings of ED MEDIA, 94. Vancouver, BC, Canada.

Paulson, M. F. (1995, August). *The online report of pedagogical techniques for computer-mediated comunication.* [Online document: http://www.nki.no/ ~morten]

Riel, M. (1991, June). *Transcribed lecture on children, learning, and computer-mediated communication.* Simon Fraser University, Vancouver, British Columbia, June 30, 1991. [Online document: http://bolt.lakeheadu.ca/~facedwww/Kerlin/ Riel.html]

Riel, M. (1996, January). *The Internet: A land to settle rather than an ocean to surf and a new "place" for school reform through community development.* [Online document: http:// www.gsn.org/gsn/ articles/article.netasplace.html]

Riley, R. W., M. M. Kunin, M. S. Smith, and L. G. Roberts (1996, June). "Getting America's students ready for the 21st century: Meeting the technology literacy challenge." A report to the nation on technology and education. [Online document: http://www.ed.gov/Technology/ Plan/NatTechPlan/]

Rockman, S., and K. R. Sloan (1995, April). *Assessing the growth: The Buddy Project evaluation, 1994–95.* Final Report. San Francisco: unpublished.

Rogers, A. (1994). *Keys to successful projects.* [Online document: http://www.ed.uiuc.edu/ Guidelines/Rogers.html]

Savage, C. M. (1996). *Fifth generation management: Co-creating through virtual enterprising, dynamic teaming, and knowledge networking.* Boston: Butterworth-Heinemann.

Scardamalia, M., and C. Bereiter (1996). Adaptation and understanding: A case for new cultures of schooling. In S. Vosniadou, E. De Corte, R. Glaser, and H. Mandl (eds.), *International perspectives on the design of technology-supported learning environments* (149–63). Hillsdale, NJ: Lawrence Erlbaum Associates.

Scardamalia, M., C. Bereiter, and D. Lamon (1994). The CSILE Project: Trying to bring the classroom into World 3. In K. McGilly (ed.), *Classroom lessons: Integrating cognitive theory and classroom practice* (pp. 201–28). Cambridge, MA: MIT Press.

Walster, D. (1996). Technologies for information access in library and information centers. In D. H. Jonassen (ed.), *Handbook of research for eductional communications and technology.* (pp. 720–54). New York: Macmillan.

Walters, J., and B. Hughes (1995, April). *Pueblo: A virtual learning community.* Paper presented at the meeting of the American Educational Research Association, San Francisco, CA.

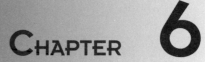

CHAPTER 6

LEARNING BY REFLECTING WITH TECHNOLOGY: MINDTOOLS FOR CRITICAL THINKING

WHAT ARE MINDTOOLS?

Traditionally, technologies have been used in schools to "teach" students, much the same as teachers "teach" students. When technologies teach, information is stored in the technology, which presents the information to the students, who try to understand and remember it. Sometimes the technology asks students questions to find out if the students understood or remembered the information. The students reply to the technology, often by selecting and pressing a key, and the technology judges the students' response and determines how well the students understood or remembered. The technology is "teaching" the students. Technologies have been developed by instructional designers and marketed to educators as *learner-proof* and *teacher-proof*, removing any meaningful control of the learning process by the learners or the teachers.

Throughout this book and especially in this chapter, we argue that this method of using technologies to teach does not exploit the capabilities of the technologies or the students. It requires the technology, for instance, to do things that learners do better and the learners to do things that technologies do better. For example, using computers to teach requires them to present information, judge answers, diagnose student understanding, and adapt the way that it is teaching to meet the needs of the student. Artificial intelligence projects have spent millions of dollars in efforts to invest the computer with enough intelligence to do these things. However, a good teacher can do them all far better than any computer. When computers teach students, students are required to memorize and recall information. Computers do that much better than humans. They are high-speed storage devices with much greater memories than humans. So, when working with technologies, why not ask learners to do what they do best—conceptualize, organize, and solve problems—and technologies to do what they do best—memorize and retrieve? That way, you'll realize a synergy from the student using the computer.

In this chapter, we argue that technologies should be used as knowledge construction tools that amplify learners' abilities to construct knowledge for themselves, rather than be "taught" by preprogrammed lessons. Through these tools, students will learn *with* the technology, not *from* it. Why is that better? Salomon (1990) asks, What effects can computers have on the minds of learners; that is, what cognitive skills will result from using technologies? The effects include not only "the cultivation, development, or even the acquisition of cognitive skills that result from the use of some technology" (cognitive residue) but also "what a computer enables the learner to do while working, planning, writing, designing, or communicating with computer software" (effects *with* technology) (Salomon 1990, pp. 29–30). Students learn *with* technologies when they use computers as cognitive tools.

This chapter describes the application of technologies, primarily computers, as cognitive learning tools (Mindtools). It is about computer applications that have been adapted or developed to facilitate critical thinking and higher-order learning. Mindtools include (but are not limited to) databases, spreadsheets, semantic networks, expert systems, multimedia construction tools (Chapter 4), microworlds, dynamic system modeling tools, visualization tools, microworlds, and computer conferencing systems (Chapter 5). These tools enable learners to represent and express what they know. In doing so, students function as designers—analyzing phenomena in the world, accessing information, interpreting and organizing their personal knowledge, and representing what they know to others. When using Mindtools, students are constructing knowledge bases that represent personally relevant and meaningful knowledge while teaching the computer. The computer constrains the ways that students are thinking, engaging them in higher-order, mindful thinking.

Mindful thinking is meaningful—that is, active, constructive, intentional, and so on. When students are using technologies mindfully, there is an intellectual partnership between the student and the computer where the computer amplifies the student's thinking. This partnership is now more "intelligent" than the student or the technology alone (Pea 1985). Mindtools engage mindful thinking. Because of that, they aren't necessarily easy. That is, Mindtools are not designed make learning easier and more efficient. They are not "fingertip" tools (Perkins 1993) that learners use naturally and effortlessly. Rather, Mindtools often require learners to think harder about the subject matter domain being studied while generating thoughts that would be impossible without the tool. Mindtools are cognitive reflection and amplification tools that help learners to construct their own realities by designing their own knowledge bases.

WHY USE TECHNOLOGIES AS MINDTOOLS?

There are several conceptual and practical reasons why computers should be used as Mindtools.

Learners Are Designers

The people who learn the most from instructional materials are the people who design and produce them, not the learners for whom the materials are intended. Jonassen, Wilson, Wang, and Grabinger (1993) reported this phenomenon while developing expert system advisers that were designed to support novice instructional designers. The process of articulating their knowledge in order to construct the expert systems forced them to reflect on their knowledge in new and meaningful ways. They began using expert systems as tools for constructing a product, but they ended up using expert systems as a Mindtools for articulating what they knew. People who design materials are necessarily engaged in a deeper analysis and articulation of the subject in order to teach it, which results in their better understanding of the subject, as opposed to learners who only read or interact with the materials.

Learners Are Intelligent; Tools by Themselves Are Not

Educational technologies have too often tried to do the thinking for learners, to act like teachers and guide the learning. Traditionally, technologies have been assumed to be more intelligent than the learners, so their job was to convey their intelligence to the learners. Derry and LaJoie (1993) argue that "the appropriate role for a computer system is not that of a teacher/expert, but rather, that of a mind-extension cognitive tool" (p. 5) or Mindtool. Cognitive tools, according to Derry and LaJoie, are *un*intelligent tools, relying on the learner to provide the intelligence, not the computer. This means that planning, decision making, and self-regulation of learning should be the responsibility of the learner, not the computer. However, computer systems can serve as powerful catalysts for facilitating these skills, assuming they are used in ways that promote reflection, discussion, and problem solving.

Mindtools Require Critical Thinking

Students cannot correctly use Mindtools without being engaged in higher order critical thing skills (Jonassen 1996), including:

1. Evaluating information by:
    Assessing information for its reliability and usefulness
    Determining criteria for judging the merits of ideas or products
    Prioritizing a set of options according to relevance or importance
    Recognizing fallacies and errors in reasoning
    Verifying arguments and hypotheses through reality testing
2. Analyzing information by:
    Recognizing patterns of organization
    Classifying objects into categories based on common attributes
    Identifying assumptions that underlie positions
    Identifying the main ideas or central ideas in text, data, or creations
    Finding sequences or consecutive order in information
3. Connecting ideas by:
    Comparing/contrasting similarities and differences
    Analyzing or developing an argument, conclusion, or inference
    Inferring deductively from generalizations or principles to specific instances
    Inferring a theory or principle inductively from data
    Identifying causal relationships and predicting possible effects

When using Mindtools, students also generate new knowledge while engaging in creative thinking activities, including:

1. Synthesizing skills by:
    Analogical thinking (creating and using metaphors and analogies)
    Summarizing main ideas and organization
    Hypothesizing about relationships between events and predicting outcomes
    Planning a process
2. Imagining processes, outcomes, and possibilities, including:
    Fluency of expression or generating as many ideas as possible
    Predicting events or actions that are caused by a set of conditions
    Speculating and wondering about interesting possibilities
    Visualizing to create mental images or mentally rehearsed actions
    Intuition or hunches about ideas are powerful strategies
3. Elaborating on information, adding personal meaning to information by:
    Expanding on information by adding details, examples

Modifying, refining, or changing ideas for different purposes
Extending ideas by applying them in a different context
Shifting categories of thinking by assuming a different point of view
Concretizing general ideas by giving examples and uses

Finally, when using Mindtools, students must solve problems and represent their knowledge by engaging in complex thinking skills, including:

1. Problem solving by:
   Sensing the problem
   Researching the problem
   Formulating the problem
   Finding alternatives
   Choosing the solution
   Building acceptance
2. Designing products or ideas by:
   Imaging a goal
   Formulating a goal
   Inventing a product
   Assessing the product
   Revising the product: expanding, extending, modifying
3. Decision making by:
   Identifying an issue
   Generating the alternatives
   Assessing the consequences
   Making a choice
   Evaluating the choice

Different Mindtools engage students in different combinations of these skills (see Jonassen 1996 for a detailed listing of critical, creative, and complex thinking skills engaged by each Mindtool).

Mindtools Are Cost-Efficient and Effort-Efficient

Mindtools are especially effective for use in schools because they use inexpensive, commonly available software. Most of the tools described in this chapter are already owned by schools or are available inexpensively or, in many cases, as freeware. The costs of using Mindtools are especially low because they can be used to represent understanding in virtually any subject in any course in any curriculum. So the cost of purchasing the software and the intellectual cost and time invested in learning how to use the software can be spread over several courses. Most of these tools are readily learned, usually in less than two hours. Readily learning how to use the tools is an important characteristic of Mindtools; that and the wide application possibilities make the mental cost and the economic cost of its use minimal. Consistently engaging learners in critical, higher-order thinking in all of their courses will easily justify the cost of purchase and the effort to learn how to use these Mindtools.

Mindtools Distribute Cognitive Processing Appropriately

Any tool may help learners transcend the limitations of their minds, such as memory, thinking, or problem-solving limitations (Pea 1985). The most pervasive cognitive tool is language. Imagine how difficult it would be to learn how to do something complex without using language. Language amplifies the thinking of the learner. Computers may also function as cognitive tools by reorganizing the way that learners think. When learners use computers as partners, they off-load some of the unproductive memorizing tasks to the computer, while the computer software requires the learner to use new ways to think about what they are studying. We should allocate to learners the cognitive responsibility for the processing they do best while we allocate to the tool the processing that it does best.

Students Learn New Languages (Formalisms) for Thinking About the World

Although language is the most common formalism we have for organizing and conveying what we know, it is not the only way. Formalisms are formal systems of rules for communicating ideas. Language is a complex formalism with many complex rules (syntax) for describing ideas. Using language to write essays, for instance, has high cognitive overhead. Many students experience difficulty in using language to think; they may profit from thinking about and representing ideas in new ways. Mindtools provide several formalisms for representing what we know, many that are more highly structured and visual. For instance, semantic networks produce visual maps of relationships between ideas. They are well liked by students for their clarity of expression. The goal of educators should be to select the formalism that is most effective for analyzing and thinking about particular content, rather than always relying on verbal accounts of understanding.

Students and Technologies Can Be Partners in Learning

Technologies, when used as Mindtools, function as intellectual partners with students. When used in this way, the technologies become intellectual toolboxes full of different tools for representing and thinking about ideas. These tools necessarily foster deeper-level, more critical thinking while engaging students in reflections on what they have learned. Using technologies as formalisms for representing what students know provides them with learning strategies for understanding content in different ways, which leads to richer understanding. The remainder of the chapter will illustrate some of the ways that computers can be used as Mindtools.

MINDTOOLS LEARNING ACTIVITIES

It is important to realize that the programs described below are not the only Mindtools in existence. Rather, the concept of Mindtools describes a way to use computer programs to foster critical thinking. Many other programs may also function as Mindtools. Computer productivity tools, such as word processors, computer-assisted design (CAD) systems, graphics programs, and desktop publishing systems are not included here because in normal use, they do not amplify the learners' thinking. They definitely make users more effective at writing, drawing, painting, and publishing, and they are used extensively in schools. They are important and useful applications. We encourage you to learn to use them and any other useful productivity tools, but they do not normally amplify the writing, drawing, painting, and publishing activities. They just make them more efficient. Can they be used as Mindtools? Probably, and we encourage you to attempt to use them in that way. Are the Mindtools described in this chapter the only ones? Definitely not. We encourage you to examine any technology application as a potential Mindtool to foster critical thinking and meaning making in your students. We realize that this position is very arguable. We encourage you to argue about it. Then our text may become a Mindtool.

Constructing Databases

Database management systems (DBMSs) are computerized record-keeping systems that were designed to replace paper-based information retrieval systems. They are electronic filing cabinets that allow users to store information in an organized filing system and later retrieve that information, just as a secretary would store documents in organized filing drawers. DBMSs consist of several components: the database, a file management system, database organization tools, and reporting (printing) functions. The database is what we want learners to produce. It consists of one or more files containing information in the form of records describing objects (e.g., an individual's account information). Each record in the database is divided into fields that describe the class or type of information in that field. The same type of information for each record is stored in each field. For example, an address database may contains hundreds of records, each with information about a different individual. These records are systematically broken down into fields (subunits of each record) that define a common pattern of information. The database might contain six fields, one for the last name, one for the first name, one for the street address, one for the city, one for the state, and one for the Zip code. The content and arrangement of each field is standardized within the records, so that the computer will know which part of the record to search in order to locate a particular kind of information.

The database manipulation tools permit the user to organize and reorganize the information in order to answer queries. The primary manipulation tools allow users to search for specific record, sort all of the record numerically or alphabetically according to one or more fields (e.g., name), and retrieve parts of the database based on a logical query. For instance, if you can use a database that contains the class schedules of each student in the school, you can access the file, change it, or search it for specific information in the database (e.g., the address of a particular student), or rearrange the database in order to develop different reports (e.g., sorted by Zip code). Most DBMSs permit you to identify multiple search criteria, that is, to search simultaneously on more than one field (e.g., if you wanted to find all the Smiths who lived in the same Zip code.

Students in most classrooms are required to read textbooks, listen to lectures, and assimilate and resolve the ideas from both into some understanding. Sometimes they are unsuccessful because the ideas from the textbook are dissonant from the ideas in the lecture, and students struggle to decide which is right. More often, however, students are unsuccessful because they do not know which ideas are most important and how they are related to each other. This is where constructing knowledge databases in groups will help them to understand the important ideas and their underlying structure. Rather than underlining or highlighting their entire textbooks or copying down every word from a lecture, students need to focus on the important concepts and ideas and try to interrelate them in an organized way. The students who produced the database in Figure 6.1 worked together to identify social and economic indicators of progress (many more could have been identified). This structured data enables students to interrelate the economic indicators. They can sort and search the database in order to answer questions such as:

- Is the relationship between wealth positively or negatively related to literacy?
- Which indicator is the best predictor of infant mortality?
- Do richer nations spend a higher percentage of their wealth on defense? Why?

country	population	pop dens	GNP $B	ave income	defense	infant mort	literacy	TVs per pers
Australia	16,646,000	5.4	220	$14,458	2.7%	8.1/1000	99	1/2.0
Brazil	153,771,000	47	313	$ 2,020	.8%	67/1000	76	1/4.0
Canada	26,527,000	6	486	$13,000	2.0%	7.3/1000	99	1/1.7
China	1,130,065,000	288	350	$ 258	4.4%	33/1000	70	1/12
El Salvador	5,221,000	671	4.1	$ 700	3.9%	62/1000	62	1/12
India	850,067,000	658	246	$ 300	3.8%	91/1000	36	1/62
Iraq	18,782,000	104	34	$ 1,950	32%	69/1000	70	1/18
Japan	123,778,000	844	1800	$15,030	1.0%	5/1000	99	1/4.1
Mexico	88,335,000	115	126	$ 2,082	.6%	42/1000	88	1/8.7
Saudi Arabia	16,758,000	15	70		12.8%	74/1000	50	1/3.5
Switzerland	6,628,000	406	111	$26,309	2.2%	6.9/1000	99	1/2.9
U.S.S.R.	290,939,000	33	2.5	$ 3,000	17%	25.2/1000	99	1/3.2
U.S.A.	250,372,000	68	4.8	$16,444	5.7%	10/1000	99	1/1.3

Figure 6.1   World statistics database

These questions are best generated by students and answered collaboratively. The queries can also serve as quizzes about the information being studied when generated by the teacher.

Databases as Study Guides   Databases may also be used as a study template for groups of students. Figure 6.2 shows three records from a database on short stories. As students read short stories in class, students in groups could generate a record that describes each of the characteristics of the story described in Figure 6.2. This type of database would act as a tool for analyzing each short story. Although this type of activity could represent nothing more than an electronic worksheet, it offers some significant advantages over traditional worksheets. First, it provides a complete and continuing record of what the students have read, but more important, it allows students to compare and contrast stories by searching and sorting the database in order to analyze short stories. What do these stories have in common? How are they different? How does the primary conflict relate to the climax of the story? Do different authors use consistent kinds of foreshadowing? How does the setting help to determine to rising action? These are the kinds of questions that literature teachers want students to answer, but because of a lack of experience in reading short stories, students are ill-prepared to think in this way. Using a database as an external corporate memory for the students, they can search their databases for such answers. The goal is to get them to see relationships among literary techniques. Databases assume some of the cognitive load for

Story Title	Author	Setting Detail 1	Setting Detail 2
Bargain	A.B. Guthrie	Old West	Baumer's Store
The Open Window	H. H. Munro	RUral area– England	At dusk, in house surrounded
All Summer in a Day	Ray Bradbury	Planet Venus/rains constantly	school classroom

Primary Conflict	Conflict 2	Rising Action Event 1	Rising Action Event 2
Man vs. Man	Man vs. Himself	Slade and Baumer fight until Slade smashes	Baumer's hand doesn't heal.
Man vs. Man	Man vs. Himself	Vera is a fifteen year old looking for some f	Framton is visiting as part of a "ne
Man vs. Man	Man vs. Nature	Margot is apart from the other children.	Children become vicious when Mar

Climax	Page	Explanation	Falling Action
Slade drinks the wood	214	Up to this point the reader is not certai	"Is good to know to read."
Framton bolts from tl	5	After being set up by Vera, he is sure l	"I expect it was the spaniel...he told n
Children let Margot o	242	The conlict of man vs. man (Margot vs.	The last sentence is thefalling action.

Foreshadowing 1	Page F1	Line F1	Explanation F1	Foreshadowing 2
Baumer tells Al educa	205	"Is good to know to r	If Baumer had known how to r	Baumer knows Slade will drir
Framton is a nervous	3	"Privately he doubtec	He's a perfect candidate to se	Vera makes sure Framton knc
Margot's aloneness.	237, 238	"Margot stood apart	The children don't like her and	Children's reaction to Margot

Figure 6.2   Short story database template

this process, enabling students to think in ways they probably otherwise would not be able to.

Analyzing Stories Using Databases We argued in Chapter 1 that constructive learning requires learners to articulate and reflect on what they have learned. Quite often, we describe what we know by telling stories. Replay and analyze most any conversation, and it will probably be comprised of a series of stories. One person tells a story to make a point, which reminds other conversants of related events, so they tell the stories that they were reminded of, which in turn remind others of stories, and so on. Why do we use stories to foster conversation? Because we remember so much of what we know in the form of stories. Stories are a rich and powerful formalism for storing and describing memories. So, one way of understanding what people know is to analyze their stories. The means for analyzing stories is called case-based reasoning (CBR).

CBR is a formalism, based on artificial intelligence techniques, for representing what people know. It argues that what people know is stored in memory as stories (Schank 1990). In any new situation, people examine the situation and attempt to retrieve a previously experienced situation that resembles the current situation. Along with information about the situation, we retrieve the lessons that the situation provides. New problems are solved by finding similar past cases and applying the lessons to the new case. So learning is a process of solving a problem in ways that make it available to help solve future problems. As a teacher, when you are confronted by a discipline problem, you are reminded of students that you disciplined last week or several years ago based on the similarity of the student, the infraction, the situation, and so on. If your method of discipline was effective, you are likely to reuse it in this situation. If it failed, you will likely search out other cases that shared similarities with the current one that were successfully resolved.

To use databases for capturing stories, you must identify cases. Cases are problem situations. Problem situations consist of a description of the problem situation (e.g., student cursing at the teacher), the solution that was selected (detention), and the outcome when the solution (student cursed again later) was carried out (Kolodner 1993). The problem situation is defined by the goals to be achieved in solving the problem (gain respect of student), the constraints on those goals (time left in the class to deal with it), and any features of the problem situation (attitude and family values of student, kind of class it occurred in). As stories are collected from students or teachers and analyzed, they must be indexed by identifying some combination of the goals, constraints, situational descriptions, themes, solutions, outcomes, and lessons in a database. For instance, Figure 6.3 illustrates a single record from a database of teachers' stories about their parent–teacher conferences. The database includes a separate field for describing the type of conference, the classroom placement, reason for the conference, goal of the conference, the teacher's plan, the result of the conference, reflections by the teacher, alternative actions that could have been taken, and a narrative of the story. Different fields could have been included to describe the teacher stories. Database programs allow you to add new fields as ideas occur. Learning, from a CBR perspective, is a

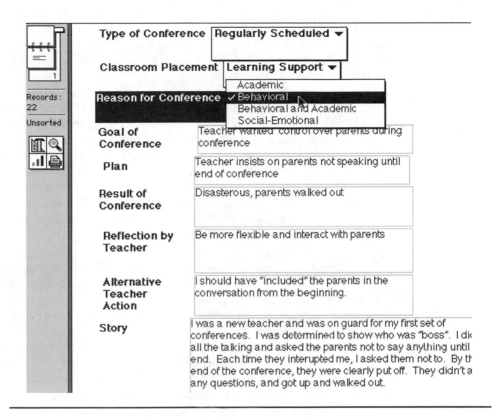

Figure 6.3   Database of teacher stories

process of indexing and filing experience-based lessons and reusing those in similar situations in the future. In this example, teachers learn about how to conduct parent–teacher conferences by examining how others have conducted them and the experiences that they have had. Databases facilitate this learning process by allowing teachers to sort on any field to locate similar cases or results.

Story databases can be developed with students, as well. Find an important story or a problem-solving event or a current or historical event where someone was faced with a dilemma (e.g., a politician's reaction to negative campaign tactics) and ask your students' "What does this story remind you of?" Collect their stories verbatim and then analyze them, trying to determine the goals being pursued by whom, situational descriptions, constraints, and so on. Identify each of these in the fewest, most descriptive words possible. Insert each reminding into a data field and sort the database on the various factors to see where the similarities exist. The more fields that two records contain in common, the more accessible and usable it is to a new situation and the better the lesson it will provide.

Learning Processes   Building knowledge databases is primarily constructive. It requires that learners articulate the underlying structure of the content that they are studying. The content structure is then translated into the database structure. Learners then reflect on the content they are studying by formulating searches and generating questions that require their peers to conduct searches in order to answer the relational questions.

Building databases is also an intentional learning strategy for studying course content. Learners must establish a higher-order learning goal and regulate their learning by monitoring how well their databases reflect the content being studied. Learners can use these sophisticated strategies in nearly any course.

It is important to note that building databases focuses on semantic relationships among the concepts being studied. Understanding content requires that learners understand the relationships between the concepts in the domain. Having learners define concepts most often invokes memorization strategies with little or no understanding. Having them compare and contrast concepts using databases provides evidence of deeper understanding.

Student Roles   The point of using each of the Mindtools is to engage students in representing what they know, including the concepts and relationships that they have identified as important. That is, students need to analyze reading or other information sources to determine the most important ideas and how they are structured. This is best accomplished in collaborative groups of three to five students. Students work to identify important concepts and brainstorm possible relationships. Some students will input the information into the databases. Others will check it for accuracy. All students should work together to develop questions that they could assign to other students to answer using their database. This is an important synthesis activity that is exemplified in the first database shown.

Teacher Roles   Allowing students to represent what they know means that teachers have to relinquish control of the content. Rather than telling students which are the important concepts and what their underlying relationships are, teachers must help students learn how to use the database program and then provide feedback about their data structures. Our experience has shown us that teachers too often direct-teach the content structures, so student databases all look the same. As a teacher, allow the student groups to construct their own databases. Prompt them or ask them questions about the underlying semantic relationships that they are trying to convey. You may also want to compare and contrast the databases in class, showing how different groups developed different data structures, asking each group about the assumptions they were making.

Assessing Learning   The databases that students produce and the questions that they ask of other students are clear indicators of students' understanding of the content being learned. You can evaluate the databases by asking questions about them, such as:

- Is the information in the database accurate (consistent with standards)?
- Have all of the instances (all important records) been identified?
- Do the fields describe all of the important characteristics/attributes/ aspects of the records? Can the database answer all meaningful queries?

It is important to describe the instances (records) in as many ways as possible.

* What relationships are implied by the queries that student write?

Constructing Semantic Networks

Concept mapping is a study strategy that requires learners to draw visual maps of concepts connected to each other via lines (links). These maps depict the semantic structure among concepts in a domain. There are a number of paper-and-pencil methods for eliciting and representing these concept maps (Jonassen, Beissner, and Yacci 1993).

Recently, several computer-based concept mapping tools (referred to here as *semantic networking tools*) have become available. Semantic networking programs are computer-based visualizing tools for developing reqresentations of the semantic networks in memory. Computer programs such as Learning Tool, SemNet, and Inspiration for the Macintosh, and VisiMap, MindMan, Axon Idea Processor, and Inspiration for Windows machines have become available as powerful Mindtools for organizing and integrating content ideas. These programs provide visual and verbal screen tools for developing concept maps (otherwise known as cognitive maps or semantic nets). Semantic nets or concept maps are spatial representations of ideas (concepts) and their interrelationships that are stored in personal memories (see Figure 6.4). These tools enable learners to identify the important ideas or concepts in a knowledge domain and interrelate those ideas in multidimensional networks of concepts by labeling the relationships between those ideas.

Semantic networks are composed of nodes (concepts or ideas) and links (statements of relationships) connecting them. In computer-based semantic networks, nodes are represented as information blocks or cards (e.g., "Cretaceous Period" in Figure 6.4) and the links are labeled lines (e.g., "moved on" in Figure 6.4). Most semantic network programs also provide the capability of adding text and pictures to each node, making them more like hypermedia (see Chapter 4). Note that the map in Figure 6.4 is but one screen in a semantic network consisting of more than 100 screens describing different dinosaurs and their relationships. Semantic networks help learners to organize their ideas and to convey that organization of ideas to others. Children love dinosaurs. They enjoy creating semantic networks such as the one in Figure 6.4 while studying dinosaurs.

Semantic nets provide one of the easiest to learn and most popular Mindtools. Whenever students are studying and analyzing new content in order to make sense out of it, semantic networks provide a rich visual tool for depicting the structure of ideas in that domain, which is essential to depicting it. Because they require learners to analyze the underlying structure of ideas they are studying, semantic networks are tools for intentionally organizing what they learner knows by explicitly describing the concepts and their interrelationships. Semantic networking specifically engages learners in relating new ideas to what they already know, which is the basis for meaning making. Even professors need to study.

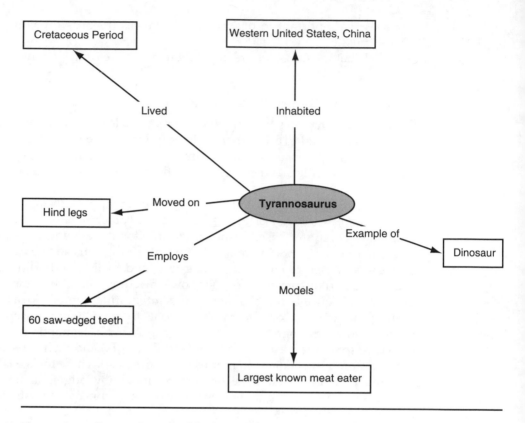

Figure 6.4 Semantic network about dinosaurs

Figure 6.5 represents a semantic net that we constructed to help us understand the influences of a new theory.

Semantic networks are also effective intentional planning tools, as well as analysis tools. When planning a paper or a speech, semantic networks can help you to organize your ideas and plan the production. Figure 6.6 depicts the organization of a recent conference presentation about Mindtools. Not only did the semantic networking program Inspiration act as a powerful tool for planning the talk, but it was also used as a presentation tool. That is, the talk was made using the semantic network as a projected visual to highlight the structure of the argument underlying the presentation. The argument made more sense to the audience by using such a visualization.

Learning Processes   Learners who build semantic networks are actively seeking important ideas from information sources that they need to construct their nets. They are evaluating information for its relevance and the ways that it fits together. They are also constructive—building visual–verbal representations of their own ideas. In this way, they are being intentional, using an intentional strategy for studying course content. That requires that students reflect on what they know

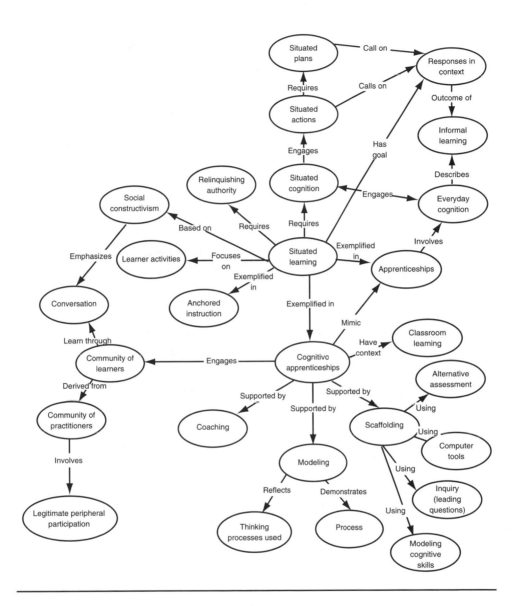

Figure 6.5 Semantic network as a study strategy

and how new ideas relate to it. Contrast those behaviors with the repetitive rehearsal strategies that students normally use to memorize information.

Student Roles Students must actively evaluate ideas as they are studying them. To create semantic networks, students need to first identify important concepts. That means reading through texts or lecture notes to identify the ideas that are important to understanding the content. Rather than defining these concepts, stu-

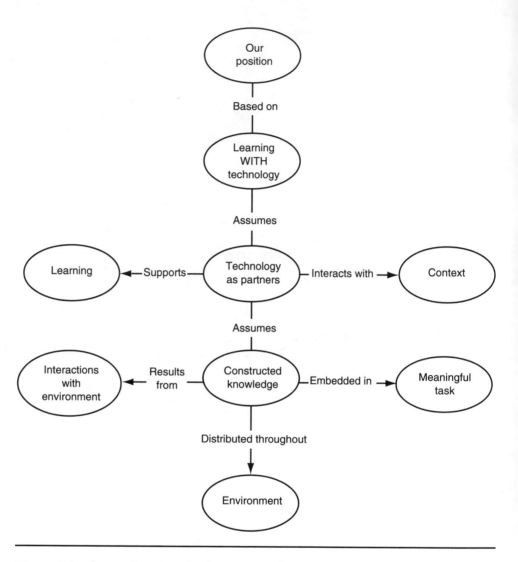

Figure 6.6 Semantic network of a presentation

dents need to describe how they relate to the other ideas that they have identified. They need to decide how clear and how descriptive those relationships are. This process will probably be enhanced by collaboration with other students.

Teacher Roles   As with constructing databases, it is important to allow students to represent what they know rather than telling students which are the important concepts and what their underlying relationships are. Teachers must help students learn how to use the semantic networking program and then provide feedback about their semantic nets without showing them the "correct" structure. Our experience has shown that, because teachers show students how to construct them, student semantic nets tend to look the same. It is important to allow student groups to construct their own nets. Prompt them or ask them questions about the underlying semantic relationships that they are trying to convey. They will need the greatest amount of coaching in describing clear and concise relationships.

Assessing Learning   In addition to functioning as study and planning tools, semantic networks are also powerful assessment tools. They can be used to assess a learner's cognitive structure, the pattern of relationships among concepts in memory (Preece 1976) or, more specifically, the organization of the relationships of concepts in long-term memory (Shavelson 1972). Semantic networking activities have been shown to be an accurate means for representing cognitive structure (Jonassen 1987). That is, semantic networking, as described in this chapter, helps learners map their own cognitive structure. The completeness and accuracy of students' semantic nets have been positively related to a variety of learning outcomes, including examination performance, memory, problem solving, and inferential thinking (Jonassen 1996). Learners with better-structured knowledge are better thinkers, rememberers, and problem solvers.

Semantic nets can also be used as evaluation tools for assessing changes in thinking by learners. If we agree that memory is organized as a semantic network, then learning can be thought of as a reorganization of semantic memory. Producing new versions of semantic networks on the same topic over time reflects those changes in semantic memory, since the networks describe what a learner knows. Thus, having learners generate semantic nets before and after instruction should reflect growth in their knowledge structures as reflected in the nets that they produce.

The following questions can be used to assess and evaluate learners' semantic networks:

- Are all important concepts represented in the semantic network as nodes?
- Are the relationships between nodes (links) descriptive? Links like "are related to" are meaningless. Describing clear relationships is the hardest part of constructing semantic networks.
- Are the concepts (nodes) interrelated to each other? Try to eliminate orphans (concepts with only one link to them).
- What are the most important concepts (those with the most links to them)?

Using Visualization Tools

Humans are complex organisms that generally possess well-balanced sensory systems. We humans have finely tuned counterbalanced motor receptor and effector systems, which enable us to feel things and to respond to those environmental stimuli with a complex combination of gross and fine motor activity. Swatting a mosquito or scratching an itch requires millions of sensory receptors and motor actions to direct the hand to strike the location of the irritating stimuli. Likewise, humans have reasonably keen aural perception, allowing us to hear a large range of sounds. Those sounds can be replicated or at least responded to orally by forcing air through the diaphragm, palate, and lips to create an infinite variety of sounds. However, our most sophisticated sensory system, vision, where the largest amount and variety of data are received, has no counterpoising effector system. We can receive visual input, but we have no output mechanism for visually representing ideas, except in mental images and dreams. Unfortunately, these visions cannot be shared. Therefore, we need what Hermann Maurer calls "visual prostheses" to visually represent what we are thinking. Some might think that draw-and-paint packages are powerful visualization tools. To some degree, they are, because they provide sophisticated tools that enable us to draw and paint objects electronically. However, in order to represent our mental images using paint/draw programs, we have to translate those images into a series of manual operations, which only *some* people do well.

Although it is not yet possible to dump our mental images directly from our brains into a computer, a new and growing class of visualization tools is mediating this process by providing us tools that allow us to reason visually in certain areas. These tools automate some of the manual process for drawing objects. Unlike the generalized representational capabilities of most Mindtools, visualization tools tend to be very task- and domain-specific. That is, there are no general-purpose visualization tools. Rather, these tools closely mimic the ways that different images must be interpreted in order to make sense of the ideas.

As we describe later in this chapter, an individual's mental models of objects, systems, or other phenomena possess visual–spatial components. In order to understand a system, it is necessary for humans to generate a mental image of the system. Visualization tools help humans to represent and convey those mental images, usually not in the same form they are generated mentally, but as rough approximations of those mental images. We next describe two different kinds of visualization tools that learners use to make sense of ideas. As with other Mindtools, these are only representative of a large and growing class of visualization tools.

Weather Visualizers

The Collaborative Visualization (CoVis) Project (described in greater detail in Chapter 7) provides scientific visualization software to students to help them to observe climatological patterns. The *Weather Visualizer* provides a graphical interface to real-time weather data. The *Weather Visualizer* provides customized weather maps that are downloaded from the World Wide Web. It generates current satellite images, both visible and infrared from the GOES-7 weather satellite. A point-and-click palette allows students to select the variables they want drawn on their customized map (Figure 6.7). These maps may be saved into the student's notebook as part of ongoing research. Additionally, the Weather Graphics Tool allows students to draw high-quality weather maps that resemble those produced by the *Weather Visualizer*. The maps are used by students for making weather predictions.

In addition to predicting weather, students can use visualization tools to observe climatological changes around the globe. The Climate Visualizer provides a front end to the Spyglass Transform scientific visualization software, which is designed to support student examination of authentic scientific datasets. The interface (Figure 6.8) visually represents scientific assumptions and knowledge that allow students to ask advanced questions without requiring complex interpretation.

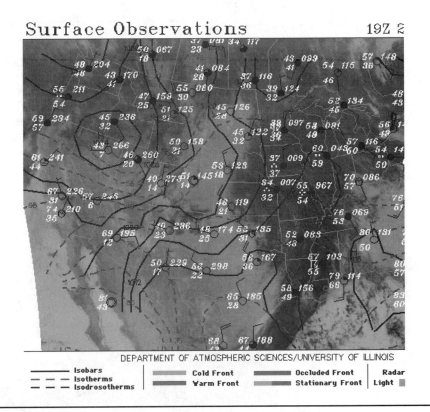

Figure 6.7 *Weather Visualizer* output

The Climate Watcher supports students' examination and manipulation of scientific visualizations in order to construct explanations of weather phenomena as well as the design of their own visualizations to communicate a result or point of view. Perhaps most significantly, the Climate Watcher visually represents complex mathematical relationships between climate variables such as insulation, absorbed and reflected solar energy, surface temperature, precipitation, greenhouse effect, outgoing long-wave radiation, net energy balance, elevation, ground cover, plant energy absorption, soil type, population density, carbon emissions, and so on. With this combination of data, students can investigate some very interesting hypotheses. Students in schools all over the world regularly record and contribute meteorological information to the *Climate Watcher* (Figure 6.9). The CoVis suite of visualization and collaboration tools enables students to function like scientists by helping them to interpret complex data that they would not otherwise be able to interpret.

Chemical Visualization Tools   A growing number of tools for visualizing chemical compounds are available. Understanding chemical bonding is difficult for most people, because the complex atomic interactions are not visible and therefore

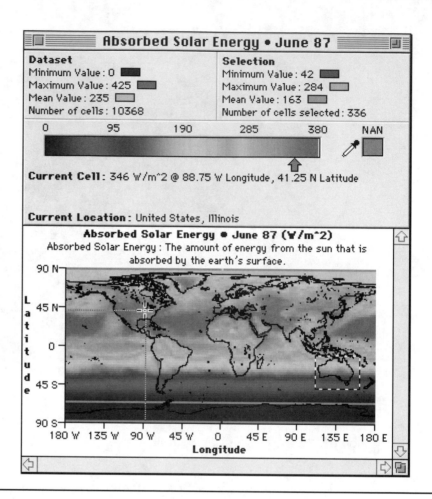

Figure 6.8   Visualization window from the *Climate Watcher*

seem abstract. Static graphics of these bonds found in textbooks may help learners to form mental images, but those mental images are not manipulable and cannot be conveyed to others. Tools such as MacSpartan enable students to view, rotate, and measure molecules using different views (see Figure 6.10), and allow them to modify or construct new molecules (see Figure 6.11), testing their structure and bonds as they construct. These visualization tools make the abstract real for students, helping them to understand chemical concepts that are difficult to convey in static displays.

Learning Processes   Visualization tools facilitate active and constructive learning. They enable students to manipulate representations of ideas and observe the results—that is, to see things in new ways. That manipulation process, in

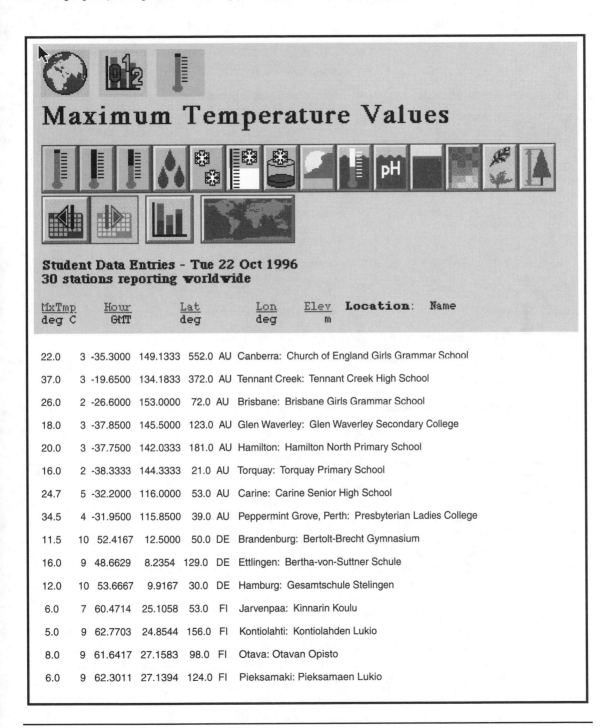

Figure 6.9 Student reporting using the *Climate Watcher*

3.0	10	66.7631	26.4153	80.0	FI	Utajarvi:Utajarven Ylaaste
13.0	10	45.7667	15.9833	120.0	HR	Zagreb: Geodetska Tehnicka Skola
13.0	10	45.7667	15.9833	20.0	HR	Zagreb: Geodetska Tehnicka Skola
21.5	4	33.8028	130.7472	48.0	JP	Fukuoka: Chiyo Junoir high School
20.0	2	34.5006	133.5764	16.0	JP	Hiroshima: Fukuyama Junior High School
18.0	0	35.8636	139.7758	3.0	JP	Saitama: Musashino Junior High School
21.0	2	35.3408	132.9011	35.0	JP	Shimane: Kamo Junior High School
20.1	4	35.7417	138.5908	48.0	JP	Oizumi Junior High School, Tokyo Gakugei University
14.9	10	53.1917	6.5758	1.0	NL	Groningen: Zernike College I
9.0	10	59.5667	9.2667	114.0	NO	Notodden: Hoegskulen I Telemark
4.0	11	64.6285	16.6562	381.0	SE	Vilhelmina: Malgomajskolan
26.0	12	41.9867	-83.8311	196.0	US	Britton: Britton-Macon Area School
26.0	12	42.4400	-85.6489	259.0	US	Plainwell: Gilkey Elementary School
15.0	12	41.1272	-79.5411	413.0	US	Easton: Easton Area High School
30.0	11	40.4822	-78.5519	407.0	US	Gallitzin: Penn Cambria Middle School

Figure 6.9   Continued

turn, enables learners to articulate or better represent underlying principles. The combination of these manipulation and representation activities fosters better understanding.

Students use visualization tools for interpreting information. What they do with those interpretations is very specific to the kind of tool being used and the expected outcome. In the CoVis Project, students make weather forecasts, have issue-based discussions (see Chapter 5), and create essays to describe weather processes. The chemical visualization tools could be used to create new compounds, make predictions about chemical reactions, or a variety of other activities. Because of the diversity of tools and applications, it is impossible to identify specific student and teacher roles or propose evaluation criteria.

Exploring Microworlds

Microworlds are a class of Mindtools that assume many forms, depending on the skills they are trying to engage. All microworlds, however, are exploratory learn-

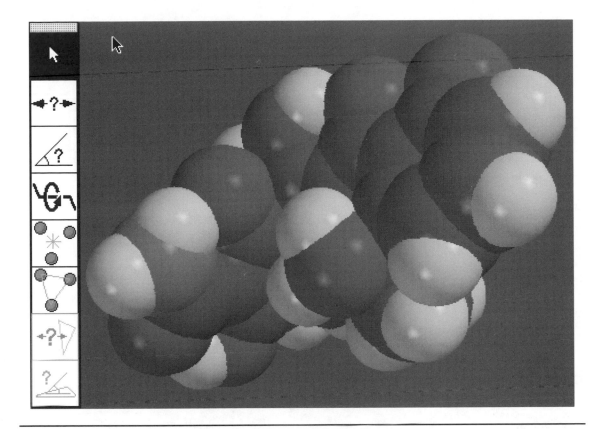

Figure 6.10   MacSpartan Molecular Visualization Tool

ing environments or discovery spaces in which learners can navigate, manipulate or create objects, and test their effects on one another. Microworlds contain constrained simulations of real-world phenomena that allow learners to control those phenomena. "Microworlds present students with a simple model of a part of the world" (Hanna 1986, p. 197) while they provide the capability needed to explore phenomena in those parts of the world. "The ideal associated with this approach is the feeling of 'direct engagement,' the feeling that the computer is invisible, not even there; but rather, what is present is the world we are exploring, be that world music, art, words, business, mathematics, literature or what ever your imagination and task provide you" (Draper and Norman 1986, p. 3).

Microworlds are not necessarily computer-based. Burton, Brown, and Fischer (1984) use skiing instruction as a pretext for developing a model for designing skill-based "microworlds." They believe that a microworld is a controlled learning environment where a student is able to try out new skills and knowledge. It is a practice-oriented simulation. Complexity is controlled by manipulating the equipment (e.g., the length of the skis), the task, and the environment (e.g., making easy turns on the "bunny" slope and later making more difficult turns on steeper terrain). All microworlds, computer-based and others, are exploration

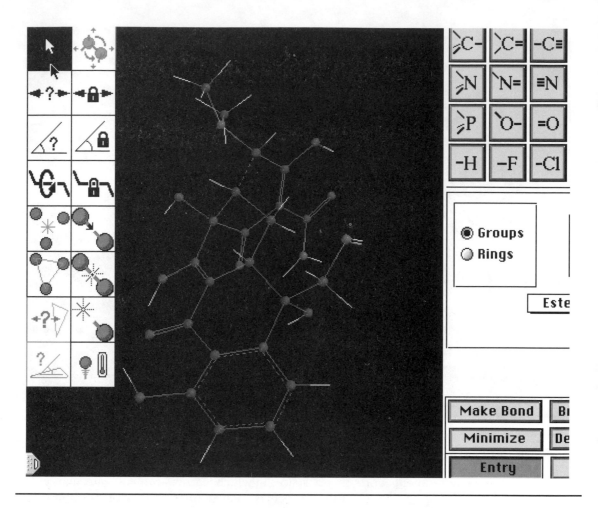

Figure 6.11   MacSpartan Molecular Construction Tool

environments that rely on the interest and curiosity of the learner. Video-based adventure games are microworlds that require players to master each environment before moving onto more complex environments. They are compelling to youngsters, who spend hours transfixed in these adventure worlds. Microworlds are perhaps the ultimate example of active learning environments, because the users can exercise so much control over the environment.

Microworlds are based on powerful ideas. The concept of microworlds was coined by Seymour Papert, the developer of Logo, a simple procedural computer language for manipulating a turtle object and drawing and creating objects that became components of larger, more complex objects. Logo was designed to be an exploratory environment in which students learn by doing, instead of just watching or listening to a description of how something works. The research on Logo has not supported the hopes of its developers. Although it is a potentially powerful environment for creating microworlds, it requires that students learn how to program a computer. Logo is a highly structured language with a simple syntax, but the language is still an impediment for many learners and it mitigates some of the potential benefits of the environment.

Many object-oriented microworlds are now available that require no programming skills in order to manipulate the objects in the microworld. One of our favorites is *Interactive Physics.* This microworld provides teachers and students the tools to create experiments in physics, such as the classic inclined plane in Figure 6.12. The experimenter can monitor aspects of the experiment (e.g., normal, friction, and gravity force) as the block slides down the plane. They can change any aspects of the microworld (e.g., stickiness of the surface, friction, gravity level) and rerun the experiment to test the effects. This microworld allows learners to create or run an infinite number of different physics and play "what-if" games in order to understand the dynamics of physical objects. *Interactive Physics* engages active and interactive learning by allowing the learner to manipulate any aspect of the environment. That is the essence of interactive learning.

The second experiment (Figure 6.13) is a motion in a plane problem that focuses on vector forces and trajectory required to intercept the falling monkey. Again, every aspect of the environment is manipulable, making it a highly interactive form of instruction.

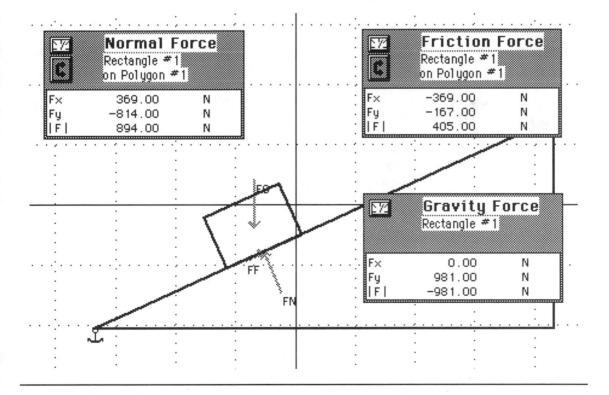

Figure 6.12   Inclined plane experiment in *Interactive Physics*

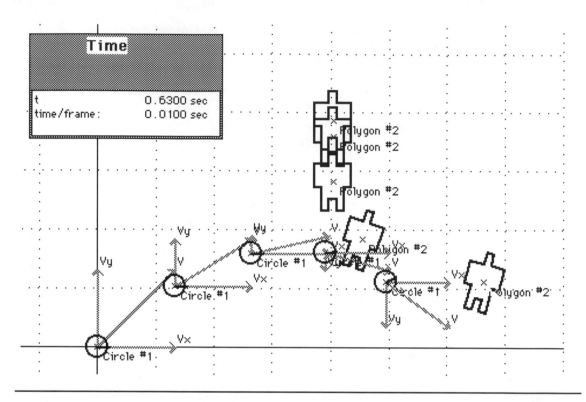

Figure 6.13 Motion in a plane experiment in *Interactive Physics*

Many microworlds are being produced and made available from educational research projects, especially in math and science. In mathematics, the Geometric Supposer and Algebraic Supposer are standard tools for testing conjectures in geometry and algebra by constructing and manipulating geometric and algebraic objects in order to explore the relationships within and between these objects (Schwartz and Yerulshamy 1987). The emphasis in those microworlds is the generation and testing hypotheses. They provide a testbed for testing students' predictions about geometric and algebraic proofs.

The SimCalc project teaches middle and high school students calculus concepts through *MathWorlds*, which is a microworld consisting of animated worlds and dynamic graphs in which actors move according to graphs. By exploring the movement of the actors in the simulations and seeing the graphs of their activity, students begin to understand important calculus ideas. In the *MathWorlds* activity illustrated in Figure 6.14, students match two motions. By matching two motions, they learn how velocity and position graphs relate. Students must match the motion of the green and red graphs. To do this, they can change either graph. They iteratively run the simulation to see if you got it right! Students may also use MathWorlds' link to enter their own bodily motion. For example, students can

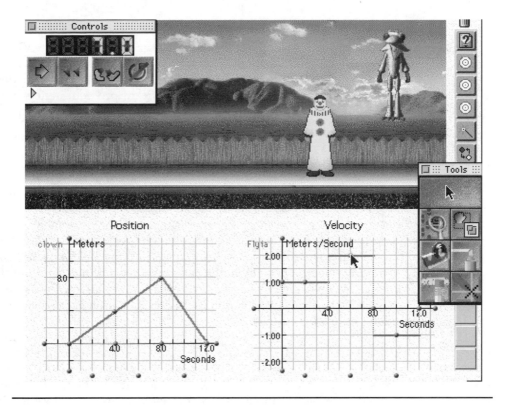

Figure 6.14   Experiment in *MathWorlds*

walk across the classroom, and their motions would be entered into *MathWorlds* through sensing equipment. MathWorlds would plot their motion, enabling the students to explore the properties of their own motion.

Learning Processes   Microworlds, better than nearly any technology-based activity or tool, enable learners to manipulate variables and observe the results of this manipulation. Microworlds provide the essence of active learning strategy. However, manipulation is not enough for meaningful learning. Microworld learning projects should be followed up with the kinds of reflective thinking that are enabled by expert systems and system modeling tools (described next in this chapter).

Microworlds are also very specific to the kind of environment being simulated and the expected learning outcome. *Interactive Physics,* for instance, can be used to provide canned physics labs as an environment for students to simulate processes or create their own microworld. *MathWorlds* also provide a wide variety of experimental simulations that, in general, require students to speculate about mathematical phenomena. Because of the diversity of microworlds and their applications, it is impossible to identify specific student and teacher roles or propose evaluation criteria.

Constructing Expert Systems

We have argued throughout this book that students should work on meaningful real-world or simulated tasks, observing phenomena in their natural settings. Why? Because ideas that are related to real-world objects are better understood and transferred to new situations. A significant problem in actively solving real-world problems is that learners do not stop to reflect on what they have learned from solving those problems. Expert systems can be used to get students to reflect on these contextualized learning situations. First, what are expert systems?

Expert systems, evolved from research in the field of artificial intelligence, are computer-based tools that are designed to function as intelligent aids (experts) to facilitate decision making in all sorts of tasks. Expert system builders attempt to develop programs that simulate the human capacity to reason and to learn so that these expert systems may perform functions that resemble human thinking. Expert systems have been developed to help geologists decide where to drill for oil, fire fighters decide how to extinguish different kinds of fires, computer sales technicians decide how to configure computer systems, and employees decide among a large number of company benefits alternatives. Problems in which the solution includes recommendations based on a variety of decisions are good candidates for expert systems.

Like a human expert, an expert system cannot put its knowledge and skills to use unless a need arises. The computer must wait for input from a user with a need or problem who is seeking advice from the system. For example, imagine that a novice loan officer in a bank must decide whether an individual should be granted a personal, unsecured loan. There are many factors to consider when making the decision (e.g., income, amount of loan, past credit record, reason for the loan, size of monthly payment, etc.)—so many factors that it may take months or years of training to prepare the loan officer to consider everything involved. An alternative is to build an expert system that asks the loan officer to input all data necessary for making an informed decision. The expert system, which is composed of facts and rules that an experienced or expert loan officer uses in making a decision, relates the information provided by the loan applicant to the rules and presents a decision that provides valuable advice to the loan officer. In this way, the expert system increases productivity because it saves both analysis time and training time.

The data about the user's problem is collected and entered into the computer's memory to help guide the expert system to a solution. For example, the expert system designed to help a novice loan officer might ask the officer the following questions:

- **Question:** Is the applicant employed? For how long? In what job? At what salary?
- **Question:** Does the applicant have other loans? Credit cards? What are their balances? What is his/her record of loan repayment?
- **Question:** Does the applicant own/rent a home? What is his/her monthly mortgage/rent payment?

The questions asked by the expert system gather information that changes with each individual situation. The answers to these questions are integrated within an existing knowledge base of information (facts and rules) that remains relatively stable.

The computer asks the user questions; the user inputs data, usually via the keyboard; and the computer records the user's input, storing it in a knowledge base for the expert systems to evaluate. The knowledge base consists of facts and rules that represent knowledge used by human experts to reach a decision. The most important part of the knowledge base is the rules, which consist of conditions and decisions. That is, rules state that IF a set of conditions exists, THEN some decision is reached. Conditions may be combined in a number of ways into sets. Sets of IF conditions may be combined using conjunctions (condition1 AND condition2 must exist), disjunctions (condition1 OR condition2 does exist), and negations (condition1 but NOT condition2 must exist) in order for a decision to be reached. A decision may be an action (do something) or it may state another condition, which is then combined with other conditions to reach another decision.

Rule: IF applicant has defaulted on a loan within the past ten years, THEN deny the application.

The inference engine contains the logical program that examines the information provided by the user, as well as the facts and rules specified within the knowledge base. It evaluates the current problem situation and then seeks out rules that will provide advice about that situation. The expert system then presents its solution and allows the users to ask "why" they were asked for information or why a particular decision was selected by the program. The expert system will retrieve that information from the knowledge base and display it for the user.

An expert system, then, is a computer program that attempts to simulate the way human experts solve problems—an artificial decision maker. For example, when you consult an expert (e.g., doctor, lawyer, teacher) about a problem, the expert asks for current information about your condition, searches his or her knowledge base (memory) for existing knowledge for which to relate elements of the current situation, processes the information (thinks), arrives at a decision, and presents his or her solution. Like a human expert, an expert system (computer program) is approached by an individual (novice) with a problem. The system queries the individual about the current status of the problem, searches its own knowledge base for pertinent facts and rules that reflect the knowledge of an expert that was stored previously, processes the information, arrives at a decision, and reports the solution to the user. The process of representing what the expert knows engages learners in deep-level analysis of the ideas in the domain. So, our goal is to have students build expert system knowledge bases—that is, to try to think like an expert and to encode that knowledge in an expert system knowledge base. This process is made easy through the use of expert system shell programs, which are user-friendly systems for writing and evaluating rules.

Expert systems can be used as Mindtools to follow up situated activities, such as labs, simulation exercises, or field trips (Figure 6.15). Having students analyze

Context: 'The following expert system knowledge base was designed to classify rocks. It was developed to follow up on field trip on observing and classifying rocks where features of different rocks were observed. The knowledge base is actually in an abbreviated form. A rock classification knowledge base could be created to include many more questions, decisions, and rules.

Dec1 : 'granite'.

Dec2 : 'syenite'.

Dec3 : 'diorite'.

Dec4 : 'gabbro'.

Dec5 : 'marble'.

Dec6 : 'schist'.

Dec7 : 'gneiss'.

Dec8 : 'conglomerate'.

Dec9 : 'breccia'.

Dec10 : 'sandstone'.

Dec11 : 'arkose'.

Dec12 : 'rhyolite'.

Dec13 : 'phonolite'.

Dec14 : 'serpentine'.

Dec15 : 'talc'.

Dec16 : 'slate'.

Dec17 : 'limestone'.

Dec18 : 'coal'.

Dec19 : 'obsidian'.

Dec20 : 'chalk'.

Dec21 : 'chert'.

Question 1 :   'Is the rock made up of crystals of roughly the same size and readily visible without magnification?'
           Answers 1 'yes'
                    2 'no'.

Question 2 : 'The pattern of the crystals are best described as:'
           Answers 1 'coarse and interlocked'
                    2 'pronounced layering/banding'
                    3 'neither of the above/no such pattern'.

Question 3 : 'The texture of the rock can be best described as:'
           Answers 1 'glassy'
                    2 'porous'
                    3 'nodular'
                    4 'uniform, microcrystalline, not layered'
                    5 'greasy'
                    6 'waxy'
                    7 'other/not as described'.

Question 4 : 'The rock is made up of firmly cemented particles that appear as:'
           Answers 1 'rounded pebbles'
                    2 'angular fragments'
                    3 'light-colored grains'
                    4 'mixture of different grains'
                    5 'unsorted volcanic fragments and pumice'
                    6 'glassy minute volcanic fragments in volcanic ash'
                    7 'not as described'.

Figure 6.15   Rock classification knowledge base

Question 5 : 'The hardness can be described as:'
          Answers 1 'soft'
                  2 'fairly soft'
                  3 'brittle'
                  4 'breaks into slabs'
                  5 'hard/tough'
                  6 'not as described'.

Question 6 : 'The color of the rock is best described as:'
          Answers 1 'frothy white/cream'
                  2 'light-colored'
                  3 'green to gray'
                  4 'dull gray'
                  5 'red to purple'
                  6 'reddish brown'
                  7 'dark green to black'
                  8 'brown to black'
                  9 'alternating dark and light bands'
                10 'not as described'.

Question 7 : 'The composition of the rock is best described as:'
          Answers 1 'quartz'
                  2 'feldspar'
                  3 'augite'
                  4 'mica'
                  5 'iron'
                  6 'calcite crystals'
                  7 'hornblende'
                  8 'not as described'.

Rule 1: IF Q1A1 AND Q2A1 AND Q6A2 AND (Q7A1 OR Q7A2) THEN D1.
Rule 2: IF Q1A1 AND Q2A1 AND Q6A2 AND Q7A1 THEN D2.
Rule 3: IF Q1A1 AND Q2A1 AND Q6A4 AND (Q7A1 OR Q7A3 OR Q7A7) THEN D3.
Rule 4: IF Q1A1 AND Q2A1 AND Q6A8 AND (Q7A2 OR Q7A3) THEN D4.
Rule 5: IF Q1A1 AND Q2A1 AND Q6A2 AND Q7A6 THEN D5.
Rule 6: IF Q1A1 AND Q2A2 AND Q7A4 THEN D6.
Rule 7: IF Q1A1 AND Q2A2 AND Q6A9 AND (Q7A1 OR Q7A4) THEN D7.
Rule 8: IF Q1A1 AND Q4A1 THEN D8.
Rule 9: IF Q1A1 AND Q4A2 THEN D9.
Rule 10: IF Q1A1 AND Q4A3 AND Q6A2 AND Q7A1 THEN D10.
Rule 11: IF Q1A1 AND Q4A4 AND (Q7A1 OR Q7A2 OR Q7A4) THEN D11.
Rule 12: IF Q1A2 AND Q3A4 AND (Q7A1 OR Q7A2) THEN D12.
Rule 13: IF Q1A2 AND Q3A4 AND Q5A4 AND Q6A3 THEN D13.
Rule 14: IF Q1A2 AND (Q3A4 OR Q3A5) AND Q5A2 AND Q6A3 THEN D14.

Figure 6.15 Continued

Rule 15: IF Q1A2 AND Q3A4 AND Q5A2 AND Q6A3 THEN D15.

Rule 16: IF Q1A2 AND Q2A2 AND Q5A5 AND (Q6A4 OR Q6A5 OR Q6A8) THEN D16.

Rule 17: IF Q1A2 AND Q2A2 AND Q5A2 AND Q6A2 THEN D17.

Rule 18: IF Q1A2 AND (Q5A1 OR Q5A3) AND Q6A8 THEN D18.

Rule 19: IF Q1A2 AND Q3A1 AND Q5A5 AND (Q6A6 OR Q6A8) THEN D19.

Rule 20: IF Q1A2 AND Q3A2 AND Q5A1 AND Q6A2 THEN D20.

Rule 21: IF Q1A2 AND (Q3A3 OR Q3A6) AND Q5A5 THEN D21.

Figure 6.15   Continued

what they observed in these settings enhances the learning experience. Developing a rule base to describe what happened in the lab exercise or to classify what they observed on a field trip causes students to reflect deeply on the experience. Figure 6.15 illustrates this use with a rock classification knowledge base that was developed after a field trip by an earth science/geology class to observe different kinds of rocks. The purpose of this rule base is to help novices classify rocks based on the physical characteristics of the rocks that were observed on the field trip. The factors, represented by the questions in this knowledge base, are based largely on physical descriptions of the rocks that students observed.

Synthesizing Knowledge About Performance   Expert systems can be combined effectively with microworlds (described earlier in this chapter) or other simulated activities to enhance the learning from those experiences. For instance, students using *Interactive Physics* (described earlier) could follow up their experiments by building rule bases to describe the outcomes of their experiments or to make predictions about the outcomes of other experiments that manipulate the variables in their experiment. So for the inclined plane experiments, they would include factors such as the angle of descent, the weight of the object, and so on. Clearly other Mindtools could serve this same purpose, but expert systems are especially good for describing and predicting events with cause–effect structures. In any case, the process of reflecting on what occurred in an activity will make the lessons learned from that experience much better understood and much resistant to forgetting.

Expert systems are also powerful tools for reflecting on thinking and learning—that is, ways to describe how we think. An important way of manifesting that thinking is to build a cognitive simulation of the thinking that you are reflecting on. This can be a powerfully engaging task. A few years ago, we were studying metacognition—the ability to monitor comprehension and select appropriate learning strategies for enhancing comprehension. Although the students comprehended in a general way the ideas of executive control, knowing how people actually used metacognitive strategies was still unclear. Why? Because they had made few, if any, personal references to the ideas. In order to relate these new ideas to prior knowledge (an essential ingredient in learning), we set about constructing an expert system rule base that reflected the kinds of decisions that the students themselves made in deciding how to study for the seminar they were in. That is, they constructed a cognitive simulation of their own thinking. The entire rule base is too long to illustrate, but some of the questions (factors) that we came up with are listed in Figure 6.16. Now, we could certainly discuss and disagree on whether these are the kinds of questions that you ask in deciding what and how much to study, but the students in that context chose those factors. As a result of the process, the students who worked on constructing the rule base understood more, made more significant contributions to class discussion and wrote better essays than students in the class who did not work on the rule base. Understanding the ways that we think is difficult. Expert systems provides us with a formalism for representing that thinking.

There are many programs, known as expert system shells, that facilitate the construction of expert systems. These range from freeware editors to sophisticated programs costing thousands of dollars. The state of the art in existing programs is changing so rapidly that recommending a shell in print is speculative. See the Web site accompanying the Mindtools book (www.ed.psu.edu/~mindtools).

Purpose: "Why am I studying this material?
    Assigned = Material was assigned by professor
    Related = Material is useful to related research or studies
    Personal = Material is of personal interest";
ASK Depth: "How well do I need to know this material?
    Gist = I just need to comprehend the main ideas.
    Discuss = We will discuss and interrelate the issues.
    Evaluate = I have to judge the importance or accuracy of these ideas.
    Generate = I have to think up issues, new ideas, hypotheses about the material.";
ASK Reading: "How fast of a reader am I?";
    Reading: slow, normal, fast;
ASK Hours: "How many hours do I have to study?
    None = Less than an hour
    Few = 1 - 3 hours
    Several = 4 - 8 hours";
ASK Days: "How many days until class?";
    Days: more_than_7, 2_to_6,less_than_2;
ASK Comparison:"How do I compare with the other students in the class?
    Superior = I think that I am better able than my classmates to comprehend the material.

Figure 6.16   Factors in expert system on metacognitive reasoning

Equal = I am equivalent to the rest of the class in ability.

Worse = I am not as knowledgeable or intelligent as the rest of the class.";

ASK Instructor: "What intellectual orientation does the instructor have?

Theoretical = The professor likes to focus on theoretical issues and comparisons.

Applied = The professor is interested in applications and implications for practice.

Argument = The professor likes to argue about the ideas.";

ASK Topic:" Can I identify important terms or major issues related to this topic?";

Topic: yes, no;

ASK Previous: "Have I studied this topic before?";

Previous: yes, no;

ASK Author: "Have I previously read articles, reports or books by the listed author(s)?";

Author: yes, no;

ASK Context: "Do I have a useful context (information need or situation in which I can apply this topic) for assimilating this content?";

Context: yes, no, do_not_know;

ASK STSupport: "Have I set short term goals for this study session?";

STSupport: yes, no;

Ask LTSupport: "Have I set long term goals for all of the study sessions until the class?";

LTSupport: yes, no;

Ask ConcenStrat: "Am I feeling relaxed and confident that I can study effectively?";

ConcenStrat: yes, no;

Ask Tension: "Am I feeling overly tense or anxious about studying?";

Tension: yes, no;

Ask NegFan: "Am I having negative fantasies about this study session or the course?";

NegFan: yes, no;

Ask NegSelf: "Am I engaging in negative self-talk about this study session or the course?";

NegSelf: yes, no;

Ask Comfort: "Am I able to sit and read comfortably where I am going to study?";

Comfort: yes, no;

Ask PhyTension: "Does my body feel overly tense or full of excess energy?";

PhyTension: yes, no;

Ask Food: "Do I have enough energy (food) to complete studying?";

Food: yes, no;

Ask SelfEff: "Do I feel confident that I can master the material?";

SelfEff: yes, no;

Figure 6.16   Continued

Learning Processes   Building expert system rule bases primarily engages reflection on learning. Reflective learners articulate what they are doing, the decisions they are making, the strategies they are using, and the answers that they are finding, while reflecting on the meaningfulness of it all. Reflection is an essential component of both constructive and intentional learning activities. Both of the rule bases already illustrated required learners to reflect on what they had seen or how they think. Using expert systems to construct cognitive simulations is a powerful method for getting students to regulate their own learning behavior. Having to articulate how they think when they learn will require students to become more reflective and self-regulated.

Student Roles   The learning roles that students assume depend on how expert systems are being used. In describing a real-world or lab activity, students must identify all of the causal factors involved in the experience. What are the variables? Which variables affect others? How? In which direction? Those factors must be converted into questions, and the questions must be assembled into rules that will predict results. These activities require formal operational reasoning and so may not be appropriate for learners younger than high school age. When developing cognitive simulations, learners must articulate their own study and learning behaviors. Students are not used to this kind of reflection, so it will be difficult at first. When they finally begin to self-articulate, it will be an illuminating experience for them. Because of the complexity and difficulty involved with most expert system rule bases, they should usually be constructed collaboratively.

Teacher Roles   The greatest challenge will be getting students to understand the predictive processes required for building expert systems. We have experienced most success with starting out building simple models, such as predicting whether I should take an umbrella to school, what will happen if I don't complete my chores or get decent grades, predicting the outcome of the football or basketball game, or the likely outcomes of asking different students for help or for a date. Help them to articulate all of the factors involved in these decisions while working in groups. Then help them to decide which factors affect the others and build rules. Make sure that student ideas are included in the rule bases, not yours. Following a similar activity, debrief the experience. Get students to reflect on what happened. After completing the expert system, get them to reflect on what is *not* in the expert system. Help students to show epistemological awareness.

Assessing Learning   Constructing expert system rule bases is among the most difficult of all of the Mindtools to learn how to use. The rule bases that students build at first will likely be fairly simple. As they learn how to construct them, you may use criteria such as the following to evaluate their rule bases:

- Are all factors or variables involved in the process included in the rule base?
- Do causal relationships involve the correct variable or factors?
- Are the causal factors or variables related in the correct direction; do they make the correct prediction?

- How well does the rule base describe the underlying structure or processes in the domain?

Representing Mental Models Using Dynamic Modeling Tools

Complex learning requires students to solve complex and ill-structured problems as well as simple problems. Complex learning requires that students develop complex mental representations of the phenomena they are studying. The outcome of this knowledge construction process is a mental model. Mental models are complex mental representations, composed of numerous kinds of mental representations, including metaphorical, visual–spatial, and structural knowledge that result in runnable models of the phenomena being studied (Jonassen and Henning 1996).

One of the best tools for representing mental models is Stella. Stella is a powerful and flexible tool for building simulations of dynamic systems and processes (systems with interactive and interdependent components). Stella uses a simple set of building-block icons to construct a map of a process (see Figure 6.17). The map describes the components of the system. Each component can be opened up, so that values for each component may be stated as constants or variables. Variables can be stated as equations containing numerical relationships among any of the variables connected to it. Stella enables learners to run the models they create and observe the output in graphs, tables, or animations of any of the variables. Psychologically speaking, Stella enables students to create physical runnable models of their own mental runnable models. At the run level, students can change the variable values to test the effects of parts of a system on the other. This kind of what-if logic is similar to that afforded by many microworlds (described earlier); only with Stella, students get to create the models themselves. So, in a sense, Stella is a microworld maker.

The Stella model in Figures 6.17 and 6.18 was developed by an English teacher in conjunction with his tenth-grade students to describing how the boys' loss of hope drives the increasing power of the beast in William Golding's novel, *The Lord of the Flies*. The model of beast power (Figure 6.17) represents the factors that contributed to the strength of the beast in the book, including fear and resistance. The resulting model is run (Figure 6.18), changing the values of faith building, fear, and memory of home experienced by the boys while assessing the effects on their belief about being rescued and the strength of the beasts within them. Although Stella is most frequently used to model scientific phenomena, this application illustrates that Mindtools can be used across the curriculum.

Stella provides a powerful suite of tools for representing the complexity of dynamic systems. Students can build models of those systems and test them. Observing the systems that students create is perhaps the most powerful way of assessing the viability and comprehensiveness of learners' knowledge. Stella is probably the most powerful Mindtool available to students.

Learning Processes and Student Roles   Stella and other dynamic modeling tools, such as Model-It from the Highly Interactive Computing Group at the University of Michigan, probably provide the most complete intellectual activity

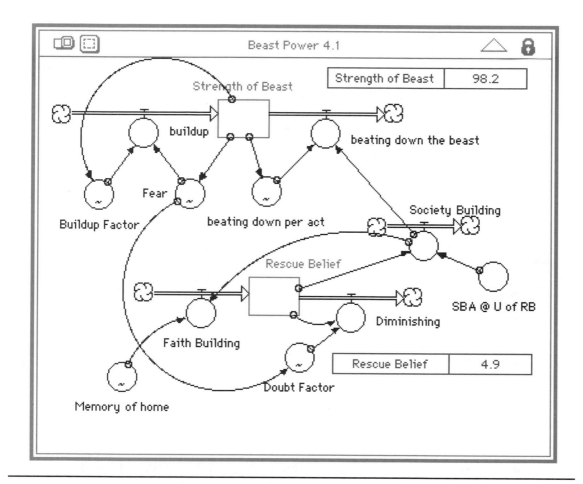

Figure 6.17   Conceptual map of the Beast

described in this book. Building Stella models engages active, constructive, intentional, authentic, and cooperative learning. They require students to articulate system components and consider their dynamic relationships. Databases and semantic networks (described earlier) require students to describe only semantic relationships between concepts. Stella requires students to define dynamic relationships (cause-effect, two-way, interactive). Building models is among the most intentional intellectual processes that students can engage in. They constantly must reflect on the system components, test them, and revise them. Stella can be used to model any kind of complex system in any kind of context. In fact, dynamic models better convey the effects of contextual variables than any other software. Finally, because of their complexity, Stella models almost necessarily must result from cooperative efforts among students. Students must spend hours conversing, checking, confirming, and collaborating on the construction of a model. Dynamic models are among the most complete activities that learners can engage in.

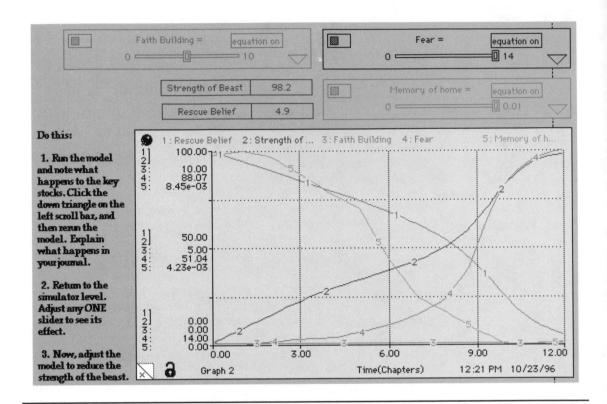

Figure 6.18   Runnable version of the Strength of the Beast

Teacher Roles   Building dynamic models will be among the most difficult yet rewarding learning activities that you can engage students in. It will require a lot of coaching—including modeling of how variables dynamically affect each other—and a lot of encouragement. We recommend starting students building simple and constrained physical systems, such as a simple refrigerator thermostat or familiar systems, such as a baseball game. Students will readily consider social systems, such as student clubs or cliques. Your role as a teacher is to perturb the student models as they are building them. "Have you thought about. . . ?" Our experience is that such interactions are very rewarding.

Assessing Learning   Viewing a student model created with a dynamic modeling tool provides perhaps the clearest and most definitive evidence of student intellectual activity available. We have experienced considerable excitement viewing student models. Some of the criteria that you might use to evaluate those models include:

- Does the model include all of the important components or objects?
- Are the values of each component appropriately defined?
- Are the direction and dimension of the relationships between components viable or accurate?

- Do the graphical outputs of the model convey viable relationships?
- Are the important variables represented as graphs?

CONCLUSIONS

Mindtools should constitute an intellectual toolbox that students use to engage them in critical thinking about what they are studying. Students should use Mindtools to construct knowledge bases that reflect on and represent their understanding. The advantage of engaging students in critical, creative, and complex thinking skills results from getting students to reflect on what they have learned. Thinking about what you know and how you came to know it defines the philosophy of epistemology. Our goal in promoting Mindtools is to make students into epistemologists who continuously think about what they have learned and what it means. In order to do that, they need a set of formalisms for representing what they know. That is what Mindtools are.

The knowledge bases or products that students construct using Mindtools can be assessed and evaluated as evidence of student learning. They are meaningful products or learning, far more meaningful, we argue, than multiple choice recall tests of knowledge. They are strong and clear indicators of what and how much students know about what they are studying.

Mindtools can also be used effectively to engage students in collaborative learning. Many efforts at collaborative learning in schools fail because the tasks that learners are collaborating to accomplish are not meaningful or engaging enough or they do not benefit from collaboration. Requiring students to collaborate in order to study for multiple-choice, recall tests probably will not result in increased learning for any of the students. Why? Because recall is an individual activity that is not effectively enhanced by collaboration. Constructing knowledge bases with Mindtools is a complex activity that will benefit in most cases from collaboration because students can share meaningful roles. The process of building knowledge bases is complex and challenging enough that learners may assume a variety of roles and provide multiple, meaningful perspective on the process.

Mindtools may also be used as planning and analysis tools. Writing reports, shooting videos (Chapter 3), building multimedia knowledge bases (Chapter 4), and other complex activities require planning and preparation in order to accomplish them. Mindtools, especially semantic nets and databases, are useful planning tools for organizing ideas and processes.

Mindtools can be used effectively in combination to represent the underlying complexity of ideas. Providing multiple representations using different Mindtools provides multiple views on the same ideas, enhancing the learners' mental model development. An example is to use a spreadsheet to calculate the process represented in a microworld. You might also use an expert system to reflect an experiment presented in a microworld. Or using a semantic net (described earlier) to plan the organization of a video production (Chapter 3) will improve the organization of the ideas in the video as well as enrich the mental models that students construct as a result of the production. Using Mindtools in combination can only add perspective.

As teachers and educators, our major intellectual responsibility to our students is to understand how learners need to think in order to function as writers, biologists, homemakers, linguists, politicians, citizens, and so on, and to provide them the opportunities to think in those ways, that is, give them meaningful tasks and problems to solve. Our other responsibility is to provide them the proper tools to help them do and think as they need to be able to in order to be writers, biologists, homemakers, linguists, politicians, citizens, and so on. Mindtools represent a class of intellectual tools that students may use to help them make sense of the world and reason about it. If you are interested in finding out more about any of the Mindtools, then we encourage you to consult *Computers in the Classroom: Mindtools for Critical Thinking* (Jonassen, in press). Information about software to use, more examples of Mindtools products, and critical-thinking skills engaged can be found in that text.

THINGS TO THINK ABOUT

If you would like to reflect on the ideas that we presented in this chapter, then articulate your responses to the following questions and compare them with others' responses.

1. Can you as a teacher really teach students what you know? Is it possible for them to know ideas in the same way that you know them?
2. Do carpenters learn *from* their hammers, saws, levels, and other tools? Can they learn anything about them without using them? Do they learn about carpentry *with* their tools?
3. If mindful thinking is active, constructive, intentional, authentic, and cooperative (as we have claimed), then what is mindless thinking? Can you describe what students do if they are mindless? Is mindless thinking even possible?
4. Recall the first time that you had to teach a new topic or skill. How well did you *know* the topic before you taught it? Did you *know* it better after you taught it? Should learners become teachers without using technology? Recall that we have argued that learners should be teaching the technology.
5. Can a tool be intelligent? What is the smartest tool that you know of? What makes it smart?
6. We claim that the goal of Mindtools is to engage students in critical thinking. Regarding question 3, is there such a thing as noncritical thinking? What kinds of things do students do when they think noncritically? Why are they not critical?
7. The distributed cognitions argument is popular these days in psychological circles. Can you think of a situation in which working with another person or a tool or technology makes you smarter than you would be if you were working alone? What makes you smarter?

8. We argue that language and software applications like databases are formalisms for representing what you know. Can you think of other formalisms for representing what you know? How is the syntax of that formalism different from language?

9. Databases and semantic networks focus on the semantics of a knowledge domain. That is, they engage learners in describing the organization of meanings in a domain. Can you think of any other semantic formalisms?

10. Semantic networks are like the frame and foundation of a house. If that is the case, how would you describe the rest of the house (plumbing, trim, decorations, walls, etc.)?

11. Visualization tools enable you to see ideas in new ways. Can you think of experiences that have enabled you to see things in new ways?

12. Microworlds are simple, virtual worlds that enable you to manipulate things in it. Can you think of other virtual world experiences that you have had? What kinds of virtual-world experiences might help students to learn, for instance, sociology or diagramming sentences?

13. Psychologists argue that IF–THEN statements, like expert systems, are the best way to represent procedural knowledge (knowledge of how to do things). If that is the case, which of the Mindtools best support the learning of declarative knowledge (knowing that things exist)?

14. Dynamic modeling tools, like Stella, enable you to represent mental models. We argued that mental models consist of many different kinds of knowledge. Pick a small topic (like your car) and write down everything that you know about it: how it works, how to drive it, what it does in different conditions, and so on. See if you can separate that knowledge into different groups. What are those groups?

15. We argue in the conclusion that Mindtools represent an intellectual toolbox that can help students learn. We do not believe that these are the only kinds of intellectual tools that students should have. What other nontechnological intellectual tools should students have or develop to help them learn?

REFERENCES

Burton, R. R., J. S. Brown, and G. Fisher (1984). Skiing as a model of instruction. In B. Rogoff and J. Lave (eds.), *Everyday cognition: Its development in social context.* Cambridge, MA: Harvard University Press.

Derry, S. J., and S. P. LaJoie (1993). A middle camp for (un)intelligent instructional computing: An introduction. In S. P. LaJoie and S. J. Derry (eds.), *Computers as cognitive tools.* Hillsdale, NJ: Lawrence Erlbaum Associates.

Draper S., and D. Norman (1986). Introduction. In D. Norman and S. Draper (eds.), *User centered*

system design. Hillsdale, NJ: Lawrence Erlbaum Associates.

Hanna, J. (1986). Learning environment criteria. In R. Ennals, R. Gwyn, and L. Zdravcher (eds.), *Information technology and education: The changing school.* Chichester, UK: Ellis Horwood.

Jonassen, D. H. (in press). *Mind tools for Critical Thinking in Schools.* Columbus, OH: Prentice Hall.

Jonassen, D. H. (1987). Assessing cognitive structure: Verifying a method using pattern notes. *Journal of Research and Development in Education,* 20 (3): 1–14.

Jonassen, D. H. (1996). *Computers in the classroom:*

Mindtools for critical thinking. Columbus, OH: Merrill/Prentice-Hall.

Jonassen, D. H., K. Beissner, and M.A. Yacci (1993). *Structural knowledge: Techniques for representing, conveying, and acquiring structural knowledge.* Hillsdale, NJ: Lawrence Erlbaum Associates.

Jonassen, D. H., and P. H. Henning (1996, July). *Mental models: Knowledge in the head and knowledge in the world.* Paper presented at the 2nd International Conference on the Learning Sciences, Evanston, IL, Northwestern University.

Pea, R. (1985). Beyond amplificiation: Using the computer to reorganize mental functioning. *Educational Psychologist, 20,* 167–82.

Perkins, D. N. (1993). Person-plus: A distributed view of thinking and learning. In G. Salomon (ed.), *Distributed cognitions: Psychological and educational considerations* (pp. 88–110). Cambridge, UK: Cambridge University Press.

Preece, P. F. W. (1976). Mapping cognitive structure: A comparison of methods. *Journal of Educational Psychology, 68:* 1–8.

Salomon, G. (1990). Cognitive effects with and of technology. *Communication Research,* 17(1): 26–44.

Salomon, G. (1993). On the nature of pedagogic computer tools. The case of the wiring partner. In S. P. LaJoie and S. J. Derry (eds.), *Computers as cognitive tools.* Hillsdale, NJ: Lawrence Erlbaum Associates.

Schank, R. (1982). *Dynamic memory: A theory of learning in computers and people.* Cambridge: Cambridge University Press.

Schank, R. (1990). *Tell me a story.* Evanston, IL: Northwestern University Press.

Schwartz, J. L., and M. Yerulshamy (1987). The geometric supposer: Using microcomputers to restore invention to the learning of mathematics. In D. N. Perkins, J. Lockhead, J. C. Bishop (eds.), *Thinking: The second international conference* (pp. 525–36). Hillsdale, NJ: Lawrence Erlbaum Associates.

Shavelson, R. J. (1972). Some aspects of the correspondence between content structure and cognitive structure in physics instruction. *Journal of Educational Psychology, 63:* 225–34.

White, B. Y. (1993). ThinkerTools: Causal models, conceptual change, and science education. *Cognition and Instruction,* 10(1): 1–100.

Yerulshamy, M., and R. A. Houde, (1986). The geometric supposer: Promoting thinking and learning. *Mathematics Teacher, 79:* 418–22.

LEARNING BY DOING: IMMERSION IN CONSTRUCTIVIST LEARNING ENVIRONMENTS

In the preceding five chapters, we have described how to use technology to facilitate learners' exploration, experimentation, construction, conversation, reflection, and knowledge representation. In this chapter, we describe two constructivist learning environments (CLEs): contexts, experiences, and learning situations in which all of the activities described in this book are combined into an integrated learning environment. In these learning environments, students learn by doing— that is, by engaging in meaningful projects that require them to explore, experiment, construct, converse, and reflect on what they are learning. The two CLEs that we describe and the many more that are being developed, we believe, engage all of the characteristics of meaningful learning that have been the focus of this book. These CLEs are archetypes of the ways that technology may be used to support meaningful learning. We challenge you to seek out, create, and use technology-based CLEs to engage your learners in meaningful learning.

WHAT ARE CONSTRUCTIVIST LEARNING ENVIRONMENTS?

This is a difficult question. Designing CLEs is an emerging science, so the state of the art is changing rapidly. CLEs are technology-based environments in which students can do something meaningful and useful. The technologies afford students the tools to explore, experiment, construct, converse, and reflect on what they are doing, so that they learn from their experiences. We have described again and again our assumptions about constructivist learning, so next we should examine what an environment is.

Environments are spaces. Wilson (1996) emphasized the spatial nature of learning environments as "a place where learners may work together and support each other as they use a variety of tools and information resources in their guided pursuit of learning goals and problem-solving activities" (p. 5). Learning environments are personal and group exploration spaces in which learners control the learning activities and use information resources and knowledge construction tools to solve problems. In traditional uses of technologies, messages in the media direct and control the learning experiences that require learners to view and retain information presented by the technology (video, computer, film, etc.). In learning environments, learners are presented with a complex and relevant problem, project, or experience that they accept or reject as a challenge. If learners are challenged by the problem, the CLE provides them with the tools and resources that they need to understand the problem and to solve it (or at least to attempt to solve it, since some problems are not readily solvable). Although learning environments are not necessarily dependent on technology, more often than not they are supported by technologies, especially computers. Learning environments may represent myriad options, from a sandbox to a space shuttle. In this book, we are interested in how technology is used to support learning, so in this chapter we will focus on technology-mediated CLEs.

Technology-supported learning environments possess several components. Perkins (1991) argued that they are comprised of information banks, symbol pads, construction kits, phenomenaria, and task managers. Although we agree with most of these components, what is needed is the glue to bind those components together. We believe that CLEs (see Figure 7.1) comprise the problem or project space (the conceptual and operational focus of the environment that functions as the glue), a set of related cases to explain the problem, information resources to support investigation of the problem, cognitive (knowledge-building) tools, and conversation and collaboration (knowledge-negotiation) tools and supports (Jonassen, 1998). We will briefly describe each of these components next.

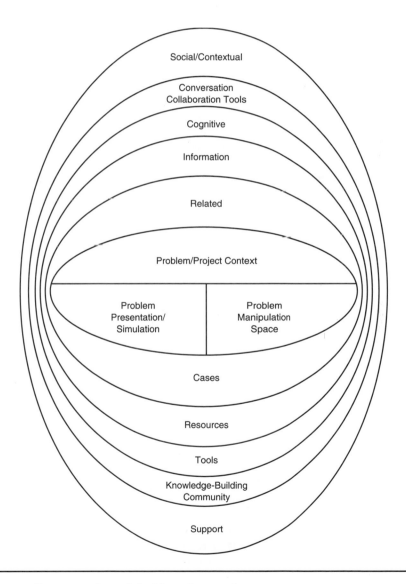

Figure 7.1   Conceptual model of learning environments

Problem/Project Space

Since the key to meaningful learning is ownership of a problem or learning goal, it is important to present learners with an interesting, relevant, and engaging problem to solve or project to complete. These problems may be conveyed by the technology or assigned by you, the teacher. It is important that the problem not be overly defined, that the problem be somewhat ill-defined or ill-structured, so that some aspects of the problem can be determined by the learners. Why? Unless some components of the problem can be defined by the students, they will have no ownership of it and so will be less motivated to deal with it. Most textbook problems engage a limited number of skills that were explained in the chapter, and they usually have a single correct answer. Students are obligated to find the correct answer, regardless of whether they care about the solution. There is little implicit motivation for solving the problem. So, problems or projects that are less prescriptive and structured allow learners define the problem or project for themselves.

Where do problems or projects come from? From the field being studied, of course. You need to ask what kinds of problems or issues practitioners in the field of study have to solve. In political science, for instance, students may construct a viable constitution for an emerging third-world democracy that can accommodate the social, cultural, political, and historical characteristics of the population and that country's relationship with other countries in the region. Or design an advertising campaign for a simulated candidate running for Congress in different districts around the country. In philosophy, apply ethical principles by rendering judgment on ethical dilemmas, such as doctor-assisted suicides or plastic surgery. In science, as will be shown in the first example, monitor a local stream and decide how it can and should be made cleaner and more ecologically viable. There are problems everywhere. Your local community is a good place to look. Read the newspaper. Visit city hall.

Next, the learning environment must describe the problem or project that represents the goal that students assume. Again, an important characteristic of these problems is that they have no convergent, "right" answer. Also, the problems should be complex enough that the solution is not readily obvious. But if we don't know what the answer is, then how do we grade students? Well, among other things, you can evaluate students on the quality of their reasoning about the problem. Not only should students recommend solutions to the problems, but they should also justify why they chose a particular approach to solving the problem. Such justifications clearly require higher-order thinking and provide ample opportunity for evaluating student performance. In Chapter 8, we present rubrics for evaluating learning from constructivist activities.

One of the major criticisms leveled against problem/project-based learning is that while being engaged in solving problems, students will not be exposed to as much important information in the curriculum. They will miss out on important stuff. That is true; they will. The issues that are raised by this criticism are quality versus quantity and depth versus breadth. Is it better to engage in higher-quality investigations or to be exposed to a higher quantity of ideas? Is it better to learn a lot about a little or a little about a lot? These are professional value judgments. There is no right answer to these questions. Teaching is an ill-structured problem, as well.

It should be obvious by now that we strongly support quality and depth of thinking over quantity and breadth of thinking. Why? The amount of information that "should" be in the curriculum is growing exponentially, while the amount of time (number of hours or days in the school year) remains the same. Rather than trying to learn everything, students need to become informed and selective consumers and users of information. Those skills can only be acquired through purposeful, meaningful investigation of ideas. But, as a teacher, you must decide.

The problem/project space in constructivist learning environments consists of three integrated and highly interrelated components: the problem context, the problem presentation or simulation, and the problem manipulation space.

Problem Context   It is important, when setting the problem, to describe the context in which it occurs. The context is so much a part of any problem that it cannot be ignored. The social, cultural, and physical context (setting, community, organization) in which a problem or project occurs or will be solved defines, to a large degree, the nature of the problem. The same problem (if that were theoretically possible) in different social or work contexts, would be a different problem. So, learning environments must devote effort to describing as clearly as possible all of the contextual factors that surround a problem. Where does it occur? What are the sociocultural expectations of the people involved? What is the history of the setting? Who sets policy? What sense of social or political efficacy do the members of the setting or organization feel? CLEs should be as descriptive as possible.

Problem Presentation/Simulation   The way in which the problem or project is introduced to the learner is critical to the amount of buy-in by the learners. The problem presentation has to be interesting, appealing, and engaging. As we described in Chapter 3, the Cognition and Technology Group at Vanderbilt (1992) insists on high-quality video scenarios for introducing the problem and engaging the learners. Other researchers are focusing on the design of virtual worlds and environments for representing phenomena. The purpose of the problem presentation is to simulate the problem in the context in which it is normally and naturally encountered. Unless the learners understand the full nature of the problems or project, they will not be able to solve it. Suppose, for instance, that the project is to design an advertising campaign for a political candidate, but your CLE forgot to mention the demographics of the candidate's constituency. How could your students design a reasonable product? Be sure to represent all aspects of the problem or project.

Problem Manipulation Space   The problem or project space must also provide students with the opportunity to manipulate or experiment with the problem. Students cannot assume any ownership of the problem unless they know that they can affect the problem situation in some meaningful way. Therefore, manipulating the phenomena in a problem and seeing the results of those manipulations are important. Perkins referred to this problem component as a *phenomenaria* (spaces for manipulating phenomena). Phenomenaria often are microworlds in which students can test their hypotheses on reasonably accurate simulations of the environment being explored. Again, the problem presentation and problem manipulation spaces are often integrated into a seamless environment. So much the better, as long as the functionality is there for learners to use.

Related Cases

As we discuss later in this chapter, understanding the world requires experiencing it and constructing mental models of how it functions. The more experiences that you have, the more you know and the more expert you become. What novice learners lack most of all are experiences. This lack is especially critical when trying to solve problems and engage in complex forms of learning. So, when you expect students to solve problems, it is important for the learning environment to provide access to a set of related experiences on which the student can draw. Related cases in learning environments support learning in at least two ways—by scaffolding memory and by representing complexity.

The richer your experience, the richer and more indelible are your memories of that experience. The things that you understand the best are probably those in which you invested the greatest amount of effort. Related cases scaffold memory by providing representation of experiences that learners have not had. Learners can examine related cases for the lessons that they should have learned. This is how experts think when they first encounter a problem—by first checking their memory for similar cases that they may have solved previously. If they can recall a similar case, they try to map the previous experiences and its lessons onto the current problem. By presenting related cases in learning environments, you are providing the learners with a set of experience to compare to the current problem or issue. The students should examine the cases to see which one(s) resemble the current problem. When they find a similar case, they can then hypothesize about its utility in solving the current case. Related cases are at the heart of goal-based scenarios (Schank 1994), where stories about previous experiences are the primary instructional medium. Stories are provided at appropriate times. For instance, if you were developing a CLE for beginning teachers on how to handle discipline problems, related cases would consist of numerous stories from novice and experienced teachers about how they handled all kinds of discipline problems. The stories would be indexed to each of the practice cases and would be made available to the learner in the CLE based on the similarities in the kind of infraction, the location of the infraction, the age of the student, the form of discipline used, the outcomes or effects of the discipline, any morals to be learned about discipline from that case, and so on. We demonstrated how a database could be used for this purpose in Chapter 6. Access to these related cases should be provided to learners, as they are trying to decided on actions in the various practice cases. Related cases function as on-demand advice. They supplant the experience that the novice teacher has not had.

Related cases also help to represent complexity in learning environments by providing multiple perspectives or approaches to the problems or issues being examined by the learners. So much instruction oversimplifies content, because teachers believe that it is impossible to convey appropriate levels of complexity to novice learners who do not have adequate prior knowledge. They simplify concepts in order to make them understandable—in order to build on the limited, relevant knowledge of the learners. So, our instruction filters out the complexity that exists in most applied knowledge domains, causing shallow understanding of domain knowledge to develop. An important model for designing learning environments, cognitive flexibility theory, provides multiple representations of content in order to convey the complexity that is inherent in the knowledge domain (Spiro, Vispoel, Schmitz, Samarapungavan, and Boerger 1987). It stresses the conceptual interrelatedness of ideas and their interconnectedness by providing multiple representations of content. The ill-structuredness of any knowledge domain is best illustrated by multiple perspectives or themes that are inherent in many cases. The extensive use of multiple cases also supports a variety of applied contexts for the acquisition of knowledge. Rather than mapping oversimplified models onto the learner, the learner needs to recognize the inconsistencies in that knowledge by applying it in different contexts or relating it to different perspectives while it is being learned. Cognitive flexibility theory conveys this complexity by presenting multiple representations of the same information and different thematic perspectives on the information. In order to construct useful knowledge structures, learners need to compare and contrast the similarities and differences between cases.

Information Resources

In order to investigate phenomena, you need information about the phenomena. So, when designing learning environments, you need to ask yourself, "What kinds of information will the learner need in order to make sense of the topic?" Then provide information banks, repositories of information about the subject, that includes the needed information. Information banks may include text documents, graphics, sound resources, video, animations, or any other medium of information that is appropriate for helping learners understand the content well enough to be able to use it to solve problems. The World Wide Web is becoming the storage medium of choice, as powerful new plug-ins enable users to access multimedia resources from the Web.

In order to be accessible and useful, information banks, regardless of their form, need to be organized in meaningful ways, preferably in ways that support the kind of thinking that you want your learners to do. Hypermedia is the most appropriate method for storing and retrieving information for most environments. Why? Because hypermedia has a malleable, associative structure onto which any kind of organization can be mapped, so that the information can be accessed through learner-controllable links that resemble the requirements of the task, the organization of the content, or any other knowledge structure (Jonassen 1991). Providing learners with the information they need helps them make meaning when it is provided in a timely manner. On the other hand, requiring learners to memorize information that they perceive no need for does not enhance meaning making. Most school curricula focus on the knowledge that students should acquire, even though they do not provide any good reason for acquiring it. CLEs provide learner-selectable information just-in-time (when they need it) to support some meaningful activity by the learners.

Cognitive (Knowledge-Construction) Tools

We have stated earlier that learning environments ought to represent the complexity of the real-world task that it represents. However, that complexity often calls on skills that learners do not possess. So it is necessary to support (scaffold) their performance of those activities. In order to do that, it is necessary to identify the skills that are required to solve the problem or complete the mission that is embedded in the problem representation. Having identified those skills, it is necessary to determine if those are skills likely to be possessed by the learners. If they are not, then it is necessary to build in cognitive tools (or Mindtools, as described in Chapter 6) that scaffold the learners' abilities to perform those tasks. Cognitive tools can assume many forms. In Chapter 6, we described visualization tools that enabled learners to "see" weather phenomena by colorizing different weather events. In the next section, we describe tools for representing mental models of phenomena that are being studied. All of the Mindtools described in Chapter 6 provide tools for constructing and representing what the learners know. So, learning environments also attempt to embed a suite of tools to help learners think in appropriate ways.

Conversation (Knowledge-Negotiation) Tools

A common misconception about learning, we believe, is that it ought to be accomplished by individuals in isolation. CLEs, on the other hand, use a variety of computer-mediated communication methods to support conversation and collaboration among communities of learners. Why? Learning most naturally occurs not in isolation but by teams of people working together to solve problems. CLEs provide access to shared information and shared knowledge-building tools to help to collaboratively construct socially shared knowledge. Many science educators have emphasized the goal of consensus building among scientists. That is, problems are solved when groups of scientists work toward developing a common conception of the problem, so their energies can be focused on solving it. In order to support collaboration, CLEs should also provide for computer conferencing, chats, UseNet groups, MUDs, and MOOs (see Chapter 5) to facilitate dialogue and knowledge building among the community of learners. In the learning environment examples described later in this chapter, students are connected with other students via electronic mail, computer conferences, and shared workspaces around the country or around the world. They share the same goal—to solve the problem or reach some scientific consensus about an issue. We have argued throughout this book that conversation and collaboration are important characteristics of meaningful learning. It is therefore critical that CLEs support conversation and collaboration among students. That is likely to become the major role for technology in the next century.

Social/Contextual Support

Throughout the history of instructional design and technology, the weakest part of the process has been implementation of the technology. Too many good instructional ideas have failed because they were poorly implemented. Why? Because the designers or technology innovators failed to consider environmental and contextual factors. That is, they tried to implement their innovation without considering important aspects of the physical environment or social, organizational, and cultural aspects of the environment. For instance, implementations of film and video failed because the physical environment couldn't be darkened sufficiently, adequate equipment wasn't available, or the content of the film or video was inimical or culturally insensitive to the audience. So the message was either not received or it was rejected by the learners.

In designing and implementing CLEs, accommodating social, contextual, and environmental factors is essential. This includes ensuring that adequate computers and networking are available and accessible and that the physical environment does not inhibit learning. More importantly, the people who will be implementing the materials (probably you, the teacher) must be philosophically amenable to the innovation and adequately skilled to implement it. Why is that essential? Because to most teachers, CLEs and project-based curriculum are new, and the teaching skills that best support the environments are different from those traditionally employed by teachers. If any support personnel are required by the project, then be sure that they are prepared as well. Not only will social and contextual support better prepare the educators, such support will likely result in greater, more meaningful learning by the learners.

These components of CLEs are contained in the two CLEs described in the remainder of this chapter. These CLEs engage learners in active, constructive, intentional, authentic, and cooperative learning.

EXAMPLES OF MEANINGFUL LEARNING ENVIRONMENTS

ScienceWare: Supporting Scientific Thinking With Technology

Think about the way that you make sense of a new piece of software, a new computer system, or a new tool or toy that you acquire. In trying to understand how to use it, you first search your memory for similar devices or systems that you have experienced and try to map your model of that system onto the new one. Using that model, you test out the functionality of the new system. If the old model works, you are up and running. If it does not (which is so often the case), you have to begin to revise your old model or construct a new mental model of the new system—what is it, what does it do, what are the parts of the systems and how do they fit together, how is the system operated? Your initial model is simplistic, but with each new experience you have with the system (especially those where you correct an error in thinking), you add a piece to the mental puzzle that describes your understanding of the system. As you become more skilled, your model grows to match the complexity of the system. Some of the processes required of the system become automated with practice, so your mental model consists of larger and more complex operations. This model-building process to explain real-world phenomena is at the center of understanding, particularly for science-related systems, and it can be facilitated by CLEs.

The ScienceWare project conducted by the Highly Interactive Computing Group (HI-C) at the University of Michigan has developed a suite of thinking tools to support project-based science learning in the classroom. RiverMUD is a multiuser dimension (see Chapter 5) containing computer-based modeling, discourse, and decision-making activities and tools.

Problem Space The key to modeling, discourse, and decision making is to provide students with a meaningful and authentic problem to solve, such as a scientific context. The context in which these tools are used is project-based science. Essentially, project-based science means engaging learners in the same kind of scientific processes that real scientists do, including solving complex and ambiguous problems over extended periods of time, using tools, and collaborating with each other (Soloway, Krajcik, and Finkel 1995). Project-based science is focused on a driving question (Are local water sources safe to drink? What effects will a new mine have on the ecology? How can we produce a safer passenger restraint system?). These questions usually require understanding and integrating different disciplines (chemistry, biology, physics, etc.). The questions may come from the teacher or be generated by the students. They need to be feasible for the students, worthwhile (authentic, complex), and contextualized (realworld and nontrivial).

Project-based science requires that students develop and carry out authentic investigations that engage a rich set of activity structures. Students must ask and refine questions, debate ideas, make predictions, design plans and experiments, collect and analyze data, draw conclusions, make inferences, communicate their findings to other, and ask new questions based on previous findings. The HI-C group has worked extensively with groups of students carrying out water quality studies, where they conduct field studies to collect samples to analyze (see Figure 7.2) in order to answer questions like: What is the condition of Traver Creek? Is the Huron River safe? How to improve a local pond?

Project-based science typically produces a variety of artifacts (solution reports, videos, computer models, etc.). These artifacts are sharable and critiquable, so they can be used to reflect emergent understanding by the students (Soloway et al. 1995). For the HI-C group, the common form of artifact is student reports. These can be evaluated. But you are evaluating complex student models and experiments, not the recall of scientific facts. The artifacts are incisive evidence of student thinking, which is the goal of project-based science. ScienceWare has provided a powerful context and suite of tools to support meaningful learning among students. It is an example of the kind of learning environment that you should seek out to use, we believe.

Related Cases Related cases are provided by students in other schools, who share stories about their problems and their findings with students in other schools via the Internet. Groups of students produce multiple related cases.

Information Resources Information is collected by student as part of the inquiry. The students use probes and tools to collect data (e.g., pH, nitrates, etc.) about the phenomena they are investigating. Additionally, students have access to information via the World Wide Web as well as knowledge bases of information provided by the HI-C group.

Figure 7.2　Collecting water samples to analyze

Cognitive Tools　RiverMUD uses one of the most powerful cognitive tools available: a dynamic modeling tool called Model-It. Building models of real-world phenomena is at the heart of scientific thinking and requires diverse mental activities such as planning, data collecting, collaborating and accessing information, data visualizing, modeling, and reporting (Soloway et al 1995). The process for developing the ability to model phenomena requires defining the model, using the model to understand some phenomena, creating a model by representing real-world phenomena and making connections between its parts, and finally analyzing the model for its ability to represent the world (Spitulnik, Studer, Finkel, Gustafson, Laczko, and Soloway 1995). So, HI-C built tools to support these activities.

In order to build a model, students are required to identify the measurable, quantifiable factors that are used to predict the outcome they are seeking. For example, the HI-C group has experimented with classes assessing water quality in local creeks. They need to identify the potential contaminants, measure them, and then enter them into equations that describe their effects on water quality. Students can take digital photographs to include in the model in the Simulation

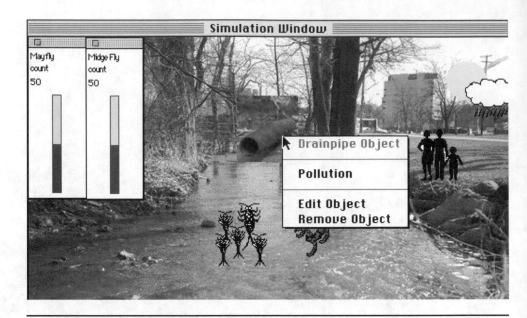

Figure 7.3   Simulation Window in Model-It

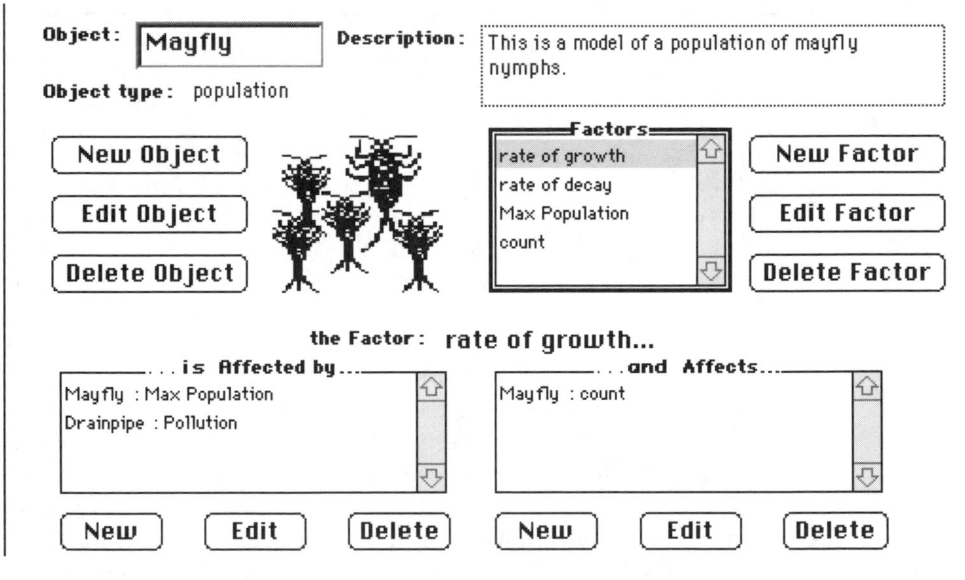

Object: **Mayfly**   Description: This is a model of a population of mayfly nymphs.

Object type: population

New Object

Edit Object

Delete Object

Factors
rate of growth
rate of decay
Max Population
count

New Factor

Edit Factor

Delete Factor

the Factor: **rate of growth...**

...is Affected by...
Mayfly : Max Population
Drainpipe : Pollution

...and Affects...
Mayfly : count

New   Edit   Delete   New   Edit   Delete

Figure 7.4   Object Editor

Window in order to describe the factor and its sources (Figure 7.3). Each object in the simulations can be described using the Object Editor (Figure 7.4). In the Object Editor factors affecting and effected by the object are defined. Each factor may be further described in terms of it measurement units, initial values, minimum, average, and maximum values in the Factor Factory (Figure 7.5). Students then build factor maps (Figure 7.6) showing the interactive effects of factors on each other. They then must define the relationships between those factors using Relationship Maker (Figure 7.7). In real scientific work, this is typically done with advanced mathematics, such as calculus. Dynamic modeling tools, such as Stella (described in Chapter 6), support modeling of these kinds of relationships. Since Model-It, the modeling program built by HI-C, was designed to be used with middle school students who have not mastered advanced mathematics, the Relationship Maker scaffolds their use of mathematics by providing a range of qualitative relationships that describe the quantitative relationship between the factors or by allowing them to enter a table of values that they have collected. So, students use pull-down menus to describe relationships such as "As fecal coliforms increase, stream quality decreases/increases by about the same/a lot/a little/more and more/less and less." After describing all of the factors, students can test their models by running a simulation (Figure 7.8). They can change values and rerun the simulation to test the effects of different values. Through inferring and speculating about the effects of variables on each other, these students are thinking like scientists—that is, building working models of phenomena and testing them against the real world.

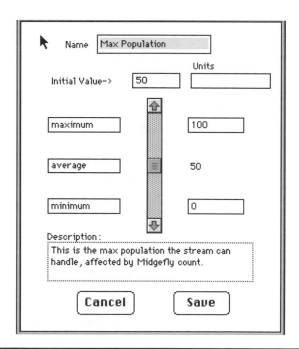

Figure 7.5 Factor Factory in Model-It

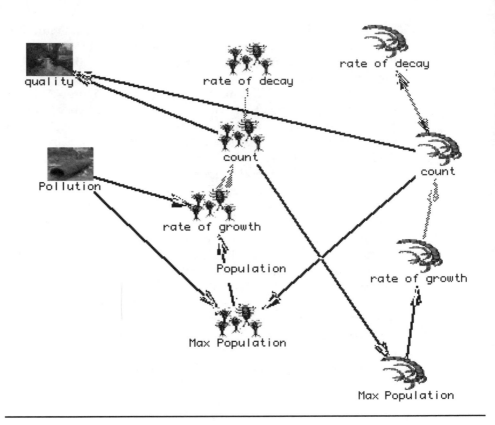

Figure 7.6 Factor map in Model-It

The whole point of constructing models and discussing them is to enable students to engage in scientific decision making. That makes science a process, as opposed to a collection of unconnected facts and concepts to memorize. Providing students with the responsibility of making decisions should be the goal of scientific literacy. To make decisions, each student must determine his or her own opinion and state a position based on scientific knowledge; comprehend the implications, advantages, and disadvantages of that position; and also understand the effects of such a position (Spitulnik et al. 1995).

Conversation/Collaboration Tools   ScienceWare was designed to be used by collaborative groups of students participating in knowledge-building communities around the country (see Chapter 5). Knowledge-building communities consist of groups of individuals who are interested in sharing what they know and who want to build a shared group understanding of processes within the cultural and historical context they exist in. A good example of this is the description of the collaborative construction of a multimedia product by Navajo children in Chapter 4. Their cultural context supports this kind of activity. However, knowledge-build-

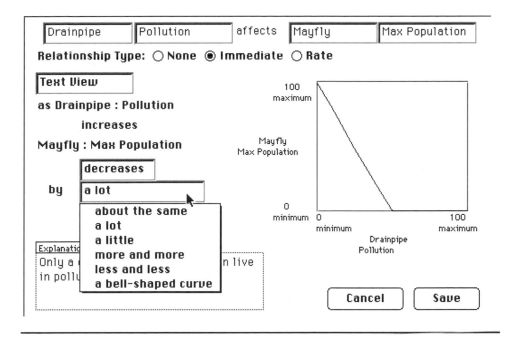

Figure 7.7   Relationship Maker in Model-It

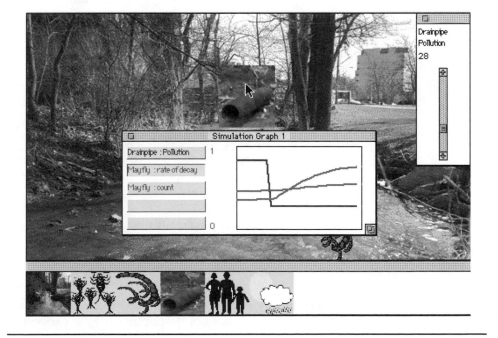

Figure 7.8   Running the simulation

ing communities are harder to facilitate in traditional American classrooms that are based on individual accountability and competition. Ann Brown and her colleagues (1990) have developed a model for reorganizing classrooms into communities of learning.

The most important activity in the discourse processes is articulating what the students know and then arguing for or against various points of view. Socially shared meaning requires that collaborative groups achieve some degree of consensus about which interpretation of phenomena is the most viable. That requires that students present information, questions, plans, and evidence and then justify their beliefs based on scientific principles, evidence, and experiences (Spitulnik et al. 1995).

Social/Contextual Support   The context for implementing ScienceWare was a series of high school courses called Foundations of Science, which were designed to be interdisciplinary approaches to science instruction. English, math, and social studies teachers collaborated with the science teachers to plan courses. In addition to supporting these planning efforts, the HI-C group also provided a portable computer for every two students in these classes through a grant, as well as Internet access, microcomputer-based laboratory interfaces, and video microscopes. Not only did this support guarantee the success of the project, but it also provided a model for successful project implementation.

Learning Processes   As we proposed earlier, CLEs such as ScienceWare and RiverMUD engage all forms of meaningful learning. Students are actively engaged in sampling streams or other environments and construct models of those environments that represent their own understanding. Students are intentional; they define their own problems to investigate. Those problems are authentic; they are in the students' own community. Students cooperatively work in scientific teams to collect, analyze, and make sense out of the data they are gathering.

Student Roles   As with most of the other activities described in this book, students assume personal responsibility for most of their learning. They select problems, conceive of experiments, conduct the experiments, analyze the results, build models that incorporate those results, and report those results and their recommendations about corrective actions. This represents a very complete set of student-initiated activities.

Teacher Roles   The HI-C group believes that teachers should be coaches, avoiding intervening in the learning process unless necessary. They also believe that many of the teachers' roles can be supported by the tools that are available. The Model-It tool, for instance, supports a very difficult process to teach.

Assessing Learning   As described earlier, the primary form of assessment is student reports. The reports consist of descriptions of the experiments, the models they built, and descriptions and arguments for solution to the problems posed. These are evaluated for the complexity of the experiments that they conduct and the accuracy of student models that describe those experiments. Questions about the reports can be asked:

- Were all of the variables identified?
- Were the data collected reliable, viable?
- Were the values believable?
- Were the variables accurately represented in the model?
- Were the hypotheses internally consistent, descriptive, and testable?
- Were the causal relationships among variable accurately represented in the model—were the correct cause–effect relationships identified?
- How likely were student solutions to work?
- Were there factors in the environment that students missed?
- Were the arguments sound?

Science teacher should be able to provide many other criteria for evaluating the project reports.

CoVis: Visualizing Science

The Learning Through Collaborative Visualization (CoVis) Project seeks to foster collaboration among students, teachers, scientists, and educators in the design and use of a scientific collaboratory (Edelson, Pea, and Gomez 1996) and to become a benchmark project for reforming science education while learning and using the geosciences. Like ScienceWare, it combines project-based science and provides a rich set of information resources, scientific visualization (cognitive) tools, networked classrooms to support conversation and collaboration, and social/contextual support in the form of teacher workshops and conferencing facilities. Like ScienceWare, it is a good model of a technology-supported learning environment for engaging contextualized, active, intentional, constructive, complex, collaborative, conversational, and reflective meaning making.

Problem Space CoVis provides project-based problems to science students studying atmospheric and environmental sciences. As with most constructivist approaches to learning, students work on authentic problems, just like geoscientists. In doing so, they learn how science applies to the real world and how it raises social and political issues. Questions that have been addressed by students include the effects of global warming on the climate, immediate and long-term weather forecasting, the role of ocean temperatures on continental climate, and many others. The focus of the CoVis curriculum is projects, not topics.

Related Cases CoVis provides no database of related cases, but it does provide access to a vast array of case-based experiences by connecting students in the classrooms with science experts in universities and industry who are willing to volunteer time to assist CoVis students with their projects. The Mentor Database on the WWW matches these volunteers with teams of students for Web conferences students. Research shows that mentors usually provide advice in the nature of stories about their experience, that is, related cases.

Information Resources   In order to support student inquiry, CoVis calls on the information-rich Geosciences Web Server at the University of Illinois. The server provides up-to-the-minute satellite imagery and a collection of multimedia instructional modules in the atmospheric sciences. This enables the students in the CoVis classroom to be working with the same data sets as professional meteorologists. Additionally, students access other data sets from the WWW, such as the Web sites for each of the Environmental Research Laboratories sponsored by the National Oceanic and Atmospheric Association (Figure 7.9). Students also create Web sites to share their findings with other classrooms.

Cognitive Tools   In order to help students understand the data that they are provided, CoVis has developed a suite of tools for visualizing weather phenomena, including the *Weather Visualizer,* the *Climate Visualizer*, and the *Greenhouse Effect Visualizer.* These tools incorporate massive amounts of data and represent those data by colorizing portions of weather maps to convey different aspects of the weather and climate. Different colors represent, for instance, different temperatures or radiant energy, making it easier to understand the interrelationships between variables.

The *Weather Visualizer* displays current satellite imagery from the Web in many different forms (see Figure 7.10). It can also convey temperature, wind velocity and direction, atmospheric pressure, dew point, and other data using traditional graphic symbols used in weather maps (illustrated in Chapter 6).

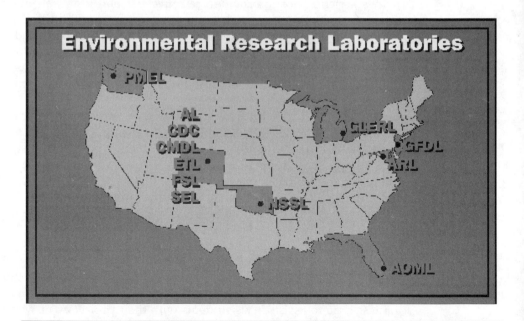

Figure 7.9   Environmental Research Labs available to CoVis students

The *Climate Visualizer* draws its data from a historical database of weather data. It allows students to display temperature as colors, wind as vectors, and pressure as contours along with latitude/longitude and continent overlays (Edelson, Pea, and Gomez 1996). Students can convert any numerical values to colors in order to enhance their understanding of the data and subtract values from map to map in order to see seasonal effects over time (illustrated in Chapter 6).

The *Greenhouse Effect Visualizer* allows students to call up maps of the levels of sunlight, reflectivity, reflected sunlight, absorbed sunlight, surface temperature, Earth's emissions, greenhouse effect energy, and radiation for different seasons or different months of the year. Comparing the output of these enables students to make conjectures about the greenhouse effect (Gordin, Edelson, and Pea 1994). Students call up weather data sets from the WWW and plot the effects using the visualizer (see Figure 7.11), allowing them to better conceptualize the relationships embedded in the data.

This powerful suite of tools enables students to see long-term trends in weather in addition to Nowcasting. The students use the tools to answer sophisticated questions like the effects of volcanoes on weather or predictions about temperatures far into the future (Edelson, Pea, and Gomez 1996). These are the kinds of questions that geoscientists are asking as well. They are able to consider those questions because they are using the same research tools and data sets used by meteorologists.

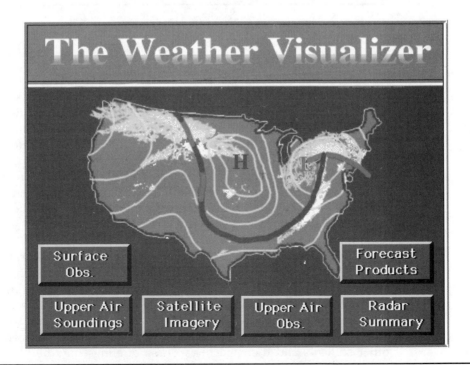

Figure 7.10 *The Weather Visualizer*

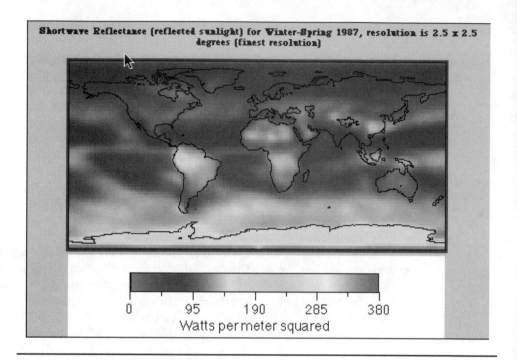

Figure 7.11 Greenhouse Effect Visualizer output

Conversation/Collaboration Tools The CoVis Project provides students with a range of collaboration and communication tools, including desktop video teleconferencing; shared software environments for remote, real-time collaboration; desktop videoconferencing; a collaborative notebook; electronic mail for connecting learners in different classrooms around the country; a UseNet news service for sharing ideas; telephone and fax machines; and, as a last resort, the U.S. mail service. The purpose of all of these communication tools is to interconnect learners in classrooms around the country, enabling them to work together to achieve scientific goals—that is, to build a community of learners. To date, more than 150 teachers in 50 schools with several thousand students have joined the CoVis community of scholars.

CoVis also supports conversation through the Collaboratory Notebook, a collaborative hypermedia composition system. The notebook is described in Chapter 5. The CoVis Project also uses videoconferencing systems for face-to-face communication among students who are forecasting weather around the country. This communication takes different forms: "interactive weather briefings" and virtual field trips. In the weather briefings, students report weather data to other students and their teachers. These briefings may be Nowcasts (real-time weather reports) or weather consultations (student consulting with atmospheric scientists about problems they are having interpreting data). In the virtual field trips, students visit the Exploratorium in San Francisco, where museum staff, guided by students in remote classrooms, move around the museum floor with videocameras that are connected to the classrooms via a video link, allowing them to interact with exhibits at the museum.

Social/Contextual Support　The CoVis Project supports teachers by sponsoring workshops and conferences where teachers can seek help from and establish a consensus with the researchers. Not only do researchers help the teachers, but the teachers also provide valuable input on the design of new technologies and activities.

Additionally, the project supports teachers by supporting online professional development forums (using electronic mail) where teachers can explore the theoretical foundations of the CoVis Project, as well as deal with practical questions about classroom issues. The goal is to create a self-sustaining professional community. The forums offer an inexpensive way for teachers to establish and maintain their own community of practice.

The CoVis Project also uses a listserv to provide technical support for the project. Teachers can pose questions, which are answered by peer teachers or by technical staff. It also offers the CoVis staff valuable information about the kinds of problems encountered in the classroom.

Learning Processes　The learning activities in CoVis are thorough. Students are actively engaged in analyzing weather data and making forecasts, and using visual representations to construct their own models about the environment. Like ScienceWare, students are intentional, because they define their own problems to investigate. Those problems are authentic; the data they use are live from the satellite. Students work in scientific teams to collect, analyze, and make sense out of the data and to share forecasts with each other via the Internet.

Student Roles　Students decide on issues and projects to investigate, collect data, analyze that data, write reports, issue forecasts, and debate weather-related issues with other students from around the country. They function collaboratively and independently.

Teacher Roles　As with ScienceWare, the major teachers' role is coaching. They recommend resources, provide feedback on student conjectures, and evaluate student activities. As with nearly every learning activity described in this book, teachers should avoid direct teaching roles.

Assessing Learning　There are multiple ways to evaluate the multiple outcomes from CoVis classrooms. The forecasts can always be assessed for their accuracy. The student reports and environmental models can be evaluated using criteria similar to those listed for the ScienceWare projects earlier. The collaboratory discussions are also useful for assessment purposes. The accuracy and viability of student conjectures, plans, and arguments can be evaluated using criteria such as:

- Do data that student provide support their explanations?
- Were the data challenged?

- Were student questions based on accepted laws and principles?
- Were student conjectures testable?

Again, science teachers could suggest many other criteria, depending on what problems students are investigating.

CONCLUSIONS

The CLEs illustrated in this chapter are the embodiment of meaningful learning. They engage learners in active, constructive, intentional, authentic, and cooperative learning. All of the other technologies described in this book may be combined to develop rich learning environments, such as those described in this chapter. These CLEs represent the goals of learning *with* technology.

You may have noted that the two examples of learning environments that we provided in this chapter both supported science learning. It is true that the most CLEs are found in the sciences. Why is that? We believe that is largely because there is more funding to support the development of science education materials, although many in the science education field might argue that it is because science education is ahead of the other disciplines. That may be, but with adequate funding, powerful learning environments certainly could be developed in the humanities and social sciences. It is also the case that technology is more familiar to scientists, so technology-supported learning environments have been more likely to be developed in the sciences. Future development, we hope, will support the development of learning environments such as ScienceWare and CoVis in all of the disciplines. Because they are publicly funded, access to the tools, environments, and activities in both ScienceWare and CoVis are available to schools. Information is available from the project staff. However, the important point is not how to gain access to these environments, but rather to search for environments that possess these characteristics as you surf the World Web Web or technology catalogs for ideas. Also, think about developing your own CLEs, using materials available from different sources. Engaging students in CLEs may well be the most rewarding experience possible, both for students and teachers.

THINGS TO THINK ABOUT

If you would like to reflect on the ideas that we presented in this chapter, then articulate your responses to the following questions and compare them with others' responses.

1. Can you think of constructivist learning environments that do not use or include technology? In what contexts would you find such environments?
2. What factors produce student ownership of a problem or project? Why do students find them relevant and meaningful enough to accept as a challenge?

3. The sciences and social sciences provide a wealth of problems and projects, while some of the humanities provide more of a challenge for redefining in a learning-by-doing way. Can you think of projects and problems that could be used to develop CLEs in history and English classes?

4. Some constructivists claim that nothing can be understood outside of its context of use. Can you think of learning outcomes where students can really understand ideas without understanding how they can be used?

5. Schank argues that intelligence is largely a matter of being able to recall and adapt stories in new situations. Can you think of a current problem? What stories does that problem remind you of?

6. CLEs argue that information is not meaningful unless it is being used to help solve a problem. Can you think of a situation when students should be forced to memorize information with using it? What are those situations? Why do they need to remember that information?

7. Cognitive tools do some of the intellectual work for the students. Isn't that cheating? Why should students receive cognitive help in performing learning activities?

8. How can student conversations be evaluated? What makes a good conversation?

9. Schank argues that every learning goal in schools can and should be learned using a goal-based scenario (a kind of CLE). Do you agree or disagree? Why?

REFERENCES

Brown A. L.,and J. C. Campione (1990). Communities of learning and thinking, or a context by any other name. In D. Kuhn (ed.), *Developmental perspectives on teaching and learning thinking skills* (pp. 108–126). Basel: Karger.

Cognition and Technology Group at Vanderbilt (1992). Technology and the design of generative learning environments. In T. M. Duffy and D. H. Jonassen (eds.), *Constructivism and the technology of instruction: A conversation*. Hillsdale, NJ: Lawrence Erlbaum Associates.

Edelson, D., R. Pea, and L. Gomez (1996). Constructivism in the collaboratory. In B. G. Wilson (ed.), *Constructivist learning environments: Case studies in instructional design*. Englewood Cliffs, NJ: Educational Technology Publications.

Gordin, D. N., D. C. Edelson, and R. D. Pea (January 1995). The Greenhouse Effect Visualizer: A tool for the science classroom. *Proceedings of the Fourth American Meteorological Society Education Symposium.*

Jonassen, D. H. (1991). Hypertext as design. Educational Technology: Research and Development, 39(1).

Jonassen, D. H. (1998). Designing case-based constructivist learning environments. In C. M. Reigeluth (ed.), *Instructional design theories and models*, vol. 2. Mahwah, NJ: Lawrence Erlbaum Associates.

Jonassen, D. H., D. R. Ambruso, and J. Olesen (1992). Designing a hypertext on transfusion medicine using cognitive flexibility theory. *Journal of Educational Hypermedia and Multimedia*, 1(3): 309–22.

O'Neill, D. K., and L. M. Gomez (1992). The Collaboratory Notebook: A distributed knowledge building environment for project learning. *Proceedings of ED MEDIA, 94*: Vancouver, BC, Canada.

Perkins, D. N. (1991). Technology meets constructivism: Do they make a marriage? *Educational Technology*, 31(5): 18–23.

Schank, R. C. (1994). Goal-based scenarios: A radical look at education. *Journal of Learning Sciences* 3(4), 429–53.

Soloway, E., J. Krajcik, and E. A. Finkel (April 1995). *The ScienceWare project: Supporting science modeling and inquiry via computational media & technology*. Paper presented at the annual meeting of the America Educational Research Association, San Francisco, CA.

Spiro, R. J., W. Vispoel, J. Schmitz, A. Samarapungavan, and A. Boerger (1987). Knowledge acquisition for application: Cognitive flexibility and transfer in complex content domains. In B. C. Britton (ed.), *Executive control processes*. Hillsdale, NJ: Lawrence Erlbaum Associates.

Spitulnik, J., S. Studer, Finkel, E. Gustafson, J. Laczko, and E. Soloway (1995). The RiverMUD design rationale: Scaffolding for scientific inquiry through modeling, discourse, and decision making in community based issues. In T. Koschman (ed.), *Proceedings of Computer Support for Collaborative Learning*. Hillsdale, NJ: Lawrence Erlbaum Associates.

Wilson, B. G. (1996). Introduction: What is a constructivist learning environment? In B. G. Wilson (ed.), *Constructivist learning environments* (pp. 3–8). Englewood Cliffs, NJ: Educational Technology Publications.

CHAPTER 8

LEARNING BY REFLECTING: WHAT HAVE WE LEARNED?

This final chapter serves three purposes. First, it summarizes the ideas about constructivist uses of technology that were described throughout this book. Second, it discusses some of the implications of adopting a constructivist philosophy to teaching. There are numerous implications, both for teachers and students. Third, this chapter elaborates on how to assess learning from constructivist uses of technology by suggesting rubrics for evaluating learning outcomes.

CONSTRUCTIVIST USES OF TECHNOLOGY

Technologies should be used in the pursuit of meaningful learning. Nearly a century's worth of research and experience in implementing learning technologies have proven that they teach no better than teachers. That is, when used to deliver instructional messages, students generally learn no differently from technologies or teachers. Richard Clark has for many years argued that technologies are "mere vehicles" that deliver instructional messages to learners, much the same as trucks deliver groceries to supermarkets. It doesn't matter which vehicles you use. They are all equivalent in their ability to deliver instructional groceries. We have claimed that instructional delivery is the wrong issue. We argue that technologies should not be used as conveyors and deliverers of the designer's message to a passive learner. Rather, they should be used as tools that students learn with. Why? Because when learners are passive receptacles of technology-delivered messages to be consumed and regurgitated, they are not learning meaningfully. When students learn by using technologies as tools for growing and sharing their own groceries, they are learning meaningfully. We have argued throughout this book that technologies should engage students in meaningful learning, where they are intentionally and actively processing information while pursuing authentic tasks together in order to construct personal and socially shared meaning for the phenomena they are exploring and manipulating. Using technologies to help them articulate and reflect on what they know is the glue that holds personally constructed knowledge together. Technologies should be used by learners to engage in:

- **Active learning,** where they explore and manipulate the components and parameters of technology-based environments and observe the results of their activities
- **Constructive learning,** where they articulate what they know and have learned and reflect on its meaning and importance in larger social and intellectual contexts
- **Intentional learning,** where they determine their own goals and regulate and manage their activities
- **Authentic learning,** where they examine and attempt to solve complex, ill-structured, and real-world problems
- **Cooperative learning,** where they collaborate with others and socially negotiate the meanings they have constructed

This has been our agenda in this book. These are the beliefs that we have constructed about technology use. They do not represent "the truth." You must construct that for yourselves. Many educators disagree with our beliefs and have constructed alternate theories based on different beliefs about learning and technology. Yet, in our view, these beliefs make the most sense. Before you accept our beliefs, if you are so inclined, consider some of the impediments to constructivist uses of technology that we discuss next.

IMPLICATIONS OF CONSTRUCTIVISM

Using technologies as constructivist tools assumes that the educational process will change, that schools or classrooms (at least those that use technologies in the ways that we have described) will reform the educational process. Although few people would ever publicly admit that schools should not emphasize meaningful learning, most people in our society tacitly accept that schools do not. Intentional learning presupposes that parents, students, and teachers will realize this and demand more. They will demand change, so that thinking is valued as much as memorizing. Technologies will not be the cause of the social change that is required for a renaissance in learning, but they can catalyze that change and support it if it comes.

Schooling is a social process, and like most social processes, it is about power (according to post-modern beliefs). That power has historically been used to impose values and beliefs on students in the name of learning. Institutions of education have a vested societal interest in retaining that power. Let's briefly examine the implications.

Implications for Teachers

In order for students to learn *with* technology, teachers must accept a new model of learning. Traditionally, teachers' primary responsibility and activity have been directly instructing students, where teachers were the purveyors of knowledge and students the recipients. That is, the teacher told the students what they knew and how they interpreted the world according to the textbooks and other resources they have studied. Teachers are hired and rewarded for their content expertise. This assumes that the ways that teachers know the world are correct and should be emulated by the students. Students take notes on what teachers tell them and try to comprehend the world as their teachers do. Successful students develop conceptions more similar to teachers'. Learners will not be able to learn *with* technology in this kind of learning context. They will not be able to construct their own meaning and manage their own learning if the teacher does it for them.

So, first and foremost, teachers must relinquish at least some of their authority. That includes their management authority and their intellectual authority. If teachers determine what is important for students to know, how they should know it, and how they should learn it, then students cannot become intentional, constructive learners. They aren't allowed. In those classroom contexts, there is no reason for students to make sense of the world—only to comprehend the teacher's understanding of it. We believe that the students' task should not be to understand the world as the teacher does. Rather, students should construct their own meaning for the world. If they do, then the teachers' roles shifts from dispensing knowledge to helping learners construct more viable conceptions of the world. We said in Chapter 1 that we believe that not all meaning is created equally. So the teacher needs to help students to discover what the larger community of scholars regards as meaningful conceptions and to evaluate their own beliefs and understandings in terms of those standards. Science teachers should help students comprehend the beliefs of the scientific community. Social studies teachers should examine with their students the values and beliefs that societies have constructed. In this role, the teacher is not the arbiter of knowledge but rather is a coach that helps students to engage in a larger community of scholars.

Teachers must also relinquish some of their authority in their management of learning. They cannot control all of the learning activities in the classroom. If teachers determine not only what is important for students to know, but how they should learn it, then students cannot be self-regulated learners. They aren't allowed.

Finally, teachers must learn how to use the technology themselves. They must gain skills and fluency with the technology. They will be most successful in helping students to learn *with* technology if they do not learn about the technologies in order to function as the expert. Rather, they should learn to coach the learning of technology skills. In many instances, teachers will be learning with the students. We have worked in many school situations where the students were constantly pushing our understanding of the technology. Often, we were barely keeping ahead of the students. They can and will learn *with* technologies, with or without the help of the teacher. That does not mean that as a teacher, you can abdicate any responsibility for learning the technologies. Rather, teachers should try not to be the expert all of the time.

These implications are very problematic for teachers. They require that teachers assume new roles with different beliefs than they have traditionally pursued. Most teachers in most schools will find these implications challenging. We believe that the results will justify the risks. And just as teachers must assume new roles, learning *with* technology requires that students also assume new roles.

Implications for Students

If teachers relinquish authority, learners must assume it. Learners must develop skills in articulating, reflecting on, and evaluating what they know; setting goals for themselves (determining what is important to know) and regulating their activities and effort in order to achieve those goals; and collaborating and conversing with others so that the understandings of all students is enriched. Many students are not ready to assume that much responsibility. They do not want the power to determine their own destiny. It is much easier to allow others to regulate their lives for them. How skilled are students at setting their own agendas and pursuing them? Many students believe in their roles as passive students. However, our experience and the experiences of virtually every researcher and educator involved with every technology project described in this book show that most students readily accept those responsibilities. When given the opportunity, students of all ages readily experiment with technologies, articulate their own beliefs, and construct, co-construct, and criticize each others' ideas. When learners are allowed to assume ownership of the product, they are diligent and persevering builders of knowledge.

Constructivist approaches to learning, with or without technology, are fraught with risks for students, parents, teachers, and administrators. Change always assumes risks. Many of the activities described in this book entail risks. We encourage you to take those risks. The excitement and enthusiasm generated by students while they construct their own understanding using technology-based tools is more than sufficient reward for taking those risks.

EVALUATING LEARNING FROM CONSTRUCTIVIST USES OF TECHNOLOGY

We have argued throughout this book that meaningful learning should be authentic and therefore complex. Educators are finally understanding that in order to evaluate authentic learning, we must use *authentic assessments*. In the last decade, calls for authentic assessment have encouraged educators to discard outdated evaluative methods designed to *sort* students, in favor of *assessment systems* designed to provide important information required to *improve performance*. How do we improve performance while assessing it? The simplest answer is that complex learning cannot be assessed or evaluated using any single measure. Rather, we must examine both the processes and products of student learning. Throughout this book, we have provided criteria for evaluating students' uses of different technologies. These criteria can be used to develop rubrics for evaluating performance. Rubrics have become a popular method for authentic assessment.

Rubrics and Meaningful Learning Environments

By definition, a *rubric* is a code, or a set of codes, designed to govern action. In educational settings, the term has evolved to mean a tool to be used for assessing a complex performance. In schools, rubrics often take the form of a scale or set of scales. In a typical classroom, for example, oral reports are mysteriously *graded* (neither students nor teachers can really tell you where the grades come from) and a few comments generally accompany the grade. Little substantive feedback about the performance is made available to the student, who cares only about the grade received.

Consider, instead, a meaningful learning environment in which the students and teachers work together to develop a rubric that will promote intentional learning by identifying important aspects of the performance, use the rubric to gather information about the learner's performance, and use the information as input for reflection on the performance. That reflection provides evidence to improve the performance. However, while rubrics can be an important tool for innovative educators who set out to create and enhance technology-rich, meaningful learning environments, rubrics are often created and used in ways that defeat their purpose. In this section we will show how to develop good rubrics and to think about using rubrics to assess not only student performance but also the power of the learning environments you create.

The "Anatomy" of a Rubric

A rubric is generally represented as a set of *scales* used to assess a complex performance and to provide rich information used to improve performance. For example, consider the task of making an effective oral presentation. There are several *elements* (components) that combine to form an effective oral presentation, including (but certainly not limited to) organization, pace, vocal qualities, and use of visual aids. So, a simplified, but useful, rubric used to assess an oral presentation might include scales for these four elements, something like Figure 8.1.

This rubric is clearer and more informative than simply assigning a letter grade, but there are several ways to enhance the value of this rubric. First, let's establish a common vocabulary to use when discussing rubrics: A rubric is a set of scales, one for each element that is considered important. The scale for each element consists of several *ratings* that describe the different levels of performance that might be expected.

Organization			
Disorganized	Weakly Organized	Well Organized	Strongly, Explicitly Organized

Vocal Qualities		
Weak	Good	Excellent

Visual Aids			
Inadequate	Adequate	Good	Excellent

Pace		
Inappropriate	OK	Good
_____ too fast	—— too slow	

Figure 8.1   A basic rubric for assessing oral presentations

Characteristics of a Good Rubric

The most effective and useful rubrics tend to display certain important characteristics. We will discuss these characteristics briefly, along with the most common
pitfalls experienced by novices. Finally, we will develop a Rubric for Developing
Effective Rubrics in order to demonstrate these characteristics.

- **In an effective rubric, all important elements are included.** If something is important enough to assess, consider it an element and develop a scale
with ratings that describe it. By definition, the rubric identifies (both for the asses-
sor and the student) the aspects of the performance that are considered important.
Consider the rubric a sort of contract between educator and student, and resist the
temptation to assess anything not included in the rubric. If you forgot an important element, then renegotiate the rubric.

- **In an effective rubric, each element is unidimensional.** Avoid using
elements that are really *molecules*. In chemistry, an *element* is irreducible. Water is a
molecule, composed of both hydrogen and oxygen—it can be separated into these
elements, which cannot be further separated. Likewise, in the preliminary example given in Figure 8.1, the so-called element "Voice Qualities" is really a combination of things that should be broken down more completely, perhaps into
separate elements of "Volume" and "Intonation." The penalty for attempting to
assess molecules rather than elements is that assigning ratings is more difficult, as
is deriving specific feedback upon which to base attempts to improve performance. Just what was it about the voice quality that was not adequate?

- **In an effective rubric, ratings are distinct, comprehensive, and descriptive.** The ratings should cover the range of expected performances. Some elements
are best assessed in a simple, two-rating scale—a yes/no distinction—while others
might require as many as seven distinct ratings. For example, the "Volume" element
in an oral report might simply be assessed as "too quiet" or "loud enough," while an
element like "social interaction" might justifiably involve five or more ratings.

A common problem in rubric design involves an attempt to use a similar scale
for all elements; for example, using a standard five-point scale like Figure 8.2.

Although it might seem cleaner to use such a scale for each element, can you
really describe the difference between ratings of "Weak" and "Poor," or between
"Good" and "Excellent," say, for example, for the volume of an oral presentation?
Would these assessments be defensible, or too subjective? Also, when a standard scale
is used for multiple elements, you lose a lot of information that is better transmitted
by descriptive ratings rather than generic labels. For example, a student might learn
more from a presentation that had been rated as "Boring" than from one that received
a "Weak" rating in an element titled "Motivation." Use labels that make sense and
describe the behaviors, and use just enough of them to cover the range of possibilities.

- **An effective rubric communicates clearly with both students and parents.** The ultimate purpose of a rubric is to improve performance. This is accomplished by clarifying expectations and by providing important information about
progress toward the desired goal states. Rubrics convey the complexity of the task
and focus intentional learning. The feedback their use provides serves as an important baseline for reflection by both learners and educators. For these purposes to be
realized, the rubric must communicate clearly with those it is to serve. Make sure that

Figure 8.2   Establishing ratings for a rubric

all who use the rubric (learners, parents, and educators) share a common understanding of all of the terms used. This common understanding is often achieved as
the educators and students develop the rubric collaboratively, after which students
explain it to their parents. This is a great way to develop metacognition (understanding of cognitive processes used), and it helps students regulate their learning as they
proceed through the complex tasks offered by meaningful learning environments.
Avoid educational jargon and words with weak or several meanings. Consider
developing, preferably with students, descriptions of each element and each rating,
or using elaborate, full-sentence rating labels instead of single terms.

•   **An effective rubric provides rich information about the multiple
aspects of the performance and avoids the temptation to create a contrived summary score.** Despite the fact that the real value of a rubric lies in its ability to provide information on the separate elements that comprise a complex task, novice
users (especially teachers in the public schools) seem compelled to turn the ratings
given on individual *elements* into *scores* for each element, and then to combine these
scores to form a total score and then, worse yet, a *grade*. When individual elements
are combined, information that could improve performance is lost. When ratings
are treated as numeric scores and combined, elements of more and less importance
are generally treated as if they were of equal value, and an inaccurate picture of the
performance is created. For example, suppose that ratings for "Organization" and
"Intonation" are combined after using a rubric to assess an oral presentation. Generally, the scores are added in a way that makes the two appear equally important.
Even when the different elements are combined using some sort of weighting
system that assigns different numbers of points based on the importance of the element, when scores are combined, attention is paid to the total at the expense of the
information about how to improve performance on each element.

A Rubric for Assessing the Effectiveness of a Rubric

Developing rubrics is a complex task. As is the case in most complex tasks, there's
no single "right answer." For most activities for which a rubric might be an appropriate assessment device, it is quite likely that different people would develop different rubrics, each with its own set of advantages and shortcomings. A rubric is
effective to the extent that it helps learners focus on the important elements of a
performance and provides information on which they can reflect and base strategies for growth. Most rubrics can be improved by a sincere attempt to assess them
against the criteria just discussed.

For example, although the rubric for the oral presentation provided in Figure
8.1 was a step in the right direction and would be useful to learners, it was not fully

developed (important elements were missing and ratings were undefined) and it included an element, "Voice Qualities," that was really a *molecule*—a combination of components that should have been addressed separately. That rubric can be improved. Other rubrics have serious flaws as well. For this reason, we offer a rubric that you can review and improve on as you develop. (Figure 8.3)

Rubric for Assessing and Improving Rubrics

ELEMENTS

Comprehensiveness: Are all of the important elements of the performance identified?

Important elements are missing (attach list of missing elements).	All important elements are identified.

Unidimensionality: Are the elements irreducible, or do they represent factors that are better addressed separately?

More than one element should be broken down (attach list). _____	One element should be broken down.	All elements are unidimensional.

RATINGS

Distinctiveness: Do the ratings represent clearly different categories, or is there overlap or ambiguity?

Ratings for one or more elements seem to overlap. (attach list of elements)	Ratings for each element are distinct from one another.

Comprehensiveness: Do the ratings cover the full range of expected performances?

Ratings are missing (attach list of suggested additions).	All important ratings are identified.

Descriptiveness: Do the ratings provide meaningful input for reflection?

Several ratings have generic or minimally useful labels (attach list).	Few ratings have generic or minimall useful labels (attach list).	All ratings communicate clearly.

CLARITY
(the extent to which key stakeholders will understand)

Among Students

Few students will understand all of the terms used in elements and ratings (attach list of suggestions).	Few students will understand all of the terms used in elements and ratings (attach list of suggestions).	All students will understand.

Figure 8.3   Rubric for assessing and improving rubrics

Among Parents

Few parents will understand all of the terms used in elements and ratings (attach list of suggestions).	Few parents will understand all of the terms used in elements and ratings (attach list of suggestions).	All parents will understand.

QUALITY OF INFORMATION PROVIDED

Richness

Misses many opportunities to communicate clearly about the quality of the performance.	Adequate information is provided to serve as the basis for growth.	Lots of specific information is provided to facilitate development.

Resists Temptation of Generic Scales

"Generic" scales seem to compromise the value of the rubric (attach list of offending elements).	The scale for each element reflects a sincere effort to identify distinctive ratings.

Resists Temptation to Summarize

Information of value may be overlooked because a summary collapsing categories is used (attach list of suggested additions).	No attempt to create an overall score or grade is evident.

Figure 8.3 Continued

Using Information Rubrics

In order to gain the maximum power that rubrics offer, innovative educators creating meaningful learning environments should consider the following "tips":

- Develop rubrics collaboratively with learners. This is an outstanding opportunity to get students thinking about what expert performance looks like, and to help students learn how to learn.
- Encourage learners to use the rubrics to guide them during the learning process. Throughout this book, we have promoted the idea of intentional learning. When rubrics are made public before the learning activity begins, students can use the content of rubrics to focus their activities.

- Encourage students to explain the rubrics to parents and other interested individuals, perhaps in the context of student-led conferences during which they describe the progress they're making and the lessons they have learned.
- View rubrics as providing important information educators and learners can use to select learning activities, rather than as evaluative devices with which to label, sort, or grade students. Gaps between what is reported and what is desired on a single element should be viewed as opportunities for growth.
- View rubrics as powerful tools in your own professional development. Consider designing a rubric that will help you become a more effective educator in promoting meaningful learning. Ask peers to develop it with you, and perhaps to use it to assess your progress from time to time. These assessments, combined with your own, can be the most important factor in your development as an innovative educator.
- Use rubrics to help you assess the quality and power of the learning environments you create, as well as the progress of individuals. In the following section, we create a rubric you might wish to modify and use to help you assess the environments you create. Using such a tool, you are likely to identify additional ways to enhance the educational experience you provide for your students.

Rubric for Understanding and Improving Meaningful Learning Environments

Throughout this book we have described the attributes of meaningful learning environments, proposing that such learning environments are active, constructive, cooperative, authentic, and intentional, and we have exemplified what is meant by each of these terms. Now, we offer a rubric you might find useful in refining the environments you create (Figure 8.4). We offer it as a starting point, not as a definitive answer. We anticipate that you will modify this rubric to help you answer the questions of greatest importance to you, to your students, and to their parents.

Assessing Activity

To what extent does the environment you have created promote manipulation of real-world objects and observations based on these activities?

Learner Interaction with Real-World Objects

Little of the learner's time is spent engaged with tools and objects found outside school.	Learners are often engaged in activities involving tools and objects found outside school.

Figure 8.4 Rubric for improving meaningful learning environments

Observation and Reflection

Students rarely think about or record the results of actions taken during activities.	Students often stop and think about the activities in which they are engaged.	Students share frequent observations about their activity with peers and interested adults.

Learner Interactions

Students manipulated none of the variables or controls in environment.	Students manipulated some variables and controls in environment.	Students manipulated all or nearly all variables/ controls in environment.

Tool Use

Students used no cognitive tools.	Students used some cognitive tools to support explorations/manipulations.	Students used nearly all cognitive tools effectively.

Assessing Construction

To what extent does the environment you have created cause learners to perceive puzzling dissonance and form mental models to explain the incongruity?

Dissonance / Puzzling

Students engage in learning activities because activities are required, rather than being an intrinsic interest.	Learners frequently seem to be operating based on a sincere curiosity about the topic of study.	Learners are consistently striving to resolve disparity between observed and what is known, operating on a sincere desire to know.

Constructing Mental Models and Making Meaning

Learners rarely create their own understandings of how things work..	Learners are often expected to make sense of new experiences and develop theories.	Learners routinely wrestle with new experiences, becoming experts at identifying and solving problems.

Assessing Cooperation

To what extent does the environment you have created promote meaningful interaction among students and between students and experts outside of school? To what extent are learners developing skills related to social negotiation in learning to accept and share responsibility?

Interaction Among Learners

Little of the learners' time is spent gainfully engaged with other students.	Learners are often immersed in activities in which collaboration with peers results in success.

Figure 8.4 Continued

Interaction with People Outside of School

Little of the learners' time is spent gainfully engaged with experts outside of school.	Learners are often involved in activities in which there is significant collaboration with experts from outside of school.

Social Negotiation

Little evidence that learners work together to develop shared understanding of tasks or of solution strategies.	Learners are often observed in the process of coming to agreement on the nature of problems and on best courses of action.	Learners collaborate with ease. Negotiations become almost invisible, yet the ideas of all team members are valued.

Acceptance and Distribution of Roles and Responsibility

Roles and responsibilities are shifted infrequently; most capable learners accept more responsibility than the less capable.	Roles and responsibilities are shifted often, and such changes are accepted by both the most and least capable.	Students make their own decisions concerning roles and responsibilities, freely giving and accepting assistance as necessary.

Assessing Authenticity

To what extent does the environment you have created present learners with problems that are naturally complex and embedded in a real-world context? To what extent do the problems you present cause higher-order thinking?

Complexity

The tasks learners face have been designed for schools (i.e., separated into "subjects" and developed to simplify learning).	The tasks learners face are embedded in theme-based units that cross disciplines and present issues in context.	Students accept challenges as they exist in real world, using language, math, science, and technologies to accomplish important tasks.

Higher-Order Thinking

A large percentage of what is expected is memorization. Students are rarely asked to evaluate, synthesize, or create.	Students are often asked to develop ideas and solutions, often in groups, and demonstrate the abilities to create and reason.	Learners routinely generate hypotheses, conduct investigations, assess results, and make predictions.

Recognizing Problems

Students are not expected to be problem finders, but are instead expected to be able to solve occasional well-structured problems	Students occasionally face ill-structured challenges and are expected to refine their problem as well as solve it.	Students frequently face ill-structured challenges and develop proficiency in identifying and defining problems.

Figure 8.4   Continued

"Right Answers"

The "problems" presented to learners tend to have "right answers," "correct" solutions that the students are expected to eventually reach.

The problems presented are new to the learners, and generally involve complex solutions of varying quality, rather than "right answers."

Assessing Intentionality

To what extent does the environment you have created cause learners to pursue important, well-articulated goals to which they are intrinsically committed? To what extent can learners explain their activity in terms of how the activities relate to the attainment of their goals?

Goal Directedness

Learners are often pursuing activities that have little to do with the attainment of specified goals.

Learners are generally engaged in activities that contribute to the attainment of specified goals.

Setting Own Goals

Learning goals are provided by educators.

Learners are sometimes involved in the establishment of learning goals.

Learners are routinely responsible for developing and expressing learning goals.

Regulating Own Learning

Learners' progress is monitored by others.

Learners are involved as partners in monitoring and reporting progress toward goals.

Learners are responsible for monitoring and reporting progress toward goals.

Learning How to Learn

Little emphasis is placed on metacognition. There are few opportunities to discuss the learning process with peers or educators.

The culture of the learning environment promotes frequent discussion of the processes and strategies (both successful and unsuccessful) involved in learning.

Articulation of Goals as Focus of Activity

Learners don't see the relationship between the activities in which they are engaged and specified learning goals.

Learners describe the activities in which they are engaged in terms that relate directly to the specified learning goals.

Figure 8.4   Continued

Technology Use in Support of Learning Goals		
The use of technology seems unrelated to the specified learning goals.	The use of technology contributes to the attainment of specified learning goals.	The use of technology makes a powerful contribution to the attainment of specified learning goals.

Figure 8.4   Continued

Index